D1337003

JEAN GREENHOWE'S
FAVOURITE DOLLS & TOYS

JEAN GREENHOWE'S
FAVOURITE DOLLS & TOYS

GUILD PUBLISHING
LONDON

Acknowledgements

The designs in this book were originally featured in WOMAN'S WEEKLY magazine and the author would like to express her thanks to the editor and the knitting and home department staff for their assistance and cooperation.

The author and publishers also wish to thank IPC Magazines Ltd, publishers of WOMAN'S WEEKLY for their kind permission to reproduce their photographs.

This edition published 1988 by Guild Publishing
by arrangement with The Hamlyn Publishing Group Limited

Some material in this book was previously published in *Cuddly Toys and Dolls, Favourite Toys* and *Knitted Toys*.

First impression 1988
Copyright © Jean Greenhowe 1982, 1985, 1986, 1988

The toys described in this book are copyright and may not be reproduced in whole or in part for commercial or industrial purposes.

All rights reserved. No part of this publication may be reproduced, stored in a retrieval system, or transmitted, in any form or by any means, electronic, mechanical, photocopying, recording or otherwise without the prior permission of the Publisher and the copyright holder.

Printed by Mandarin Offset, Hong Kong

CONTENTS

INTRODUCTION

Calling all toymakers! This bumper book is guaranteed to give hours of creative enjoyment, and the results are certain to delight and amuse children of all ages. The contents make available again a wealth of playthings from my previous Hamlyn books, Cuddly Toys and Dolls *and* Favourite Toys, *and also some patterns for knitted toys, among which is a super-sized teddy bear.*

Simply leaf through the pages to discover irresistible furry animals, rag dolls to dress and undress, colourful rosette toys, big sit-upon cuddlies, Wendy houses and miniature houses, a child-sized Punch and Judy puppet booth complete with puppets, and many more appealing novelties.

The only problem is, you'll be spoilt for choice!

TIPS FOR TOYMAKERS

Instructions

Firstly, do take time to read through the instructions before making a start on any project, so that you are familiar with what is involved. If you then follow the instructions at each stage of making, your toy should turn out just like the one shown in the illustration.

Safety first

Common sense should always be used regarding the safety aspect when making toys for children. It is obvious that very young children and babies should not be given toys containing potentially dangerous items such as buttons, beads, wire, or any other parts which could cause injury or become detached and swallowed.

Adhesive

When adhesive is quoted in the instructions, this means an all-purpose clear glue such as UHU. This adhesive dries very quickly and also remains flexible after it is dry.

Before cutting out felt facial features (or any other small felt pieces which are to be sewn or stuck in place on the toy), first spread the back of the felt with adhesive, then work it into the felt with fingertips and leave it to dry. When felt is treated in this way the cut-out shapes will have smooth well-defined edges. This method should not of course be used for pieces of felt which are to be stuffed.

To cut out tiny pieces of felt, such as eyes and noses, first stick your paper pattern to the glued side of the felt with a dab of adhesive. Cut out the felt level with the edge of the paper pattern, then peel off the pattern before the adhesive dries completely.

To stop the cut edges of trimmings (ribbons, braid and lace) from fraying,

proceed as follows. Cut the trimming a little longer than required, spread a little adhesive across the wrong side and leave to dry. Cut the trimming through the glued portion.

Unwanted smears of UHU can be removed by dabbing with a cloth dipped in a little acetone. Take care when using acetone as it is highly flammable.

Measurements

On some of the diagrams only metric measurements are given, although the imperial equivalents may be quoted in the text. Where you find that metric sizes appear in the diagrams *only*, refer to the table below for the appropriate conversions.

Metric – Imperial Conversion Chart

Metric	Imperial	Metric	Imperial
5 mm	$\frac{1}{4}$ in	24 cm	$9\frac{1}{2}$ in
1 cm	$\frac{3}{8}$ in	25 cm	10 in
1.5 cm	$\frac{5}{8}$ in	27 cm	$10\frac{3}{4}$ in
2 cm	$\frac{3}{4}$ in	28 cm	11 in
2.5 cm	1 in	30 cm	$11\frac{3}{4}$ in
3 cm	$1\frac{1}{4}$ in	32 cm	$12\frac{3}{4}$ in
5 cm	2 in	34 cm	$13\frac{1}{2}$ in
6 cm	$2\frac{3}{8}$ in	35 cm	$13\frac{3}{4}$ in
7 cm	$2\frac{3}{4}$ in	43 cm	17 in
8 cm	3 in	46 cm	18 in
10 cm	4 in	47 cm	$18\frac{3}{4}$ in
11 cm	$4\frac{1}{4}$ in	50 cm	$19\frac{3}{4}$ in
12 cm	$4\frac{3}{4}$ in	74 cm	$29\frac{1}{4}$ in
13 cm	5 in	79 cm	31 in
14 cm	$5\frac{1}{2}$ in	87 cm	$34\frac{1}{4}$ in
15 cm	6 in	90 cm	$35\frac{1}{2}$ in
16 cm	$6\frac{1}{4}$ in	91 cm	36 in
17 cm	$6\frac{3}{4}$ in	96 cm	38 in
18 cm	7 in	110 cm	$43\frac{1}{2}$ in
20 cm	8 in	140 cm	55 in
21 cm	$8\frac{1}{4}$ in	150 cm	59 in
22 cm	$8\frac{3}{4}$ in		

Opposite Punch and Judy Booth. Instructions begin on page 184

See also note top page 8.

Important note: The imperial measurements given in the table are *not* simply straight conversions of the metric sizes. They have been worked out individually to suit each design where they appear in the book. Use this table *only when* no other imperial conversions are given, either in the instructions or on the diagrams.

Making the stitched toys

Equipment required

Dressmaking equipment: You need all the ordinary items as used for dressmaking – sewing machine, sewing threads, sharp scissors (both large and small pairs), sewing needles, tape measure, thimble, and so on.

Ruler: Marked with metric and imperial measurements.

Pins: Large glass- or plastic-headed pins are the best kind to use when making soft toys, as they are much easier to see and handle than ordinary pins. To avoid the danger of any pins being left in the toy accidentally, use a limited number and count them at each stage of making.

Tweezers: These can be very useful when handling small pieces of fabric or felt – for example, when glueing facial features in place. Tweezers can also be used to turn very small pieces right side out after stitching.

Compasses: A pair of inexpensive school compasses will be found invaluable for drawing out small circular patterns. Very large circles outside the span of your compasses can easily be drawn as described in the section headed *Copying the patterns* below.

Old Scissors: It is a good idea to keep an old pair of scissors just for cutting card and paper because these will blunt your good scissors.

Leather punch: Although this is not essential, a punch is extremely useful for cutting perfect tiny circles from felt, for small dolls' and animals' eyes. The felt should first be treated with adhesive as described on page 7.

Copying the patterns

If full-size patterns are given for a toy, these can be traced directly off the pages on to thin strong paper, such as ordinary writing paper. First follow any special notes in the instructions regarding the patterns, then after tracing and cutting out the patterns, mark on all details and lettering.

Patterns for the larger toys are given scaled down on grids ruled to represent 1 cm, 2 cm or 5 cm squares, etc. For drawing out such patterns to full size, you can buy packets of dressmaker's metric graph paper from dress fabric shops or haberdashery departments. This paper is usually divided into 1 cm squares with a heavier line ruled at 5 cm intervals.

If the scaled-down diagram states 'one square = 2 cm', then use a coloured pen or pencil to over-rule the graph paper every 2 cm. Now, following the scaled-down pattern outlines square by square, draw the same shapes on to the 2 cm graph paper as shown in diagram 1 (*opposite*). For USA readers, refer to the metric – imperial conversion chart (page 7) for the equivalent sizes of squares required when drawing diagrams on to imperial graph paper.

For circular patterns the measurement given is usually the diameter (the distance across the centre) of the circle. When drawing circles set your compasses to the radius measurement, i.e. *half* the diameter. To draw circles which are larger than your compasses can make, take a length of thin string and knot one end around a pencil point. Now tie a knot in the string, the required radius measurement away from the pencil point, keeping the string taut as you measure. Now draw the circle as shown in diagram 2 (*opposite*).

When measurements for simple shapes are given in the instructions (such as squares, rectangles or triangles), you can draw these directly on to the wrong side of the fabric before cutting out. However, if the toy is to be made more than once, it is a good idea to cut paper patterns for such shapes and mark on all the details for future use.

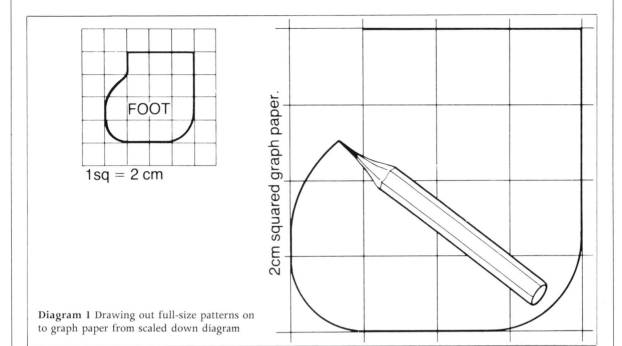

1sq = 2 cm

2cm squared graph paper.

FOOT

Diagram 1 Drawing out full-size patterns on to graph paper from scaled down diagram

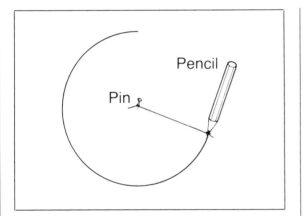

Pencil

Pin

Diagram 2 How to draw large circles using pencil, a pin and a length of string

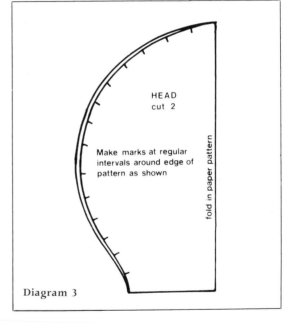

HEAD
cut 2

Make marks at regular intervals around edge of pattern as shown

fold in paper pattern

Diagram 3

Seams

Seams and turnings are allowed on the pattern pieces as stated in the instructions for each toy. Join fabric pieces with right sides facing unless otherwise stated.

To join the edges of large fabric or fur fabric pieces together accurately, proceed as follows. First of all, if the pattern is symmetrical, fold it in half as shown in diagram 3 (*right*). This shows the head pattern for the Best-dressed Doll on page 39. Now make pencil marks around the edge of one half of the pattern at intervals as shown on the diagram. Mark the other half of the

pattern in the same way, matching the marked lines. If the pattern is not symmetrical, simply make marks at intervals all round the edge.

Now pin the pattern on to the fabric and cut out the shape. Before removing the pattern, lift it away from the fabric at each marked point and make a mark on the fabric at these positions. When pinning and stitching the fabric pieces together, match the marked points all round.

To mark dart lines, or other points on the paper pattern, on to the fabric, simply pierce the pattern along the dart lines at intervals with a sharp pencil point, pushing the point of the pencil into the fabric.

Fur fabric

There are various types of fur fabric available, with long or short pile and polished or unpolished surfaces. Short-pile fur fabric is used for the toys in this book unless otherwise stated. If you have difficulty obtaining fur fabrics, see the list of suppliers at the end of the book.

On fur fabric, the fur pile lies smooth and flat if stroked in one direction, and will lift up if stroked in the opposite direction. On patterns for fur fabric toys, the direction of the 'smooth stroke' of the fur pile is indicated by an arrow on each pattern piece. Always take care to cut out the pieces so that the smooth stroke of the fur pile follows the direction of the arrows.

Fleecy fabric is also required for some of the toys. This fabric, sold for making dressing gowns, etc., has a knitted backing and is brushed on the right side to form a soft furry surface. It does not have a pile with a smooth stroke like the other fur fabrics.

To cut out fur fabric pieces, pin the patterns, one at a time, to the wrong side of the fabric then snip through the back of the fabric only, so as not to cut through the fur pile on the right side. When cutting a pair of pieces, always take care to remember to reverse the pattern before cutting the second piece.

To join fur fabric pieces, place the pieces right sides together, tucking in the fur pile at the raw edges, then push in pins at right angles to the raw edges all round, as shown in diagram 4 (*above*). After sewing, remove all the pins, then turn right side out and pick out the fur pile trapped in the seam with the point of a pin.

Working with felt

Because felt is a non-woven fabric, it is often

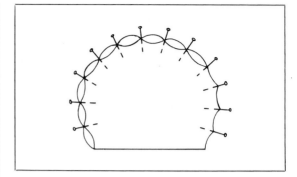

Diagram 4 Holding fur fabric pieces together with pins before sewing seams

supposed that it has no grain. However, it does have varying amounts of stretch when pulled lengthways and sideways, as well as stretch across the bias. When using felt for stuffed toys, always cut any identical pieces so that they lie in the same direction, parallel with the selvedge, or a straight edge if a square of felt is being used.

Diagram 5A (*below*) shows an example of the correct way to cut the pieces for a doll's feet. If the feet are cut as shown in diagram 5B (*below*), there may be differences in size

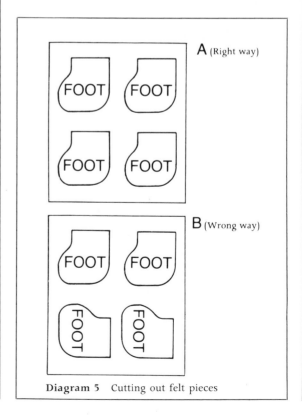

Diagram 5 Cutting out felt pieces

Sit-upon elephant. Instructions for this giant-size soft toy begin on page 174

after stuffing due to the felt stretching more in one direction than the other.

If the 'maximum stretch' of the felt is marked by arrows on the pattern pieces, be sure to cut out the pieces of felt accordingly.

Knitting yarn

When yarn is quoted in the instructions for a stitched toy or doll, this means knitting yarn, usually double knitting unless other plys are mentioned. Some of the dolls in the book have yarn hair and yarn is sometimes required for working facial features on the toys.

Making rag dolls

Using woven fabrics: Any fine, closely-woven calico, cotton or poly/cotton fabric is suitable for doll-making. While pink and peachy shades look best, cream or white can also be used. Pale pink is sometimes difficult to get in a dress fabric, but may be obtainable as sheeting. Many shops now have sheeting by the metre for making duvet covers, etc. If you do a lot of doll-making it is worth looking out for sale or bargain offers of sheets in the larger chain stores. A sheet bought in this way can work out cheaper than buying fabric by the metre.

Always cut out the doll pieces on the straight grain of the fabric unless the pattern indicates otherwise. Use a small machine stitch, and trim seams around all the curved parts to about 3 mm ($\frac{1}{8}$ in). After stuffing, any puckers in the seams can be ironed out as follows. Pinch the toy tightly between finger and thumb to force the stuffing against the puckered seam, then rub the seam against a warm iron.

Using stockinette: Cotton stockinette, in flesh or cream colour, is available by the metre specifically for making dolls. If you have difficulty obtaining stockinette, see the list of suppliers on page 254. Alternatively, discarded plain white stockinette vests or T-shirts can be used instead. These can be tinted pink if desired, following the dye-maker's instructions. When dyeing fabric remember that the colour always looks darker when the fabric is wet. Test a small cutting in the dye solution first.

Although stockinette will stretch in any direction when pulled, it usually stretches most across the width, as in hand-knitted fabric. The direction of 'most stretch' is indicated by arrows on each pattern piece or in the instructions when making dolls from stockinette.

Use a small machine stitch when sewing stockinette, stretching the seams slightly as you stitch, so that the threads will not snap when the pieces are stuffed. Trim the seams around all the curves to about 3 mm ($\frac{1}{8}$ in).

Dolls' hair

Cutting a number of equal lengths of knitting yarn for a doll's hair is a simple matter if you first wind the yarn into a hank. Select an object of suitable size to wind the yarn around – for example, a large book or the back of a chair. Note that the object should be somewhat longer than the required lengths, because the yarn will stretch slightly as it is wound.

After winding your hank, any kinks in the yarn can be removed as follows. Using two wooden spoons or any similar long-handled cooking utensils, slip the handles through each end of the hank. Stretch the hank tightly and steam it, by holding it over a pan of boiling water. Finally, cut through the hank at each end and trim the yarn strands to the length required.

Colouring cheeks

Use an orange-red pencil for colouring a doll's cheeks and always try the effect on an oddment of fabric first. For dolls made from woven fabric, gently rub the side of the pencil tip (not the point) over the cheek area. If the colour is too strong or uneven, some of it can be removed by rubbing gently with a soft eraser. For stockinette dolls which are very firmly stuffed, use the same method. For lightly stuffed stockinette dolls, moisten the pencil tip and apply a little colour at the centre of each cheek. Blend the colour over the cheek area with a bit of damp fabric.

Rosette Dolls

The bodies, arms and legs of these dolls are made from fabric circles of different sizes gathered up round the edges then threaded onto lengths of thin cord elastic. This type of elastic, sometimes known as hat elastic, is obtainable in various thicknesses. Elastic of about 2 to 3 mm ($\frac{1}{16}$ to $\frac{1}{8}$ in) in diameter is about the right thickness for the dolls.

You can use any oddments of lightweight plain or printed fabrics for the circles, such as dressmaking leftovers or pieces cut from discarded garments. If you haven't enough fabric on hand, pay a visit to your local thrift shop or jumble sale where cast off items of clothing can usually be purchased more cheaply than buying fabric by the metre.

The fabric circles can be strung on the lengths of elastic mixing the colours at random; but to achieve a prettier effect, try grouping similar colours together for each different part of the doll, as shown in the illustrations. Sort your fabric into piles before cutting out the circles, for example place greens and blues in one pile, reds and oranges in another.

Thin card is required for making the circle templates. You can use card from large breakfast cereal or washing powder packets or any similar cardboard grocery packages. **To make the card templates:** Draw the circles onto the card with compasses (or string and pencil for larger circles) to the sizes given for each doll. Cut out the card circles then mark the diameter size on each

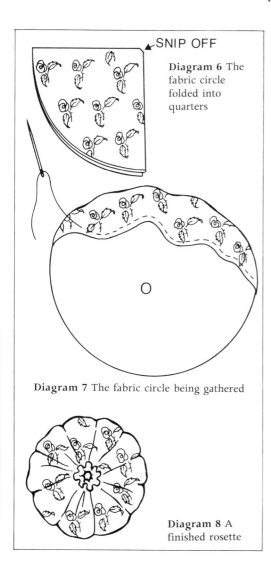

Diagram 6 The fabric circle folded into quarters

SNIP OFF

Diagram 7 The fabric circle being gathered

Diagram 8 A finished rosette

because the circles are stuffed.

For all the other gathered circles, first fold each one into quarters then snip off the corner at the centre to make a tiny hole as shown in diagram 6. Run a gathering thread all round about 3 mm ($\frac{1}{8}$ in) from the edge of the circle as shown in diagram 7. Pull up the gathers until the raw edges meet then fasten off. Flatten the gathered circle into a rosette having the gathers lying on top of the centre hole as shown in diagram 8.

Group the same size circles together as you make them and add a paper label to each pile, marked with the letter of the alphabet given for that size of circle in the instructions for each doll.

Stuffing the toy

Many types of filling are available for toy-making. Foam chips should be avoided because they can be highly flammable. Kapok is very good, but rather messy to work with as the fibres fly everywhere. Man-made fibre fillings are very clean to work with, and they have the added advantage of being washable. These fillings come in several grades, ranging from luxury high bulk white polyester to inexpensive multi-coloured filling, for use only when the colour will not show through the 'skin' of the toy.

For rag dolls and small to medium-sized soft toys, the most expensive polyester filling is really the best buy. Since it goes further (due to its high bulk quality) this filling can be just as economical to use as a cheaper type, where more filling would be required. For larger items, such as the sit-upon toys which need to be firmly stuffed, the cheaper fillings are very good.

Lumpy toys are usually the result of uneven stuffing, because small gaps are left where one piece of filling ends and the next begins. This happens most frequently in narrow pieces such as the limbs of a rag doll. When stuffing these, take a large handful of filling (polyester, not kapok which falls apart), and tease it into an elongated shape. Push one end of the filling into the end of the limb, then gradually feed in the filling with the fingers, trying to keep it in a continuous piece. Keep feeling the limb as it

one. Keep all the card circles after making your doll because some of them will come in useful for another doll. To cut out the fabric circles, draw round one of the card templates onto a piece of fabric then cut out the circle. If you need a number of circles of the same size, several can be cut at the same time as follows. Pin the cut-out fabric circle round the edge, onto three or four layers of fabric, then cut through all the fabrics level with the edge of the first circle.

To gather the circles: The circles for the rosette dolls are all gathered as described below, except for the Six Stretchy Dolls, (page 79) which have their own instructions

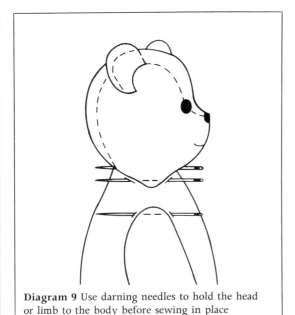

Diagram 9 Use darning needles to hold the head or limb to the body before sewing in place

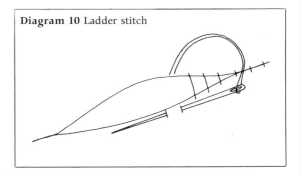

Diagram 10 Ladder stitch

diagram 10, above). Ladder stitch can also be used to make an invisible join when attaching the head or limb of a toy to the body.

Making a face

The age and character of a doll or toy are mainly determined by the positioning of the facial features. For a child-like appearance the eyes should be placed half-way down the face. If they are too close together the face will look mean, too far apart and the eyes will be frog-like. Therefore if measurements are given in the instructions for placing facial features, always follow these and your toy should look exactly like the one in the illustration.

If the eyes are made from felt, first pin them to the face, pushing the pins straight through the eyes and into the toy. Now check that they are level and centrally placed on the face by looking at the toy in a mirror. Any irregularities will show up immediately. The same method can be used if eyes and noses are to be embroidered, by pinning small paper shapes to the face before actually marking the fabric. An embroidered mouth line can be marked in the same way using a short length of thick thread or yarn pinned to the face as a guide.

When embroidering facial features, secure the knotted end of the thread in a place where it will not be seen on the finished toy – for example, at the back of a doll's head or under the position of a felt eye or nose on an animal. Use a long darning needle to take the thread through the toy to the position of the embroidered feature. Work the feature using a small sewing needle, then use the darning needle to take the thread back through the toy as before and fasten off the thread.

is stuffed, both inside and outside, taking care to fill any empty areas. When the piece of filling is almost finished, introduce one end of another piece in the same way, so the fibres of the first piece blend with the next.

If the limb is too narrow to get a finger inside, push in filling with the end of a pencil or knob of a knitting needle. To stuff very small toys, use tweezers.

Attaching a head or limb

To hold the head or limb of a toy securely to the body while sewing it in place, use darning needles instead of pins. Push the needles first into the body fabric, then into the head or limb, then back into the body fabric as shown in diagram 9 (*above*).

Ladder stitch

This stitch is used for closing the opening on a soft toy after stuffing. The raw edges of the fabric are turned in at the seam line, then the folded edges are laced together from side to side forming stitches which look like a ladder. Use strong double thread and take small, straight stitches alternately along one side then the other. After working a few stitches, pull the thread up tight, thus bringing the fabric edges together (*see*

When sewing or glueing felt features on a fur fabric toy, snip away the fur pile beneath the felt before fixing it in place.

Making the knitted toys

Knitting needle sizes

A needle conversion chart is given on page 254 with the old UK sizes, then the USA needle sizes.

Yarns

You will only need double knitting and 4 ply yarns. Any make of yarn will do, no specific brands are mentioned.

Knitters in the USA see page 254.

Tension

When knitting a garment which has to be made to fit a particular size, you must always take care that your tension is exactly the same as recommended in the knitting instructions.

However you don't need to be so precise when knitting toys. Your creation will be just as lovable even if it does turn out a bit larger or smaller than the size stated on the pattern.

The following chart is therefore intended as a *general* guide only, not to be followed slavishly, but to indicate that if you work near to these tensions then your toy will be more or less the same size given in the pattern. If your tension varies, don't worry! Just make sure that your knitting is not so loose as to allow the stuffing to escape between the stitches. Should this happen, then use a smaller size knitting needle.

Tension chart

[measured over stocking stitch and before stuffing]
Working with 4 ply yarn:
3 mm [No 11, USA 2] – 30 sts to 10 cm [4 in]
Working with double knitting yarn:
3 mm [No 11, USA 2] – 26 sts to 10 cm [4 in]
$3\frac{1}{4}$ mm [No 10, USA 3] – 25 sts to 10 cm [4 in]
$3\frac{3}{4}$ mm [No 9, USA 4] – 23 sts to 10 cm [4 in]

The making up instructions

In knitting patterns the directions for assembling the pieces normally come at the end, when all the knitting is completed. However, when making toys there can be so many bits and pieces that it is sometimes easier and less confusing to do the making up as the work progresses. Consequently, for some of the designs, the making up instructions follow after each piece is knitted.

Equipment required

Much of the equipment already mentioned on page 8 will be found useful – large glass-headed pins, tweezers and tape measure or ruler.

Knitters' sewing needles which are sold for sewing up knitted pieces are invaluable. These are usually available in two sizes for use with fine and heavy weight yarns. They have large eyes and smooth rounded points designed to pass between the knitted stitches when sewing up your work.

You will need a darning needle and ordinary sewing needles also. The darning needle for passing yarn through a toy to work the mouth stitches or other features, and the sewing needles for use with ordinary sewing threads.

Casting on and off

The first row after casting on is usually the right side of the work unless otherwise stated.

When casting on and off and also when joining on different colours, always leave a long end of yarn which can be used when making up the toy, to sew up each different coloured portion.

If the instructions say to cast on or cast off 'loosely', use a larger size of knitting needle to do this evenly.

Joining on a new ball of yarn

Instead of knotting on the yarn at the beginning of a row, join on a fresh ball in the following way. Thread a darning needle with the new yarn then take the needle point through the yarn loop of the first stitch on the previous row and also through the yarn strand coming away from the first stitch on the needle, as shown in the diagram. Pull the yarn through, leaving a long end. You must take care to pierce both the yarn loop and the yarn strand, then the first knitted stitch on your next row will hold firm and not slip open as you work.

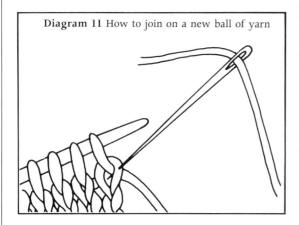

Diagram 11 How to join on a new ball of yarn

The knitted shapes

When making knitted toys it is important to remember that the knitted pieces will stretch to shape when stuffed, so don't be put off by the unattractive appearance of the pieces at the knitting stage.

Making up the toy

Do not press any part of the work unless the instructions say so. Join the seams with the wrong side of the work outside unless other instructions are given. Normally the main knitted pieces of the toy should be seamed by back-stitching or stab-stitching the row ends together, working one full stitch within each knitted edge. Some knitted pieces need to be seamed by over-sewing the edges together instead of back-stitching and this is always mentioned in the instructions. Use matching yarn when sewing seams.

When adding any extra pieces to a knitted toy, such as knitted arms, hats, or felt pieces, sew them in place with matching sewing thread instead of knitting yarn. This gives a really neat finish to the work. Alternatively you can split the yarn into single strands and use this instead.

Stuffing the toy

Man-made fibre fillings are the most suitable types for stuffing knitted toys because they are washable. Use the best quality you can afford (see page 13). Avoid kapok which is not washable and foam chips which are highly flammable.

Where only very small amounts of stuffing are needed the amount required is not quoted in the instructions.

When stuffing your toy, let the knitted fabric stretch naturally to shape and fill all parts evenly. Do not force more stuffing in than necessary. After filling, the toy should still be soft and yielding to the touch, yet firm enough to spring back into shape again.

Ladder stitch

This is worked in the same way as for the stitched toys (see page 14), using matching knitting yarn.

Making a face

The same general instructions apply to knitted toys as for the stitched toys (see page 14).

On knitted toys it is easy to make sure that the eyes are level, simply check that they are both in line with the same row of knitted stitches.

To work embroidered features

When the head of a toy is to be covered by the hair or a hat then the strand of yarn used for embroidering, for instance, the mouth can be started and finished off at the top or back of the head where it will be hidden. If the stitches can not be covered then proceed as follows. Thread a needle and knot the end of the yarn. Take the needle through the toy from the back of the head or body, passing it *between* the knitted stitches and bringing it out at the position required. Pull the yarn to draw the knotted end right inside the toy and tug, to make sure that the knot is caught in the stuffing. If the knot pulls right through the toy, try again at another place.

Now work the embroidered stitches as required, then pass the needle back through the toy to come out again at a position *between* the knitted stitches. Pass the needle back again between the *same* knitted stitches to come out at a different position. Repeat if necessary until the yarn is securely fastened off then snip off end of yarn. Take care to always pass the needle between the knitted stitches. If you split a stitch then the yarn strand will show on the surface of the toy.

Colouring cheeks

Use an orangey-red pencil the same as for the stitched toys. First try rubbing the knitted stitches with the *side* of the pencil lead using a circular motion. This works very well on most yarns. If it doesn't work then moisten the pencil lead and apply a little colour to the centre of the cheek. Now use a bit of wet fabric to blend the colour into the surrounding knitted stitches.

The colour will come off if the toy is washed but it can be applied again.

To make a twisted yarn cord

Twisted cords are useful for decoration and making little bows where a knitted piece would be too bulky.

To make a cord from a single strand of yarn proceed as follows. First cut a length of yarn, three times as long as the measurement you will require. Knot one end round a door knob and make a loop in the other end to fit loosely over the index finger of your right hand. Now keeping the yarn taut, twist your finger round and round in a clockwise direction, steadying the yarn by holding your left hand cupped around it close to your right hand. Keep twisting until when relaxed, the strand of yarn begins to curl back tightly on itself. Now fold the strand in half, keeping it taut and bringing the ends together. Stroke along the length to make it curl up evenly. Knot both ends of the cord, trimming it to the required length.

To make a cord using two or more strands, use the same method, starting off with the specified number of strands.

USA knitters see page 254.

The knitted toys (yarn weights)

Metric	Imperial
20 g	$\frac{3}{4}$ oz
50 g	$1\frac{3}{4}$ oz

Abbreviations

These are the same for all the designs and should be read before working.

K	knit
P	purl
st[s]	stitch[es]
tog	together
inc	increase [by working twice into the same stitch]
dec	decrease [by working two stitches together]
st-st	stocking stitch [K on the right side, P on the wrong side]
g-st	garter stitch [K on every row]
single rib	K 1 and P 1 alternately, on every row
*	
**	
***	a single asterisk, or group of two or more, is used to mark a place in the instructions which will be referred to later on. Meanwhile, work the row, following the instructions in the usual way
m	metre[s]
cm	centimetre[s]
mm	millimetre[s]
g	gram[s]
[in]	inch or inches
[yd]	yard or yards
[oz]	ounce or ounces

1
LARGE DOLLS

Twin Rag Dolls

Meet the Tearaway Twins, the 48-cm (19-in) high rag dolls – just the right size to play with and cuddle. They have flexible arms and legs and soft short hair that can be brushed this way and that. In addition there is a full set of removable clothes for each doll

For both dolls you need: 50 cm ($\frac{5}{8}$ yd) of 91 cm (36 in) wide pink cotton fabric; 20 cm ($\frac{1}{4}$ yd) of 91 cm (36 in) wide striped or plain fabric for legs; scraps of plain dark fabric for feet; 18 by 44 cm (7 by $17\frac{1}{2}$ in) strip of fur fabric for hair; 500 g (1 lb) of stuffing; scraps of felt and red and black thread for facial features; red pencil for cheeks; adhesive.

Note about doll pattern on page 26
The body and head is a one-piece pattern but since it is too long to fit on the page, it is printed in two pieces. Trace the body and the head patterns onto thin folded paper, placing folded edge of paper to the dotted lines on patterns when tracing. Mark on all details then cut out patterns with paper still folded. Now open up the patterns and join the head to the body at the neckline with sticky tape, to form the complete one piece pattern. Trace all other patterns off the pages and cut out.

Notes: The seam allowance is 5 mm ($\frac{1}{4}$ in) on all pieces unless otherwise stated. Join fabrics with right sides facing. Cut out all pieces with straight grain of fabric in the direction shown on patterns (the body pieces are cut on bias of fabric).

The dolls

Legs: For each leg cut a fabric strip 14 by 19 cm ($5\frac{1}{2}$ by $7\frac{1}{2}$ in). From pattern cut two pairs of foot pieces. Join them in pairs at centre front for about 3 cm ($1\frac{1}{4}$ in). Press seam open then join top edge of each foot to one short edge of each leg strip. Press seam down

towards foot then join long edges of leg and remainder of seam round foot pieces. Turn right side out.

Stuff legs firmly to within 3 cm ($1\frac{1}{4}$ in) of top edges. Put a pin through each leg to hold stuffing in place, bringing top edges together so leg seam is at centre back of leg.

Body: Cut two body pieces, making sure they are on the bias of fabric shown on the pattern.

Mark dart lines at neck on wrong side of each fabric piece, then mark positions of facial features lightly on right side of one piece. Fold each piece on neckline then stitch darts along dotted lines. Trim a little off folded edges of darts. Cut two 1 by 7 cm ($\frac{3}{8}$ by $2\frac{3}{4}$ in) straight strips of pink fabric. Place one beneath each neck dart and stitch again along dart stitching line (this straight strip prevents neck stretching as the body is stuffed).

Join body pieces, leaving top and lower edges open. Turn right side out, turn in lower edges of body 1 cm ($\frac{3}{8}$ in) and tack. Tack top raw edges of each leg together, making a tiny inverted pleat at each side of leg so leg will fit in position shown on lower edge of body pattern. Slip top edges of legs 1 cm ($\frac{3}{8}$ in) between tacked lower edges of body then stitch through body and legs as tacked.

Stuff the body and head firmly. Turn in top raw edges of head and run a strong gathering thread round. Pull up gathers as tightly as possible and fasten off, oversew securely to close any gap. Tie doubled thread tightly round neck at dart lines and sew thread ends into neck.

Arms: Cut two pairs of arm pieces. Join them in pairs round edges leaving upper edges open. Trim seam round hand. Turn and stuff to within 3 cm ($1\frac{1}{4}$ in) of top edges. Take a few stitches through arm at seams 2 cm ($\frac{3}{4}$ in)

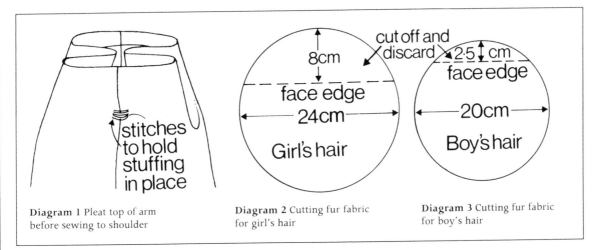

Diagram 1 Pleat top of arm before sewing to shoulder

Diagram 2 Cutting fur fabric for girl's hair

Diagram 3 Cutting fur fabric for boy's hair

down from top edge to hold stuffing in place (see diagram 1). Turn in top raw edges 1 cm ($\frac{3}{8}$ in) and bring seams together making an inverted pleat at each side (see diagram 1). Oversew top edges of each arm together as pleated then sew arms securely to shoulders where shown on pattern.

Face: Mark mouth and nose lines lightly with red pencil then work over mouth with small straight stitches in red. To colour cheeks rub pencil gently over fabric. Work eyelashes with black straight stitches. Cut 1 cm ($\frac{3}{8}$ in) diameter circles of black felt, glue them in place for eyes.

Hair: To make a pattern for girl's hair draw a 24 cm ($9\frac{1}{2}$ in) diameter circle, cut an 8 cm (3 in) section off circle (see diagram 2) and discard it. Using remaining pattern piece, pin pattern on wrong side of fur fabric and cut out carefully snipping through backing to avoid cutting fabric pile.

   Gather round edge of fur fabric, pull up gathers, place on head with straight edge around face then pull up gathers to fit head and fasten off. Adjust position of hair on head and sew to head securely all round. Sew a small ribbon bow to hair.

   Make boy's hair in same way, drawing a 20 cm (8 in) diameter circle and cutting off a 2·5 cm (1 in) section (see diagram 3).

Dolls' clothes

Notes: The seam allowance is 5 mm ($\frac{1}{4}$ in) on all pieces unless otherwise stated. Hems and all casings for elastic are turned 5 mm ($\frac{1}{4}$ in) then 1 cm ($\frac{3}{8}$ in). Join all pieces with right sides facing. Use either buttons or snap fasteners for fastening the garments.

Girl's pants and underskirt

You will need: 50 cm ($\frac{5}{8}$ yd) of 91 cm (36 in) wide white cotton fabric; 1·40 m ($1\frac{5}{8}$ yd) of lace trimming about 2 cm ($\frac{3}{4}$ in) wide; 60 cm ($\frac{3}{4}$ yd) of narrow elastic; 3 buttons or snap fasteners.

To make pants: Cut two pieces from trouser pattern, placing fold line marked on pattern to fold in fabric each time. Hem lower edges of each piece to form casings for elastic. Sew lace trim to lower edge of each casing then thread 16 cm ($6\frac{1}{4}$ in) of elastic through, securing elastic in place at each end.

   Join pants pieces at centre edges then bring these seams together and join inside leg edges. Hem waist edge and thread through a 24 cm ($9\frac{1}{2}$ in) length of elastic.

To make underskirt: Trace off bodice pattern and mark dotted lines at neck, arm-hole and side edges. Cut out pattern on dotted lines.

   Cut out one bodice front piece, placing fold edge of pattern to fold in fabric. Cut out two back pieces. Join front to back pieces at side edges. For a lining make another bodice in same way. Join both pieces round all edges, leaving shoulder and lower edges open. Clip curves in seams and turn bodice right side out. Turn in raw edges at shoulders and press, then slip stitch front and back shoulder edges together.

For skirt cut a fabric strip 24 by 91 cm (9½ by 36 in). Narrowly hem one long edge and sew on lace trim. Make two 5 mm (¼ in) tucks at 1 cm (⅜ in) intervals above hem edge. Join short edges of skirt pieces, taking 1 cm (⅜ in) seam and leaving a gap about 8 cm (3 in) at top of seam for back opening. Press seam open then stitch down turnings on the gap.

Gather upper edge of skirt to fit lower edge of bodice. Join gathered top of skirt to bodice then turn in lower raw edge of bodice lining and slip stitch it over seam. Sew on fastenings at back of bodice.

Girl's dress

You will need: 50 cm (⅝ yd) of 91 cm (36 in) wide fabric; 1·30 m (1½ yd) of narrow ric-rac braid; 24 cm (9½ in) of narrow elastic; 3 buttons or snap fasteners.

To make: Using bodice pattern cut one front piece, placing pattern to fold in fabric where shown, and two back pieces. Join them at sides and shoulders. Make another bodice in same way for lining. Join lining to bodice round neck and back edges. Clip curves in seam, turn right side out and press; tack raw edges of armholes together.

Cut two sleeves, placing fold edge shown on pattern to fold in fabric each time. Make two 5 mm (¼ in) tucks across each sleeve, the first one where shown on pattern and the second about 1·5 cm (⅝ in) below it. Sew ric-rac below second tuck. Join underarm edges of each sleeve. Hem lower edges of sleeves and thread 12 cm (4¾ in) of elastic through each one.

Run a gathering thread along armhole edge of each sleeve where shown on pattern. Pin armhole edges of sleeves into armholes of bodice, matching underarm and sleeve seams and pulling up gathers at tops of sleeves to fit. Sew sleeves in place. Clip seams at curves; oversew raw edges.

For dress skirt cut a fabric strip 26 cm by 91 cm (10¼ by 36 in). Make two tucks as for sleeves – the first about 6 cm (2⅜ in) from one long raw edge. Sew on ric-rac. Hem lower edge; complete as for underskirt.

Girl's apron

You will need: 1·10 m (1¼ yd) of 20·5 cm (8 in) wide broderie Anglaise edging fabric.

To make: For the skirt cut a fabric strip 16 by 78 cm (6¼ by 30¾ in), using broderie edging as one long edge. Hem short ends.

For waistband cut a fabric strip 4 by 28 cm (1½ by 11 in). Fold it in half along length, sew across short ends, turn right side out and press. Gather upper edge of skirt and sew to one long edge of band; turn in and sew remaining edge of band over seam. Make and sew fabric ties to ends of band.

For each shoulder strap cut a plain strip 4 by 14 cm (1½ by 5½ in), and a broderie Anglaise edging 4 by 16 cm (1½ by 6¼ in). Hem short ends of edging and gather to 12 cm (4¾ in). Sew edging centrally to one long edge of strip; sew other long edge of strip over seam.

Place skirt of apron round doll over the dress and tie at centre back. Place a shoulder strap over each shoulder and pin each end in place under waistband, leaving trimming free. Sew straps in place as pinned.

Boy's shirt

You will need: 20 cm (¼ yd) of 91 cm (36 in) wide fabric and a scrap of contrast fabric for bias collar and cuff strips; a scrap of ribbon; 4 buttons or snap fasteners.

To make: Add 5 cm (2 in) to lower edge of bodice pattern and trim 1 cm (⅜ in) off neck edge. Cut out bodice front and backs from this pattern as for girl's bodice. Join side and shoulder seams. Make another bodice in same way for lining. Join lining to bodice round back and lower edges, turn right side out and press.

Cut a 4 by 22 cm (1½ by 8¾ in) bias strip of fabric for neckband. Bind raw neck edges with this strip, stretching the strip to fit as it is sewn in place.

Cut two sleeves, shortening length to the line shown on sleeve pattern. Cut two 4 by 14 cm (1½ by 5½ in) bias strips of fabric for cuffs. Sew one long edge of each strip to lower edge of each sleeve, stretching strips to fit as they are sewn in place. Join underarm edges of sleeves then turn in remaining raw edges of bias strips and slip stitch in place over seams.

Set sleeves into bodice armholes as before. Sew a ribbon bow to front of neckband and fastenings to back edges.

Trousers

You will need: A small piece of fabric for trousers and thin fabric for lining; 2 buttons and 2 snap fasteners.

To make: Cut two trouser pieces from fabric, cutting leg length as shown on pattern. Make as for girl's pants, omitting elastic and lace trim in hemmed waist and lower edges.

For shoulder straps cut two 6 by 25 cm (2⅜ by 9¾ in) fabric strips. Join long edges of each strip and across one short end. Turn right side out and press. Place the remaining raw edge of each strap inside back edge of pants on each side of centre seam. Sew these ends in place at an angle so straps will cross over at back before passing over shoulders.

Make lining as for pants using thin fabric, but do *not* hem upper and lower edges. Place lining inside pants, wrong sides facing, and slip stitch upper edge and lower leg edges to pants, making slightly larger turnings on lining so it does not show on right side. Sew snap fasteners to fasten strap ends, sew buttons to outside of pants at same position.

For underpants use trouser pattern, cutting leg shorter as shown. Make as for girl's pants, omitting lace trim.

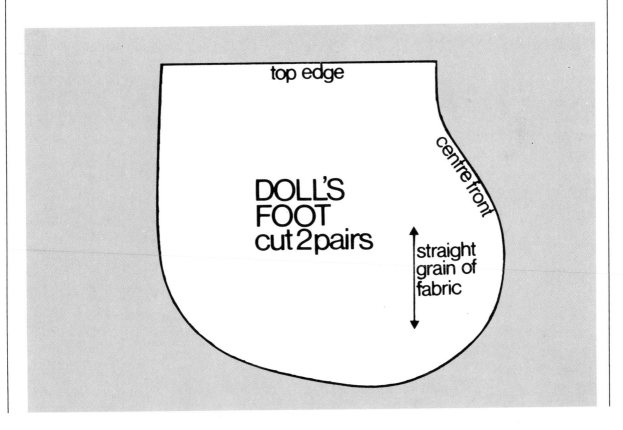

top edge

centre front

DOLL'S FOOT cut 2 pairs

straight grain of fabric

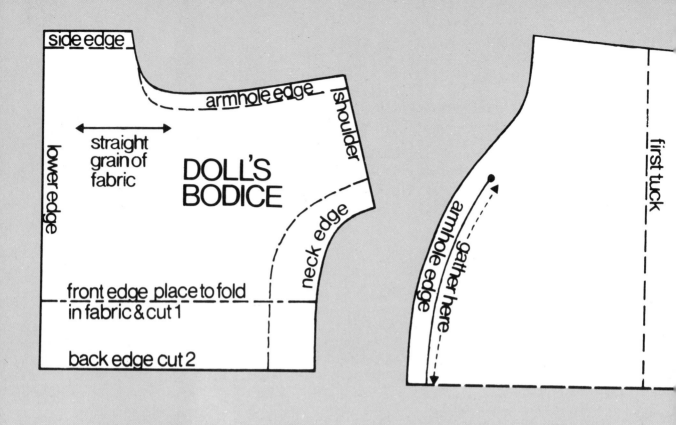

side edge

armhole edge

shoulder

straight grain of fabric

DOLL'S BODICE

lower edge

neck edge

front edge place to fold in fabric & cut 1

back edge cut 2

armhole edge

gather here

first tuck

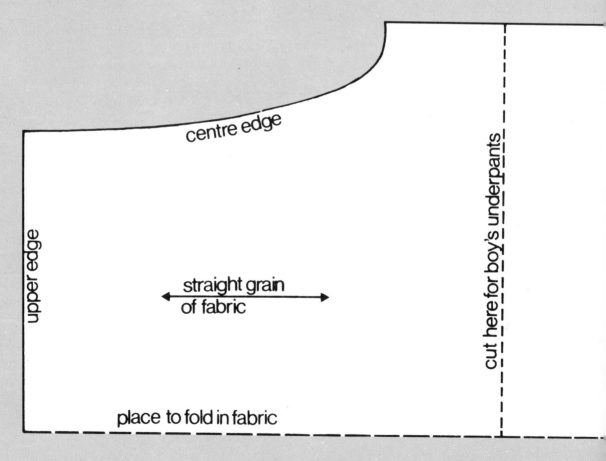

centre edge

upper edge

straight grain of fabric

cut here for boy's underpants

place to fold in fabric

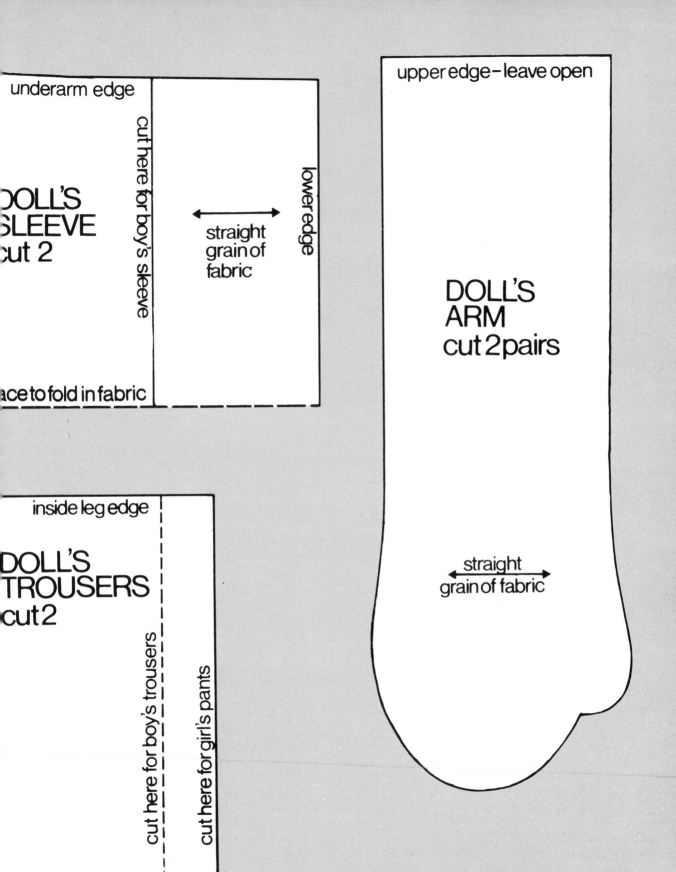

underarm edge

DOLL'S SLEEVE
cut 2

cut here for boy's sleeve

straight grain of fabric

lower edge

ace to fold in fabric

inside leg edge

DOLL'S TROUSERS
cut 2

cut here for boy's trousers

cut here for girl's pants

upper edge – leave open

DOLL'S ARM
cut 2 pairs

straight grain of fabric

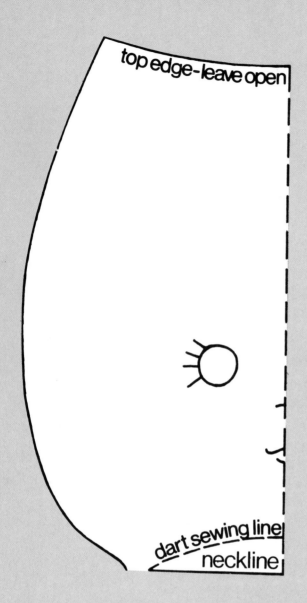

top edge-leave open

dart sewing line

neckline

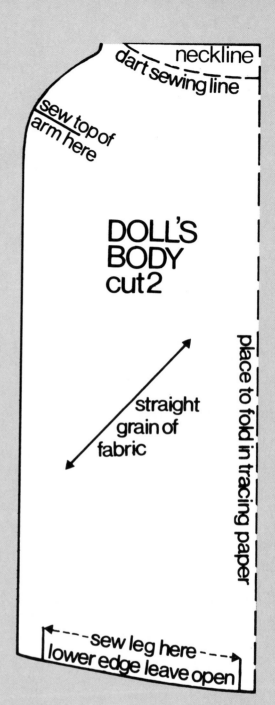

neckline

dart sewing line

sew top of arm here

DOLL'S BODY cut 2

straight grain of fabric

place to fold in tracing paper

sew leg here

lower edge leave open

The Adaptable Rag Doll

You can use the same, easy method to make these three 46-cm (18-in) high rag dolls.
One is a dressing-up doll (with removable clothes). The second is a pretty nightdress
case. The third is a topsy-turvy doll based on a popular nursery rhyme

For the doll you will need: Stockinette (the kind sold in rolls for household cleaning and polishing cars which can be bought in rolls in Woolworths, supermarkets and car accessory shops. It is about 22 cm (8¾ in) wide, and one large roll is enough to make three dolls; about 113 g (¼ lb) of stuffing; a small ball of thick-knit yarn; scraps of black felt, red pencil; black and red thread for face; white tape; adhesive.

Note: Take 1 cm (⅜ in) seams, except where stated otherwise.

Dressing-up doll

For the body and head cut a 30 cm (12 in) length off the stockinette roll. Fold it in half bringing side edges of roll together and join these edges. Gather one end of the tube, pull up gathers and fasten them securely (this will be the top of the head). Turn right side out and insert stuffing, to make a sausage shape measuring about 28 cm (11 in) around. Turn in and oversew remaining raw edges (see diagram 1).

To make the neck, tie a length of tape very tightly round the shape, 13 cm (5 in) down from top of head. Cut the tape ends short and sew them into back of neck.

For eyes, cut two 1 cm (⅜ in) diameter circles of black felt and glue them in place 5 cm (2 in) up from neck and 2·5 cm (1 in) apart. Work eyelashes in black thread. Use red thread to work a small straight stitch for mouth, 2 cm (¾ in) below eyes.

Moisten the point of red pencil and rub a little colour over cheeks. Blend colour into cheeks by rubbing with a piece of wet cloth.

For hair, wind yarn three times round two fingers, then sew these loops to head, beginning at one side of head. Continue making loops and sewing them in place across forehead to the other side of head. (The hat will cover the rest of the head.)

For each leg, cut a 24 cm (9½ in) length of stockinette. Fold it in half to bring the side edges of the roll together, then fold in half again (see diagram 2) and sew all the 24 cm (9½ in) edges together taking a 5 mm (¼ in) seam. Continue the seam round one end as

shown in diagram 2. Trim off corners and turn right side out. Stuff the leg until it measures 13 cm (5 in) around. Turn in and oversew remaining raw edges then sew leg to lower edge of body.

For each arm, cut a 19 cm (7½ in) length of stockinette. Make as for legs, but take a 1 cm (⅜ in) seam. Stuff arm to measure 11 cm (4¼ in) around, leaving 4 cm (1½ in) at top unstuffed. Turn in and oversew raw edges; sew an arm to each side of body, 2·5 cm (1 in) down from neck. For wrist tie thread round, 5 cm (2 in) from end of arm.

Doll's clothes

For patterns, copy the outlines shown on diagram square by square, on to metric graph paper (each square on diagram equals 1 cm). Join all fabrics with right sides facing.

Shoes

You will need: Scraps of felt.

To make: Cut four shoe pieces from pattern; on two of them cut out shape shown by dotted line on pattern. Join shoe pieces in pairs round curved edges, taking 5 mm (¼ in) seam. Turn right side out, fit shoes on doll's legs and sew in place.

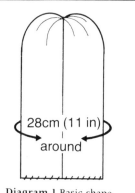 

28cm (11 in) around

Diagram 1 Basic shape for body and head. Oversew lower edges together, with upright seam placed at centre back

Diagram 2 For arms and legs, fold stockinette in half down length, then in half again, and sew seam as shown

Pantaloons

You will need: 25 cm (9¾ in) of 91 cm (36 in) wide fabric (this fabric is also used for neck and cuff bindings on the dress); elastic and lace trimming.

To make: Cut two pantaloon pieces, placing edge of pattern indicated to fold in fabric. Join pieces at centre seams; clip seams at curves. Hem lower leg edges and sew on trimming. Join inside leg edges. Hem waist edge, taking a 1 cm (⅜ in) turning twice, then thread through elastic.

Dress

You will need: 30 cm (12 in) of 91 cm (36 in) wide fabric; fabric oddments left from pantaloons for contrast edging; 2 snap fasteners.

To make: Cut one front, two backs and two sleeves as directed on the pattern. Join centre back edges of back pieces to within 14 cm (5½ in) of neck edge. Press seam open and stitch down remaining raw edges. Join armhole edges of sleeves to front and back of dress and clip curves.

Gather the lower edges of sleeves to fit doll's arms loosely, then bind them with 4 cm (1½ in) wide bias strips of contrast fabric. Gather neck edge to fit neck and bind this in same way. Join sides of dress and sleeves; hem lower edge. Sew snap fasteners to back opening.

Pinafore and hat

You will need: 55 cm (21½ in) of 91 cm (36 in) wide fabric; ribbon for the hat band.

To make pinafore: Cut a fabric strip 18 by 91 cm (7 by 36 in). Gather one long edge to measure 26 cm (10¼ in), hem other edges.

For waistband cut a fabric strip 5 by 68 cm (2 by 26¾ in); bind gathered edge of pinafore with this, leaving an equal portion of waistband at each side for ties.

For each shoulder strap cut a fabric strip 5 by 15 cm (2 by 6 in). Join long edges of each strip and turn right side out. Sew ends of shoulder straps to inside of waistband.

To make hat: Cut two 30 cm (12 in) diameter circles of fabric. Join them round edges, taking 5 mm (¼ in) seam and leaving a gap for turning. Turn right side out, slip stitch opening. Gather round hat 4 cm (1½ in) from edge, pull up gathers to fit doll's head behind hair, and fasten off. Put a little stuffing in hat, then sew it to head all round. Sew ribbon over gathers.

Nightdress-case doll

You will need: Stockinette, yarn etc. as for making the dressing-up doll.

For her clothes: 50 cm (19½ in) of 91 cm (36 in) wide fabric; contrast fabric for hat and apron; oddment of fabric for the case lining; 5 snap fasteners; 1·20 m (1⅜ yd) of lace edging.

To make the doll: For the body and head, cut a 26 cm (10¼ in) length of stockinette. Sew, stuff and slip stitch lower edges, then make neck and face, as for dressing-up doll.

For fringe, wind yarn twice round two fingers and stitch loops to centre of doll's forehead.

For hair, wind yarn three times round a 24 cm (9½ in) piece of card, slip yarn off the card and sew centre of strands above fringe then sew loops to each side of the doll's head as shown in illustration.

Her clothes

Make the hat as for dressing-up doll. For dress bodice, cut a fabric strip 8 by 30 cm (3 by 12 in). Join short edges, and turn right side out. Place bodice on doll. Turn in raw edge at neck, place lace edging round the turned-in edge and run a gathering thread round through lace and fabric. Pull up gathers round neck and fasten off. Turn in remaining raw edge at waist and slip stitch it to doll's body.

Make arms as for dressing-up doll but stuff them only halfway up. Trim 1 cm (⅜ in) off upper edge of each arm and oversew raw edges together, pulling stitches to gather. For each sleeve cut a fabric strip 16 by 17 cm (6¼ by 6¾ in). Join short edges, turn right side out and slip a sleeve over each arm. Turn in wrist edge, add lace and gather as for neck of

bodice. Turn in top edge of each sleeve and oversew, pulling stitches to gather. Sew top of a sleeve each side of doll, 2 cm ($\frac{3}{4}$ in) down from neck.

For case lining, cut a fabric strip 28 by 72 cm (11 by 28$\frac{1}{2}$ in) and join short edges. Hem one remaining raw edge then gather the other edge to fit round doll's waist and sew it, through the gathers, over the waist edge of the bodice all round. Sew snap fasteners to the lower edge of case.

For the skirt, cut a fabric strip 30 by 91 cm (12 by 36 in). Join the short edges, hem lower edge and sew on lace trim, then gather the waist edge. Sew skirt round waist on top of the case lining.

For the apron, cut a fabric piece 18 by 24 cm (7 by 9$\frac{1}{2}$ in). Gather one long edge and hem remaining raw edges. Sew gathered edge to waist. For apron waistband, cut a strip of matching fabric 4 cm (1$\frac{1}{2}$ in) wide; turn in and press raw edges then sew strip round doll's waist to cover all raw fabric edges at waist.

Topsy-turvy doll

There was a little girl, who had a little curl
Right in the middle of her forehead.
When she was good she was very, very good,
But when she was bad she was horrid!

You will need: Stockinette, yarn etc. as for the dressing-up doll.

For her clothes: 50 cm (19$\frac{1}{2}$ in) of 91 cm (36 in) wide fabric for each end of doll; pieces of contrast fabric for hats and belts; 2·30 m (2$\frac{1}{2}$ yd) of lace edging or trimming.

The doll

For her body and both heads, cut a 38 cm (15 in) length of stockinette. Join long edges, turn and stuff as for the dressing-up doll. Gather the remaining raw edges, turn them in and fasten off securely. Tie tapes tightly round the sausage shape, 13 cm (5$\frac{1}{8}$ in) away from each gathered end, to form each neck.

Make smiling face as for dressing-up doll, stitching a V-shape for smiling mouth. For the scowling face, cut a little off the top of each eye and instead of eyelashes work a single black stitch across top of each eye. Work an inverted V-shape for sulky mouth.

For each 'curl', twist a yarn strand until it curls up tightly, then sew a curl to each forehead. Make hair as for nightdress case.

Her clothes

For each dress bodice, cut a fabric strip 8 by 30 cm (3 by 12 in). Join the strips at one long edge, taking a 5 mm ($\frac{1}{4}$ in) seam. Join short edges, then fit bodice on doll and gather and trim both neck edges as for nightdress case.

Make four arms and sleeves in the same

way as for the nightdress case.

For each skirt, cut a fabric strip 30 by 91 cm (12 by 36 in). Join short edges of each strip then place them right sides together and join one long edge, at the same time enclosing a strip of lace edging between the seam so the edging will extend below lower edge of skirt when turned right side out. Turn skirt right side out, bringing raw edges together; press.

Gather each remaining raw edge separately to fit round doll's waist. Place one gathered edge round seam at doll's waist (making sure the skirt fabric matches bodice fabric) then back stitch skirt to doll through gathers all round. Turn doll the other way up and back stitch the remaining skirt in place in same way. To cover raw edges of skirts cut a 4 cm (1½ in) wide strip of contrast fabric, turn in and press raw edges then sew each band round waist.

For each hat cut two 22 cm (8¾ in) diameter circles of contrast fabric. Make each hat as for dressing-up doll, but omit the stuffing and gather 2·5 cm (1 in) from edge.

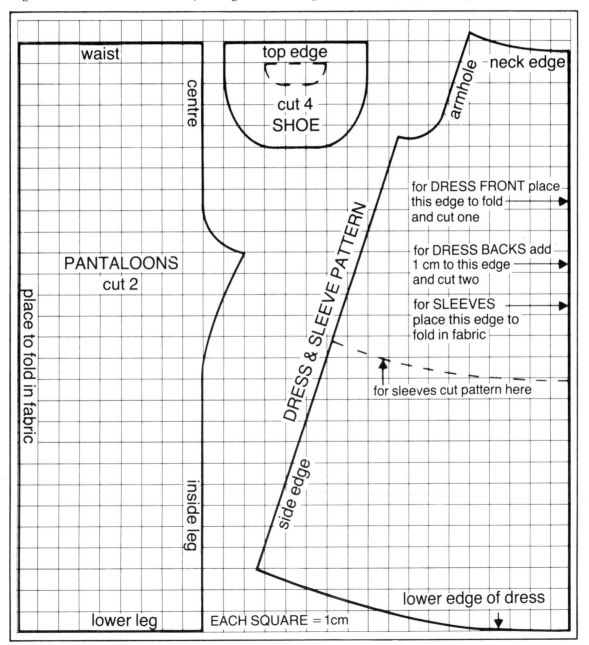

Jennifer Rag Doll

Jennifer is a big armful of a rag doll – about 61 cm (24 in) tall. She is made from cotton stockinette with yarn hair divided into ten plaits. She also has lots of removable clothes – pantaloons and petticoat, dress, apron and mob cap.

For the doll you will need: 50 cm ($\frac{5}{8}$ yd) of pink cotton stockinette – tubular knit 57 cm ($22\frac{1}{2}$ in) wide, opening out to 114 cm (45 in) width; 600 g ($1\frac{1}{4}$ lb) of stuffing; one 50 g ball of double knitting yarn for hair; short length of tape for joining hair to head; two black trouser-type buttons, about 2 cm ($\frac{3}{4}$ in) in diameter, for eyes (or if doll is for a very young child, use circles of black felt); strong black and pink thread; red pencil for colouring cheeks; pieces of felt, narrow ric-rac braid, and ribbon for shoes; red, pink, black embroidery thread; metric graph paper; adhesive.

Notes: Copy all patterns from the diagrams on pages 65–6, square by square, on to graph paper, and mark on all details. Each square on diagram = 5 cm. For body and head pieces, draw pattern for back of doll following outline, then draw pattern again for front and trim pattern along centre back dotted line as indicated.

Take care to cut out stockinette pieces with most stretch in fabric going in the direction shown on each pattern. Take 5 mm ($\frac{1}{4}$ in) seams unless stated otherwise. Use a small machine stitch when sewing stockinette, and stretch the fabric slightly as it is stitched, so seams will not snap when pieces are stuffed.

The doll

Body and head

Cut one pair of back pieces and mark dots on right side of fabric for position of eyes. Join pieces at centre back edges, taking a 1 cm ($\frac{3}{8}$ in) seam and leaving a gap in seam as indicated. Cut one front piece, placing edge indicated to fold in fabric. Mark dots on right side of fabric for eye positions and corners of mouth.

Join front to back, right sides facing, all round edges. Clip seam at neck and trim seam round lower corners of body. Turn right side out through back opening.

Stuff head, neck and body very firmly, then ladderstitch gap in seam. (When stuffed, the head should measure about 39 cm ($15\frac{1}{2}$ in) around, and the body about 37 cm ($14\frac{1}{2}$ in) around.) Tie four strands of strong pink thread round neck, pulling and knotting threads tightly at back of doll to shape neck. Sew thread ends into neck.

To sew on buttons for eyes, use a long darning needle and doubled strong black thread. Take threads through from dot at back of head to dot at front. Thread on button through one pair of holes, with upper surface of each button against face. Take thread through to back of head again and knot threads tightly to depress button into face. Repeat once more through remaining pair of holes in button. Lift button carefully away from face, and spread a little glue underneath to fix eyes firmly to face.

Indent corners of mouth as for eyes, using darning needle, single strong pink thread, and taking threads through from back of head near positions of eye threads.

Colour cheeks by rubbing fabric with the *side* (not the point) of the red pencil. Mark on eyelashes and also a shallow U-shape between indented corners of mouth. Mark on nose as shown in illustration on page 35.

When embroidering facial features which follow, start and fasten off embroidery threads at back of head. Take the threads through to face with a long darning needle, use an ordinary needle to work the stitches, then pass threads through to back of head with darning needle again. Work small back stitches in red for mouth, then work oversewing stitches through each back stitch. Work the nose in the same way, using pink, then work straight black stitches for eyelashes.

Legs and shoes

Cut two leg pieces, placing edge of pattern indicated to fold in fabric each time. Cut two pairs of shoe pieces and two soles from felt. Join centre front edges of shoe pieces and trim seams. Now stitch ankle edges of legs to upper edges of shoes, with right sides facing, raw edges level and stretching stockinette to fit edges of felt. Join centre back edges of legs and shoes and trim seams. Tack, then stitch soles to shoes, matching points A and B. Trim seams.

Turn legs right side out and stuff firmly. Turn in top edges and oversew, with leg seams at centre back of legs. Sew ric-rac round top edges of shoes and sew ribbon bows to fronts of shoes. Sew legs securely to lower edge of body.

Arms

Cut out arms as for legs. Stitch seams then turn and stuff to within 3 cm ($1\frac{1}{4}$ in) of top edges. Turn in top edges and oversew, with each arm seam at underarm, pulling stitches tightly to gather. Tie strong pink thread tightly round each arm, 6 cm ($2\frac{3}{8}$ in) from ends, to shape wrists, then sew thread ends into arms. Sew ar   to sides of body, 3 cm ($1\frac{1}{4}$ in) down from neck.

Hair

For fringe, wind a strand of yarn twenty times round an 8 cm (3 in) piece of card. Slip yarn off card and sew loops together at one end. Sew fringe to top of head to hang down over forehead.

For hair, cut remaining yarn into 70 cm (28 in) lengths. Keep aside a few lengths for knotting round ends of plaits. Now stitch centres of yarn to a 20 cm (8 in) length of tape, keeping yarn 1 cm ($\frac{3}{8}$ in) within each end of tape. Turn in ends of tape then sew hair, tape side down, to centre parting position on head, starting about 6 cm ($2\frac{3}{8}$ in)

above eyes. Now smooth all the yarn strands down sides and back of head, then tie a length of tape round head, level with eyes, to hold strands in place.

Divide strands at each side of head into five roughly equal sections. Plait each section below the tape, making plaits of equal length. Knot strands of yarn round ends of plaits. Remove the tape, then catch each plait to head with small stitches taken through tops of plaits and into head. Trim yarn ends to even lengths on all plaits.

The clothes

Notes: Take 1 cm ($\frac{3}{8}$ in) seams and turnings on all pieces, unless stated otherwise. Join fabric with right sides facing unless other instructions are given.

Pantaloons and petticoat

You will need: 90 cm (1 yd) of 91 cm (36 in) wide fabric; short lengths of narrow elastic; 60 cm (24 in) strip of narrow ribbon or tape for the elastic casing on legs of pantaloons; 6 m ($6\frac{5}{8}$ yd) of narrow frilled lace edging; three snap fasteners.

To make pantaloons: Cut two pieces, placing edge of pattern indicated to fold in fabric each time. Narrowly hem lower edges of each piece and sew on lace edging, then sew another row of lace edging above first row. Sew ribbon or tape to wrong side of each piece, as shown by dotted lines on pattern. Thread elastic through to fit legs and secure it at each side of casing with a few stitches.

Now join pieces to each other at centre edges, stitching twice at curved parts of seams to reinforce. Trim seams at curves. Bring centre seams together and stitch inside leg seams on each leg. Turn pantaloons right side out and hem waist edge, taking 1 cm ($\frac{3}{8}$ in) turnings twice. Thread elastic through to fit doll's waist.

To make petticoat: Cut bodice front, placing dotted line shown on pattern to fold in fabric. Cut one pair of back pieces to pattern outline. Turn in shoulder edges of each piece and press. Join front to backs at side edges and trim seams. Make a lining for bodice from same fabric in same way.

Join lining to bodice round neck, armhole and centre back edges. Trim seams and clip curves. Turn bodice right side out, then slip stitch front shoulder edges of bodice to back shoulder edges. Join shoulder edges of lining in same way. Press bodice, then sew lace edging round armholes and neck edge.

For petticoat skirt, cut a strip of fabric 18 by 91 cm (7 by 36 in), then cut two strips 10 by 91 cm (4 by 36 in) for skirt frill. Cut one frill strip in half across width, and join one short end of each half to ends of the other frill strip. Narrowly hem one long edge of frill and sew on two rows of lace edging as for pantaloons. Gather remaining long raw edge of frill strip to fit one long edge of skirt, then sew it in place, right sides facing and raw edges level. Join short edges of skirt, from frilled hem to within 10 cm (4 in) of waist edge. Neaten open edges for back opening of skirt.

Gather waist edge of skirt to fit lower edge of petticoat bodice. Sew it to bodice, right sides facing, raw edges level and leaving bodice lining free. Turn in lower edge of lining and slipstitch it over seam.

Sew lace edging round petticoat at waist seam, then sew snap fasteners to centre back edges of bodice.

The dress

You will need: 80 cm ($\frac{7}{8}$ yd) of 91 cm (36 in) wide printed fabric; 3 m ($3\frac{3}{8}$ yd) of broderie anglaise lace edging; 2 m ($2\frac{1}{4}$ yd) of wide ric-rac braid; 70 cm (28 in) of narrow ric-rac braid; four snap fasteners.

To make dress: For the skirt cut two strips of fabric 25 by 91 cm (10 by 36 in). Cut one strip in half across width and join one end of each half to an end of long strip. Stitch top of lace edging to skirt, about 5 cm (2 in) above one long edge (this is the hem edge of skirt). Sew wide ric-rac to top edge of lace. Now join short edges of skirt, from hem edge to within 10 cm (4 in) of waist edge. Press

seam to one side and neaten raw edges of opening. Narrowly hem lower edge of skirt.

Cut bodice front, placing dotted line shown on pattern to fold in fabric. Cut one pair of backs to pattern outline. Join front to backs at shoulder edges. Turn in centre back edges of bodice 1 cm ($\frac{3}{8}$ in) twice and stitch in place.

Cut a 50 cm (19$\frac{1}{2}$ in) length of lace edging and neaten ends. Gather it to fit round neck of bodice, then sew raw edge to raw edge of neck, with right sides of both uppermost and raw edges level. Now bind neck edge of bodice with a 4 cm (1$\frac{1}{2}$ in) wide bias strip of fabric, trimming seam before sewing second edge of binding in place. Sew narrow ric-rac to bias, next to lace edging.

Join dress front to backs at side edges. Cut two dress sleeves, placing pattern to fold in fabric each time. Run gathering threads between dots at shoulder edges of sleeves. Join underarm edges of sleeves. Tack shoulder edges of sleeves into armholes of bodice, matching underarm seams to side seams and pulling up gathers to fit bodice armholes. Stitch seams twice. Trim seams.

For each wrist frill, cut a 35 cm (13$\frac{1}{2}$ in) strip of lace edging. Join ends of each, then gather to fit wrist edges of sleeves. Sew gathered edges of lace to wrist edges of sleeves, with right sides facing and raw edges level.

Bind these raw edges with 3 cm (1$\frac{1}{4}$ in) wide bias strips of fabric, turning bias completely to wrong side when sewing second edge in place. Sew narrow ric-rac above frills.

Gather waist edge of skirt to fit lower edge of bodice, then sew it in place. Sew snap fasteners to back edges of bodice.

The apron

You will need: 60 cm ($\frac{3}{4}$ yd) of 91 cm (36 in) wide fabric; 3 m ($3\frac{3}{8}$ yd) of ric-rac braid; two hooks and eyes; four small buttons.

To make apron: Cut one apron bodice back, placing edge indicated to fold in fabric. Cut one pair of bodice fronts. Join fronts to back at side and shoulder edges. Make another bodice for lining in same way. Join bodice to

lining at centre front and around neck edges. Trim seams and clip curves and corners. Turn right side out. Tack armhole edges together.

Cut two apron sleeves, placing edge shown on pattern to fold in fabric each time. Take narrow hems on lower edges of sleeves, then sew on ric-rac. Join underarm edges of sleeves. Run gathering threads all round shoulder edges of sleeves, then pull up gathers to fit bodice armholes. Sew sleeves in place, matching underarm seams to side seams of bodice, and matching dots on sleeves to shoulder seams of bodice. Trim seams and neaten raw edges. Hand-sew ric-rac up fronts of bodice and around neck, taking care not to catch lining to bodice at centre front edges.

For apron skirt, cut two strips of fabric 18 by 60 cm (7 by 24 in). Join them at one short edge, for centre back seam of skirt. At remaining short edges, cut a generous curve from one long edge round on to short edges (this will be hem edge of skirt). Narrowly hem this long edge, round curves and up short edges. Sew on ric-rac as shown on illustration on front cover.

Gather remaining long raw edge of skirt to fit lower edge of bodice. Sew gathered edge to bodice, right sides facing, raw edges level and leaving bodice lining free. Turn in lower raw edge of bodice lining and slipstitch it over seam. Sew ric-rac round waist edge of bodice, then sew hooks and eyes to front edges and sew on buttons as shown on illustration on the frontispiece.

Mob cap

You will need: A strip of fabric 38 by 82 cm (15 by $32\frac{1}{2}$ in); 1 m ($1\frac{1}{8}$ yd) of narrow ric-rac braid; short length of elastic; scrap of fabric or felt to match ric-rac, and a little stuffing; ribbon for bow.

To make mob cap: Fold fabric strip in half down length, right side out, and press folded edge. Open up again and stitch ric-rac about 1 cm ($\frac{3}{8}$ in) away from pressed fold. Join short edges of strip for centre back seam. Fold strip in half down length as before, and tack long edges together.

For elastic casing, run a line of stitching round cap, about 4 cm ($1\frac{1}{2}$ in) above ric-rac, then stitch again 1 cm ($\frac{3}{8}$ in) above first line of stitching. On inside of cap, unpick centre back seam between stitching lines for elastic casing, then thread elastic through to fit doll's head, and slipstitch seam again.

Run a gathering thread round remaining top raw edges of cap, pulling up gathers tightly until raw edges touch. Fasten off. To cover these raw edges, gather and stuff an 8 cm (3 in) diameter circle of fabric to match ric-rac. Sew this to top of cap to cover gathered raw edges. Sew ribbon bow to front of mob cap.

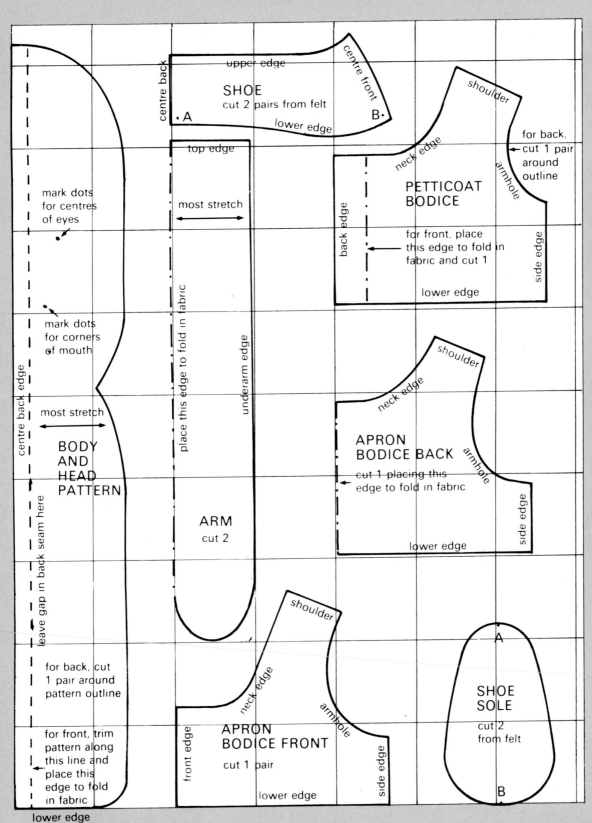

SHOE
cut 2 pairs from felt

upper edge
centre back
lower edge
. A
B .
centre front

PETTICOAT BODICE
shoulder
neck edge
armhole
for back, ← cut 1 pair around outline
back edge
for front, place ← this edge to fold in fabric and cut 1
side edge
lower edge

mark dots for centres of eyes

mark dots for corners of mouth

centre back edge

most stretch

BODY AND HEAD PATTERN

leave gap in back seam here

for back, cut 1 pair around pattern outline

for front, trim pattern along ← this line and place this edge to fold in fabric

lower edge

top edge

most stretch

place this edge to fold in fabric

underarm edge

ARM
cut 2

APRON BODICE BACK
shoulder
neck edge
armhole
cut 1 placing this ← edge to fold in fabric
side edge
lower edge

shoulder
neck edge

APRON BODICE FRONT
cut 1 pair
front edge
armhole
side edge
lower edge

SHOE SOLE
cut 2 from felt
A
B

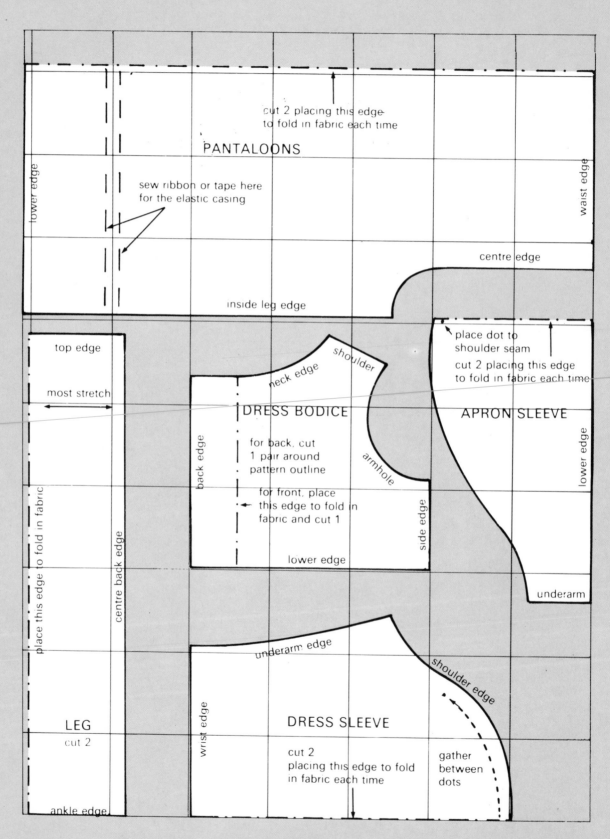

PANTALOONS

cut 2 placing this edge to fold in fabric each time

sew ribbon or tape here for the elastic casing

lower edge

waist edge

centre edge

inside leg edge

place dot to shoulder seam

cut 2 placing this edge to fold in fabric each time

DRESS BODICE

for back, cut 1 pair around pattern outline

for front, place this edge to fold in fabric and cut 1

neck edge

shoulder

armhole

back edge

side edge

lower edge

APRON SLEEVE

lower edge

underarm

top edge

most stretch

place this edge to fold in fabric

centre back edge

LEG

cut 2

ankle edge

underarm edge

wrist edge

DRESS SLEEVE

cut 2 placing this edge to fold in fabric each time

shoulder edge

gather between dots

Best-dressed Doll

This 43 cm (17 in) rag doll has six different outfits of clothes. All patterns for the doll and clothes are printed full-size for you to trace off the pages.

For the doll you will need: 30 cm ($\frac{3}{8}$ yd) of 91 cm (36 in) wide pink cotton fabric; 250 g ($\frac{1}{2}$ lb) of stuffing; small pieces of white fabric, black and white felt; 20 g ball of 4-ply yarn; red thread and red pencil for facial features; two small buttons for shoes; adhesive.

Important note about the doll patterns on page 43–5

The body and head is a one-piece pattern but since it is too long to fit on the page, it is printed in two pieces. Trace the body and the head patterns on to thin folded paper, placing folded edge of paper to the dotted lines on patterns when tracing. Mark on all details then cut out patterns with paper still folded. Now open up the patterns and join the head to body at the neckline with sticky tape, to form the complete one-piece pattern.

General notes: Trace all the other patterns off the pages. The doll's legs are straight strips of fabric, and measurements for these are given in the instructions.

The clothes are made in the same basic way using three patterns – bodice, sleeve and pants. Clothes are varied by cutting these patterns to different lengths. When making, read basic instructions, then refer to individual instructions for each garment.

5 mm ($\frac{1}{4}$ in) seams are allowed on all pieces unless otherwise stated. For all hems, turn in raw edges 5 mm ($\frac{1}{4}$ in) then 1 cm ($\frac{3}{8}$ in) and stitch down.

The doll

Legs and shoes: Cut two pairs of shoe uppers from felt. Join them in pairs at fronts then trim seams. For each leg cut a piece of pink fabric 14 by 16 cm ($5\frac{1}{2}$ by $6\frac{1}{4}$ in). For each sock top cut a piece of white fabric 5 by 14 cm (2 by $5\frac{1}{2}$ in). Fold the sock piece, right side out, bringing long edges together. Tack these edges to one 14 cm ($5\frac{1}{2}$ in) edge of

each leg piece, with raw edges level. Now join these edges to upper edges of shoes, with sock tops sandwiched between legs and shoes. Join the remaining long edges of legs and back edges of shoes.

Cut two soles from felt. Keeping legs wrong sides out, oversew edges of soles to lower edges of shoes all round, matching points A and B. Turn legs right side out and stuff firmly to within 2 cm ($\frac{3}{4}$ in) of tops. Tack top edges together, with seams at centre back.

To complete each shoe place a piece of folded white felt over dotted outline on shoe pattern, with fold against front edge then cut out. Sew these pieces to shoe fronts, then sew on buttons as shown in the illustrations on page 39.

Body: Cut two body pieces. Stitch neck darts on each piece and trim folded edges of darts. Join body pieces together round edges, leaving lower edges open. Clip seam at neck. Stitch upper edges of legs to lower edge of one body piece, with right sides facing and raw edges level. Turn body right side out and stuff firmly. Turn in remaining lower edge and slipstitch over seam at tops of legs.

Face: Work mouth in back stitch using red thread, then work back again, oversewing through each stitch. Mark on nose and colour it and cheeks by rubbing with red pencil. Cut eyes from black felt, glue in place then work eyelashes.

Hair: Sew a few loops of yarn to forehead as shown on pattern. For hair at back of head cut about forty 80 cm ($31\frac{1}{2}$ in) lengths of yarn. Backstitch ends of yarn strands to one side of face as shown on pattern. Take strands across back of head and backstitch them to face at opposite side. Repeat this, taking strands backwards and forwards, working up towards top of head until back of head is covered. For a centre parting at back of head, take a long stitch from back of head near neck, to the loops of yarn at front, using matching thread.

For front hair cut about fifty 40 cm (16 in) yarn lengths. Machine stitch through centre of strands and sew this centre parting line to top of head above fringe. Take strands to each side of head, covering ends of yarn that form back hair, and sew yarn strands in place, then plait them and trim the ends evenly.

Arms: Cut two pairs of arm pieces. Join in pairs, leaving upper edges open. Trim seams and turn right side out. Stuff firmly to within 3 cm (1¼ in) of upper edges then stuff lightly. Turn in upper edges and gather them to close. Sew an arm to each side of body, 1·5 cm (⅝ in) down from neck.

Her clothes

For all the clothes you will need: Small pieces of fabrics, stretchy fabric for track suit and T-shirt, lace edging, trimmings, narrow elastic, narrow ribbon; small snap fasteners; hooks and eyes; short open-ended zip fastener for track suit; two small buttons. For posy – card, cockleshells, silver bells, fabric flowers and adhesive.

Basic pants: Cut two pants pieces, placing side edge indicated for each garment on pattern to fold in fabric and cutting lower edges as given for each garment. Hem lower edges and if stated thread through elastic to fit legs. Join pieces at centre edges and clip curves. Bring centre seams together and join inside leg edges. Hem waist edge and thread through elastic to fit.

Basic dress: Cut bodice front, one pair of backs and two sleeves as directed on pattern, cutting lower edges as given for each garment. Cut a 2·5 cm (1 in) wide bias strip of fabric long enough to bind neck edge. Join front to backs at shoulders. Turn in and hem centre back edges. Bind neck edge. Hem lower edges of sleeves and thread elastic through to fit arms. Sew trimming to bodice as shown in illustrations. Gather armhole edges of sleeves between dots as shown on pattern and pull up gathers to fit bodice armholes. Sew armholes of sleeves to bodice. Join side and underarm edges.

Cut dress skirt strip as directed in

individual instructions for each garment. Join short edges taking a 1 cm (⅜ in) seam and leaving 6 cm (2⅜ in) open at top of seam for back opening. Neaten raw edges of opening and press seam to one side. Hem lower edge of skirt and sew on trimming as shown in illustrations. Gather remaining raw edge of skirt to fit lower edge of bodice and sew in place. Sew snap fasteners to back of bodice.

Underpants: Cut lower edges to line A and trim 1 cm (⅜ in) off waist edges. Sew lace trimming to lower edges before threading through the elastic.

Mary, Mary, quite contrary outfit

Pantaloons: Using pants pattern cut lower edges to line B. Sew lace trim to lower hemmed edges. Cut two 16 cm (6¼ in) lengths of elastic and stitch one across each pants leg 3 cm (1¼ in) up from lower edges, stretching elastic to fit as it is being stitched.

Hat: Cut a fabric strip 30 by 50 cm (11¼ by 19½ in). Fold, bringing long edges together and with right sides out, then press. Sew lace trim to folded edge.

Stitch across hat 3 cm (1¼ in) from fold then stitch again, 1 cm (⅜ in) away from first stitching line. Thread elastic through between lines of stitching, to fit head. Join short raw edges. Run a strong gathering thread round through remaining long edges. Pull up gathers as tightly as possible and fasten off. To cover gathered raw edges, gather a circle of fabric round a flat button then sew button on top of gathers.

Dress: Cut lower edges of bodice and sleeves to line A on pattern. For dress skirt cut a fabric strip 16 by 91 cm (6¼ by 36 in).

Apron: Cut a piece of fabric 12 by 16 cm (4¾ by 6¼ in). Make narrow hems and sew lace to all but one long edge. Gather this to measure 8 cm (3 in) then bind it with the centre portion of a waistband strip of fabric 5 by 30 cm (2 by 11¼ in). Sew two hooks and eyes to ends of waistband.

Posy: Cut a 5 cm (2 in) diameter circle of

card. Glue a frill of lace round edge of card at back. Thread narrow ribbon through bells and glue ends of ribbon to back of card so that bells hang down below posy. Take a length of elastic through card to form a loop at back, knotting ends together at front. Cover front of card with felt and stick on shells and flowers as shown in illustration on page 39.

Nightdress *(not shown in illustrations)*

Using pattern cut lower edges of bodice to line B and make full-size sleeves. Sew trimming to front of bodice before making up. For skirt use a fabric strip 26 by 60 cm (10¼ by 23½ in) and leave 8 cm (3 in) open at top of seam, for back opening.

Blouse and pinafore

Cut lower edges of bodice to line A and cut full-length sleeves.

For bib front join two 6 by 8 cm (2⅜ by 3 in) fabric pieces, leaving one long edge open. Turn and press then sew on trimming. Tack raw edges of bib to centre front raw edge of bodice. For straps cut two fabric strips 4 by 17 cm (1½ by 6¾ in). Fold each in half down length, right sides facing, and join long edges and across one short end. Turn and press then tack raw edges of each strap to back bodice, with raw edges level.

For skirt use a fabric strip 14 by 60 cm (5½ by 23½ in). Sew ends of straps to inside of bib at top then sew on buttons.

Track suit

Note: Take 5 mm (¼ in) seams as usual, but for all hems turn in 1 cm (⅜ in) only and stitch down raw edge to prevent fraying.

Pants: Use full-sized pants pattern, then trim 1 cm (⅜ in) off waist edges. Sew braid down centre of each pants piece before making up. Put elastic through lower edges.

Jacket: Cut full-sized bodice and sleeve pieces from pattern then trim 1 cm (⅜ in) off

underarm edges of sleeves. Note that bodice pieces will be back to front, to make the front zipped fastening.

Sew braid down the centre of each sleeve. Hem lower edge of jacket and thread through elastic. Turn in front edges and sew zip in place, trimming off any excess length of zip at top. Bind neck edges.

T-shirt: (Not shown in illustrations.) Use bodice pattern, cutting lower edges to line C. Make as for basic bodice then bind raw edges of armholes with 2·5 cm (1 in) wide bias strips of fabric.

Jeans and top *(not shown in illustrations)*

Jeans: Use full-size pants pattern and use contrasting thread for all stitching. Make two lines of stitching down centre of each piece. Cut two 5 cm (2 in) squares for back pockets. Turn in top edges and stitch, then turn in remaining edges and lower corners and sew to back of each pants piece before making up. Fake a front 'fly fastening' by working stitching lines on left front before making up.

Smock top: Using pattern cut lower edges of bodice and sleeves to line B. Cut lowered front neckline on bodice front as shown on pattern. Omit elastic at lower edges of sleeves.

For the frill cut a fabric strip 8 by 50 cm (3 by 19½ in). Hem all edges except for one long edge. Gather this and sew it to lower edge of bodice.

Party dress

Using pattern cut lower edges of bodice to line B and sleeves to line A. Cut lowered front neckline on bodice front as on pattern.

For skirt cut a fabric strip 14 by 60 cm (5½ by 23½ in). Make petticoat as for skirt and sew on lace edging to hang below skirt (*see illustration on page 39*). Catch gathered raw edge of petticoat to gathered raw edge of skirt.

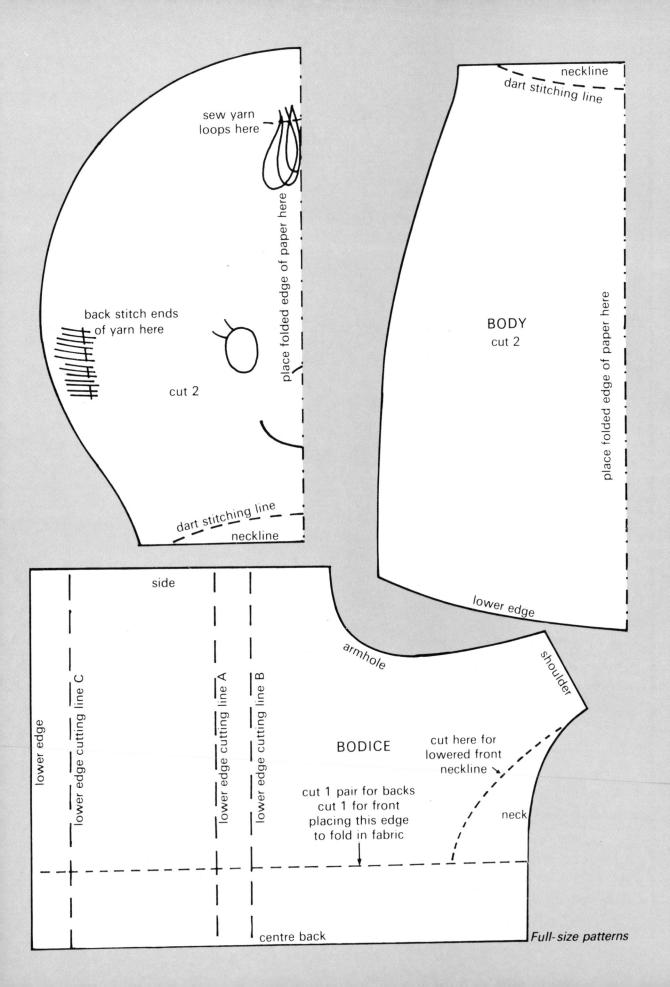

sew yarn
loops here

back stitch ends
of yarn here

cut 2

place folded edge of paper here

dart stitching line

neckline

neckline

dart stitching line

BODY
cut 2

place folded edge of paper here

lower edge

side

shoulder

armhole

lower edge

lower edge cutting line C

lower edge cutting line A

lower edge cutting line B

BODICE

cut here for
lowered front
neckline

cut 1 pair for backs
cut 1 for front
placing this edge
to fold in fabric

neck

centre back

Full-size patterns

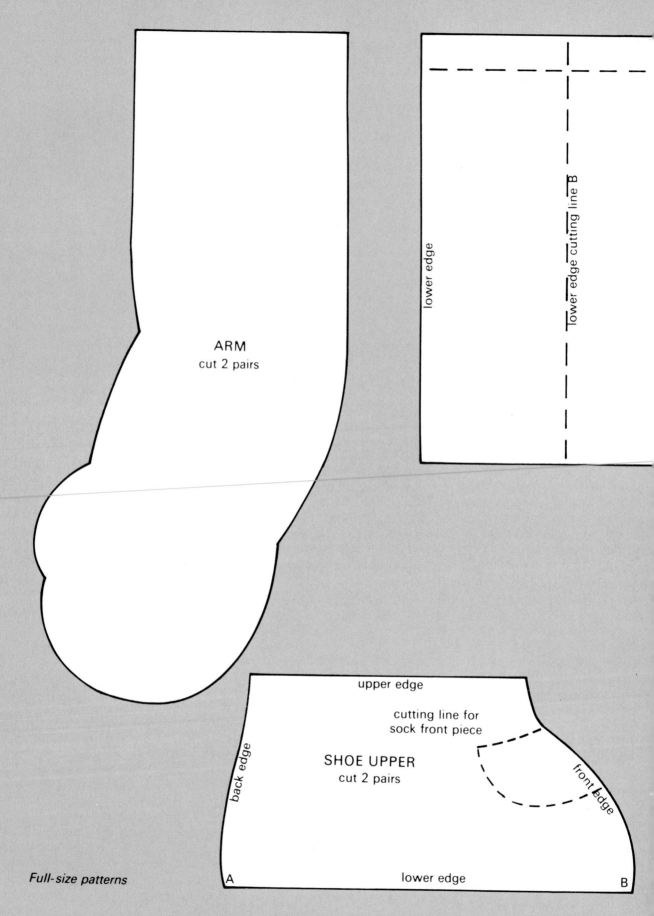

ARM
cut 2 pairs

lower edge

lower edge cutting line B

upper edge

cutting line for
sock front piece

back edge

SHOE UPPER
cut 2 pairs

front edge

A

lower edge

B

Full-size patterns

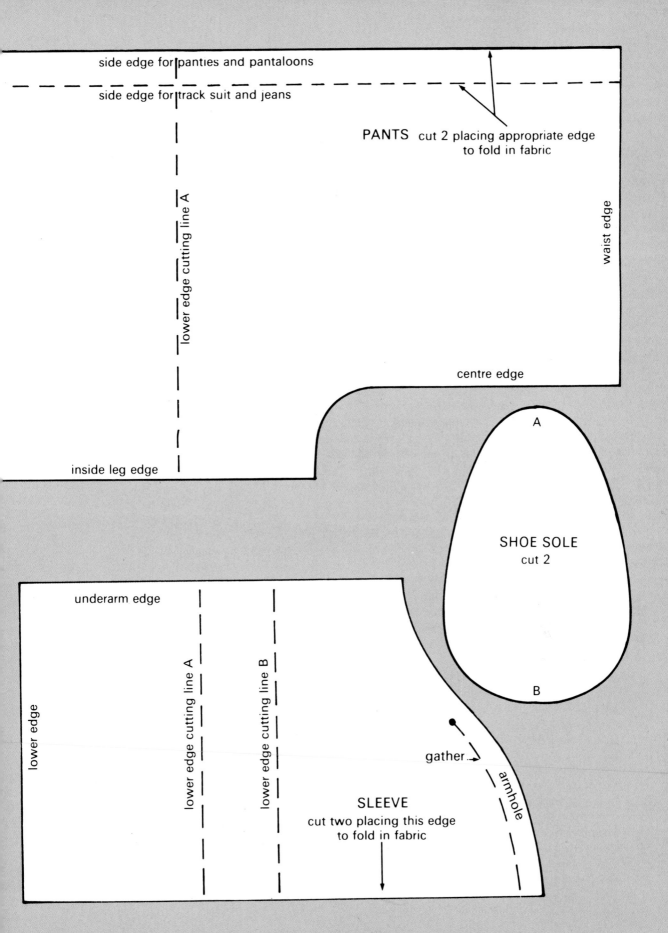

side edge for panties and pantaloons

side edge for track suit and jeans

PANTS cut 2 placing appropriate edge to fold in fabric

lower edge cutting line A

waist edge

centre edge

inside leg edge

A

SHOE SOLE
cut 2

B

underarm edge

lower edge

lower edge cutting line A

lower edge cutting line B

gather

armhole

SLEEVE
cut two placing this edge
to fold in fabric

Football Mascot

This shock-headed football mascot is about 53 cm (21 in) tall. The actual colours of his shirt, shorts and socks are left to you – just pick the colours of your favourite team! The mascot itself should be made of felt; this is firm enough to give you a fairly rigid figure, but it will need dry-cleaning from time to time.

For the mascot you will need: 45 cm of 91 cm wide ($\frac{1}{2}$ yd of 36 in wide) flesh-coloured felt (or two 46 cm (18 in) squares); 450 g (1 lb) of stuffing; a small piece of fur fabric for hair; pieces cut off a pair of medium-size children's socks; a pair of black flat shoe-laces, small pieces of black and white felt, 5 mm ($\frac{1}{4}$ in) wide white tape and thin card for boots; scraps of black and pink felt, red embroidery thread and red pencil for face; adhesive; metric graph paper.

Notes: Copy all patterns from the diagram on page 55 square by square on to graph paper and mark on all details. Each square on diagram = 2 cm.

Before cutting out mascot pieces, test the stretch of your felt by pulling a small portion gently widthways then lengthways (the maximum stretch on felt is usually across the width – i.e. from selvedge to selvedge). Cut out all felt mascot and boot pieces with the maximum stretch across the width of patterns, as shown on each pattern piece. Mark darts and neck hole on back head piece, and all other points on pieces after cutting out.

Cut hair from fur fabric, with smooth stroke of fur in direction shown on patterns.

Stuff all parts of the mascot very firmly unless otherwise stated. Join all pieces with right sides facing and take 5 mm ($\frac{1}{4}$ in) seams unless otherwise stated.

The mascot

Cut two pairs of ear pieces and join them in pairs, leaving inner edges open. Trim seams and turn right side out. Stitch round ears, about 3 mm ($\frac{1}{8}$ in) away from seam. Cut front head piece then tack inner edges of ears to positions shown, with raw edges of felt level.

Cut back head piece and stitch darts as shown on pattern. Trim darts. Cut out neck hole as shown on pattern. Now join front head to back head, matching points A, leaving upper edges open and easing front head to the back between darts on back head. Leave head, wrong side out, for the time being.

Cut one pair of body back pieces and join them at centre back edges, taking a 1 cm ($\frac{3}{8}$ in) seam and leaving a gap in seam as shown on pattern. Cut one body front piece and join it to body back at side edges. Join body front to back at inside leg edges of each leg, squaring off seam at top as on pattern. Stitch again at this point to reinforce, then clip seam to corners. Turn body right side out through gap in centre back seam.

Now slip open upper edge of head down over body. Pull the neck edge of body through neck hole on back head piece, taking care to match points B and C. Tack neck edges together all round, then machine stitch the seam twice. Turn head right side out. Stuff head then run a strong gathering thread round upper edge. Pull up gathers tightly and fasten off. Stuff neck and body, then legs. Ladderstitch opening in body back seam.

The face: Cut nose from pink felt and stick it to centre of face, 5 cm (2 in) up from seam at lower edge of face. Cut eyes from black felt and work a highlight on each one with small white stitches. Stick eyes to face slightly higher up than the nose and 3·5 cm ($1\frac{3}{8}$ in) apart. Use red thread to backstitch an irregular W shape for mouth, 2 cm ($\frac{3}{4}$ in) below nose, then work back with the thread, oversewing through each back stitch. Colour cheeks by rubbing gently with red pencil.

The hair: Cut one front and one back hair piece. On back hair piece bring edges of each dart together and oversew. Oversew front hair to back hair along upper edges, matching points D and pulling stitches as you go to gather slightly. Turn hair right side out and place on doll's head. Sew face edge of front hair to doll, and also lower edge of back. Trim fur pile slightly shorter to neaten if necessary, at sides and lower back edge of head.

The football socks: Cut a 10 cm (4 in) section off leg of each sock, measuring from top of sock downwards. Turn over about 2 cm ($\frac{3}{4}$ in) at top edge of each piece, then slip socks on to mascot's legs, with raw edges of socks level with ankle edges of legs. Sew raw edges of socks to legs.

The football boots: Cut two pairs of boot pieces from black felt. Sew three strips of tape to each piece as shown on pattern, taking care to turn two of the boot pieces over when doing this, to make pairs.

Now join boot pieces in pairs at centre front and centre back edges, leaving a gap in front seam as shown on pattern. Clip seams at front as on pattern. Turn boots right side out then turn in upper edges 1 cm ($\frac{3}{8}$ in) and tack.

Cut two soles from thin card. Place one inside lower edge of each boot, matching points E and F. Glue 1 cm ($\frac{3}{8}$ in) at lower edge of each boot on to card soles all round. Place boots in position at ankle edges of legs, with the boots overlapping ankle edges about 1 cm ($\frac{3}{8}$ in) at back, and slightly higher at front. Pin boots in place, with toes of boots turned away from each other. Sew upper edges of boots securely to legs. Stuff ankles and boots firmly through gaps in front seams of boots. Slipstitch gaps in seams.

For the band around top edge of each boot, cut a strip of black felt 2 by 16 cm ($\frac{3}{4}$ by $6\frac{1}{4}$ in). Fold each strip in half along its length then stitch long edges together. Glue strips around top edges of boots, oversewing short edges together at centre front.

For each boot cut another card sole and trim about 2 mm ($\frac{1}{16}$ in) off outer edges. Stick each card sole on to a piece of felt then cut out felt 1 cm ($\frac{3}{8}$ in) larger all round than soles. Turn and glue this surplus to other side of card. Glue card soles under boots.

For boot studs on the soles cut eight strips of white felt 5 mm by 10 cm ($\frac{1}{4}$ by 4 in). For the studs on the boot heels cut four 10 cm (4 in) strips of white felt, slightly wider than 5 mm ($\frac{1}{4}$ in). Spread each felt strip with glue then grip one end with tweezers and roll up tightly along the length. Glue four studs to each sole, and two heel studs to each heel (see pattern).

Cut two boot tongues from black felt and machine round each one, close to edge. Cut slits in each tongue as on pattern, then thread shoelace through slits and tie ends in a bow. Wind sticky tape round shoelace ends to seal. Sew tongues to tops of boots as shown in the illustration on page 46.

The arms: Cut two pairs of arm pieces and join them in pairs, leaving upper edges open. Trim seams round hands then turn arms right side out. Stuff hands and thumbs lightly then machine stitch through hands along dotted lines shown on pattern. Pull thread ends through to one side of each hand, knot them, then sew thread ends into hands. Stuff arms to within 3 cm ($1\frac{1}{4}$ in) of upper edges. Bring seams together at top of each arm and oversew the edges together, pulling thread to gather slightly. Sew an arm securely to each shoulder at the position shown on body patterns.

The clothes

For the shirt you will need: 25 cm ($\frac{1}{4}$ yd) of 91 cm (36 in) wide fabric; cuttings off a lady's or man's knee sock; oddments of fabric as required to make the colours of your favourite football team.

For the shorts you will need: 15 cm (6 in) of 91 cm (36 in) wide fabric and a little elastic.

Notes: 1 cm ($\frac{3}{8}$ in) seams are allowed unless otherwise stated. After cutting out shirt and shorts pieces and before making up the garments, stitch on any side stripes to shorts, sleeve or chest stripes to shirt, as required for the particular club colours. Join fabric with right sides facing.

To make the shirt: Cut one pair of back pieces, one front and two sleeves. Join front to backs at shoulders. Clip armhole edges of front and backs at curves. Stitch armhole edges of sleeves to armhole edges of shirt, matching points G on sleeves to shoulder seams on shirt and easing sleeves to fit. Stitch seams again, just within first line of stitching, then trim seams.

Cut the sock open along length, down centre back and under foot to toe (*see diagram 1 below*). For each sleeve cuff cut a 7 cm ($2\frac{3}{4}$ in) wide strip across width of sock above the heel area (*see diagram 1*). Trim strips to about 15 cm (6 in) long if necessary. Stitch one long edge of each cuff to lower edge of sleeve, stretching cuff to fit and with raw edges level.

For neckband cut two 5 cm (2 in) wide strips from sock as for cuffs. Join strips at one short edge, stitching seam as shown in diagram 2 (*below*), so that this seam will form the mitre at centre V-point of neckline. Trim seam.

Now clip V-point on shirt almost to seam allowance. Pin one edge of neckband V-point seam to front V-point of shirt. Pin remainder of neckband to neckline of shirt, with raw edges level and stretching band slightly as it is pinned. Trim off any excess length in band, level with centre back edges of shirt. Stitch band in place. Fold band in half to inside of shirt, then sew long raw edges of band together.

Join side seams of shirt and underarm edges of sleeves including cuffs. Clip seams at underarms. Trim seams on cuffs then fold cuffs in half to inside and sew raw edges together as for neckband.

Hem lower edge of shirt. Turn in one centre back edge of shirt 1 cm ($\frac{3}{8}$ in) and press. Put shirt on mascot with turned-in back edge overlapping the other back edge by 1 cm ($\frac{3}{8}$ in), and slipstitch neatly in place.

To make the shorts: Cut two shorts pieces and join them together at centre edges. Stitch again at curved portions of seams, then trim seams at curves. Bring centre seams together then join inside leg edges. Trim seams. Make narrow hems on lower leg edges. Hem waist edge, taking a 5 mm then 2 cm ($\frac{1}{4}$ in then $\frac{3}{4}$ in) turning. Stitch round close to fold in waist edge, thread elastic through casing to fit waist.

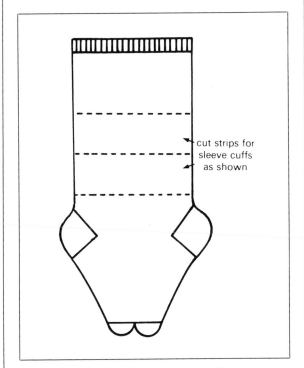

Diagram 1 Showing how to cut strips from a knee sock, for trimming football shirt

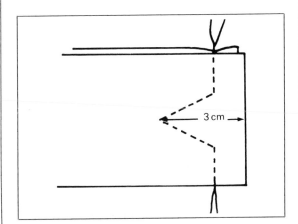

Diagram 2 Stitching the neckband seam to mitre the front point

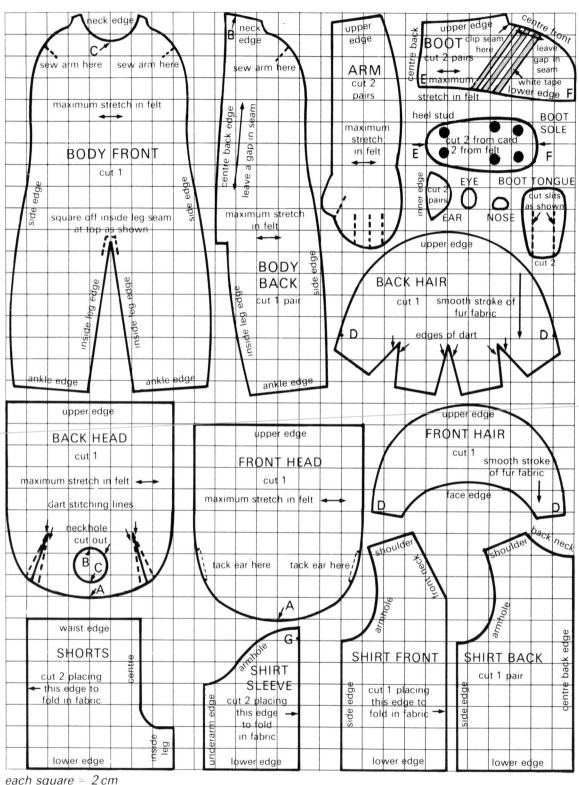

each square = 2 cm

Santa and Mrs Claus

A pair of cheery Humpty Dumpty toys just right for the Christmas season! Knitted from two strands of double knitting yarn, they measure about 30 cm [12 in] from the tops of their hats to their toes.

You will need: Oddments of double knitting yarn in red, pink, white, green and black [note that it is advisable to have several balls of red yarn on hand when making these toys, but it does not matter if the shades vary]: a pair of 5½ mm [No 5] knitting needles and a pair of 3¾ mm [No 9] knitting needles; small amount of stuffing for each toy; scraps of felt for facial features and the holly leaves.

Abbreviations: See page 17.

Important note: Please remember that the double knitting yarn is to be used *double* throughout and worked on 5½ mm [No 5, USA 8] knitting needles; tension: 16 sts to 10cm [4in]. This is taken for granted in the instructions for each piece and so will not be mentioned again.

When single yarn and 3¾ mm [No 9] needles are required for the looped fringes this will *always* be mentioned in the instructions.

Santa Claus

The body

Begin at lower edge and using red cast on 6 sts loosely then work as follows:

1st row: Inc K wise into every st – 12 sts.
2nd row: P.
3rd row: Inc K wise into every st – 24 sts.
Beginning with a P row st-st 3 rows.
Next row: Inc K wise into every st – 48 sts.
St-st 13 rows.

The head

Break off red and join on pink for head then continue in st-st and work 4 rows.

Next row: K 5, (K 2 tog, K 10) 3 times, K 2 tog, K 5 – 44 sts.
St-st 9 rows.
Next row: K 4, (K 2 tog, K 9) 3 times, K 2 tog, K 5 – 40 sts.
St-st 3 rows.

To shape top of head: *1st row:* (K 2, K 2 tog) to end – 30 sts.

2nd and every alternate row: P.
3rd row: (K 1, K 2 tog) to end – 20 sts.
5th row: (K 2 tog) to end – 10 sts.
7th row: (K 2 tog) to end – 5 sts.
Break off yarn leaving long ends, thread through remaining sts, then pull up tightly and fasten off.

The arms [make two alike]

Begin at top of arm and using red cast on 12 sts.

St-st 5 rows.

Break off red and join on white [read green here for Mrs Claus], then P 2 rows.
Next row: K.
Break off white [or green] and join on pink for hand.

Beginning with a K row, st-st 6 rows.
Next row: (K 2 tog) to end – 6 sts.
Break off yarn and finish off as for top of head.

The legs [make two alike]

Begin at top of leg and using red cast on 14 sts.
St-st 13 rows.

Break off red and join on white [read green here for Mrs Claus], then P 2 rows.
Next row: K.
Break off white [or green] and join on black for shoe.

Beginning with a K row, st-st 8 rows.

Next row: (K 2 tog) to end – 7 sts. Break off yarn and finish off as for top of head.

To make up Santa

Gather up the cast on sts of body tightly and fasten off, then join row ends of body leaving a small gap in head for turning. Turn right side out and stuff, then ladder stitch gap. Note that seam will be at centre back of toy.

Fold each arm and join the row ends leaving cast on edges open. Turn and stuff then oversew top edges together. Sew an arm to each side of body having top edge of arm level with last row of red on body and taking care that cast on edges of arms are in a vertical position as shown in the illustration.

Sew leg seams as for arms. Turn right side out and stuff lower portion of legs then stuff upper portions more lightly. Oversew top edges together having leg seams at centre back of legs. Sew legs to body at front having tops of legs two knitted rows up from last inc row at base of body, and in a horizontal position.

The face

Using a single strand of red yarn work a small V-shape for mouth about 2 cm [¾ in] up from last row of red on body, securing end of yarn under position of one felt cheek [where it will be hidden] and fastening off yarn under position of other cheek. Using the pattern cut cheeks from pink felt and sew in place.

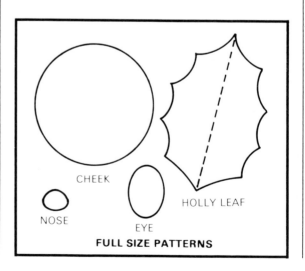

FULL SIZE PATTERNS

Cut nose from red felt and sew in place 1.5 cm [⅝ in] above mouth. Cut eyes from black felt and sew on either side of nose about 2 cm [¾ in] apart.

The beard

Using 3¾ mm [No 9] needles and a single strand of white yarn, cast on 30 sts. Work looped pattern as follows.

1st row: K 1; * insert right hand needle K wise into next st, place first two fingers of left hand at back of st, then wind yarn anticlockwise round needle and fingers 3 times, then round tip of right hand needle only, draw through the 4 loops; repeat from * until 1 st remains; K 1.

2nd row: K 1; * K 4 tog pulling loops down firmly as you go; repeat from * until 1 st remains; K 1 – 30 sts.

Cast off.

Pin, then sew beard to face as illustrated.

The hat

Note that the hat is worked in double yarn throughout, [including the looped lower edge], and on 5½ mm [No 5] needles.

Using white begin at lower edge and cast on 64 sts. Work the first row of the looped pattern as given for the beard, winding the yarn round needle and fingers twice instead of 3 times.

Break off white and join on red.

Work 2nd row of looped pattern: K 1; * K 3 tog pulling loops down firmly as you go, repeat from * until 1 st remains; K 1 – 64 sts.

Now beginning with a P row, st-st 9 rows.
** **Shape the top:** *Next row:* (K 2, K 2 tog) to end – 48 sts.

St-st 3 rows.

Next row: (K 1, K 2 tog) to end – 32 sts.

St-st 3 rows.

Next row: (K 2 tog) to end – 16 sts. ***

St-st 3 rows.

Next row: (K 2 tog) to end – 8 sts.

Break off yarn leaving long ends, thread through remaining sts, pull up tightly and fasten off. Join row ends of hat.

Make a pom-pon in white yarn and sew to top of hat. Place hat on head as illustrated and sew to head through first row of red sts. Cut

two holly leaves from green felt using the pattern. Work stitches up the centre of each one, then sew them to hat as shown in illustration.

Mrs Claus

Work body and head in exactly the same way as given for Santa.

Make arms and legs as for Santa noting variations in colour.

Make up all pieces and cut out and sew on facial features as for Santa.

The skirt

Using 3¾ mm [No 9] needles and a single strand of red yarn cast on 70 sts.

Work the two rows of the looped pattern as given for Santa's beard, winding the yarn round three fingers instead of two, to make longer loops. Join row ends of skirt and sew it round body just below the arms.

The hair

Use white yarn and wind it 30 times around a 40 cm [16 in] length of card. Take this hank of yarn off card and sew across strands at centre of hank. Sew centre, to centre parting position on head, starting 2 cm [¾ in] above the eyes.

Gather strands to each side of head just above the arms and sew there. Take ends of loops up towards centre back of head and sew in place.

The hat

Begin at lower edge and using green cast on 128 sts.

G-st 4 rows.

Next row: (K 2 tog) to end – 64 sts.

Beginning with a P row, st-st 13 rows.

Now work as for Santa's hat from ** to ***.

Next row: (P 2 tog) to end – 8 sts.

Break off yarn leaving long ends and finish and sew seam as for Santa, omitting pom-pon.

Put a little stuffing in top of hat, then put hat on head as shown in the illustration. Sew hat to head through the dec row after the first 4 rows of g-st.

2
SMALL
DOLLS

Baby Bunting Dolls

The cuddliest of baby dolls, about 18 cm (7 in) high, are so easy to sew, complete with their snuggle-down sleeping bags.

You will need: Small oddments of the following – cotton stockinette (or cuttings off a T-shirt or vest); stuffing; printed and plain cotton fabrics; black felt; trimmings; narrow ribbon; thin wadding; shirring elastic; knitting yarn; cuttings off a sock; red pencil; adhesive.

Notes: Trace the body pattern on page 58 off the page on to thin folded paper, placing fold in paper to dotted line shown on pattern. Cut out, then open up to give you a full-sized pattern. Trace hand and bib patterns and cut out.

Take 5 mm ($\frac{1}{4}$ in) seams unless otherwise stated. Join fabrics with right sides facing. When cutting stockinette pieces, make sure that the most stretch in the fabric is going in the directions stated.

The doll

Hands: Cut two pairs of hand pieces from stockinette. Join pairs, leaving wrist edges open. Trim seams, turn right side out and stuff lightly. Gather round hands 1 cm ($\frac{3}{8}$ in) from raw edges, pull up gathers tightly and fasten off.

Head: Cut two pieces of stockinette 6 by 11 cm ($2\frac{3}{8}$ by $4\frac{1}{4}$ in), with most stretch going across the narrow measurement. Join the long edges and trim seams. Gather round one remaining raw edge, pull up gathers tightly and fasten off securely. Turn head right side out and stuff firmly. Run a gathering thread round 2 cm ($\frac{3}{4}$ in) from remaining raw edge, then pull up gathers tightly and fasten off.

Body: Pin body pattern on to two layers of cotton fabric. Trim off fabric level with neck and wrist edges of pattern. Now stitch round

close to all remaining edges of pattern. Remove pattern and cut out body 3 mm ($\frac{1}{8}$ in) from seamline, clipping corners and cutting between legs.

Turn body right side out. Turn in wrist edges 1 cm ($\frac{3}{8}$ in) and run round gathering threads. Slip a hand inside each one and pull up gathers tightly round gathers in hand. Fasten off, then sew gathers to hands.

To make thumbs, take a stitch round and through one side of each hand (so that thumbs are pointing upwards); fasten off.

Stuff legs and pin through both layers of fabric across top of each leg. Stuff arms and pin them in the same way. Stuff body lightly then turn in and gather neck edge as for wrists. Insert head and finish as for wrist edges. Remove pins.

For eyes cut two 5 mm ($\frac{1}{4}$ in) diameter circles of black felt (cut these with a leather punch if available) and glue them about halfway down face and 2 cm ($\frac{3}{4}$ in) apart. Mark nose between lower edges of eyes, with red pencil. Make a small smudge with pencil for mouth, 1 cm ($\frac{3}{8}$ in) below nose. Work a stitch with double pink thread across mouth, starting and fastening off thread at top of head. Colour cheeks with pencil.

For ears, take a pinch of fabric at seam at each side of head between levels of mouth and eyes. Sew through the pinch of fabric with small running stitches. Colour ears with pencil.

For hair, split a strand of knitting yarn to make finer strands. Sew a few loops of yarn to top of head, to hang down above eyes.

Cap: Cut a strip of fabric 6 by 23 cm ($2\frac{3}{8}$ by 9 in) to match body. Cut a 3 by 12 cm ($1\frac{1}{4}$ by $4\frac{3}{4}$ in) strip of sock fabric, with most stretch across the long measurement. Fold the sock strip, bringing long edges together. Stitch these raw edges to one long edge of fabric strip with edges level and stretching the sock strip to fit fabric. Join short edges of cap, then gather round remaining raw edge. Pull up gathers tightly then fasten off. Turn right side out. Gather up a 2·5 cm (1 in) diameter circle of sock fabric, putting a little stuffing in the centre, for cap bobble. Sew this to top of cap. Now sew cap to head.

Bib: Pin bib pattern on to two layers of thin cotton fabric. Stitch round close to edge of pattern, leaving a gap in stitching as shown on pattern. Remove pattern and cut out bib as for body. Turn right side out, slipstitch gap. Sew on trimmings and ribbon ties.

The sleeping bag: Cut a 20 by 40 cm (8 by 17½ in) strip of printed cotton fabric for cover, and a strip of plain fabric the same size, for lining. Cut a strip of wadding slightly larger all round than the fabric strips.

Round off the corners of the fabric strips at one short edge. Pin fabric pieces together, right sides facing, with wadding underneath both of them. Join round edges, leaving a gap in short straight edge. Trim wadding level with edges of fabric all round. Turn right side out and slipstitch gap. Sew lace trim to right side of short straight edge.

Now, with lining outside, fold up 15 cm (6 in) at short straight edge of strip to form a pocket (*see diagram 1, below left*). Stitch along each side of pocket, taking 2 cm ($\frac{3}{4}$ in) seams. Using a double strand of shirring elastic in a sewing needle, work small running stitches all round edge of lining in the curved top edge of sleeping bag. Pull up elastic to gather and form the hood, as shown in illustration on pages 54–5, then fasten off. Turn the sleeping bag right side out and slipstitch pocket to hood at positions shown in diagram 2 (*below*).

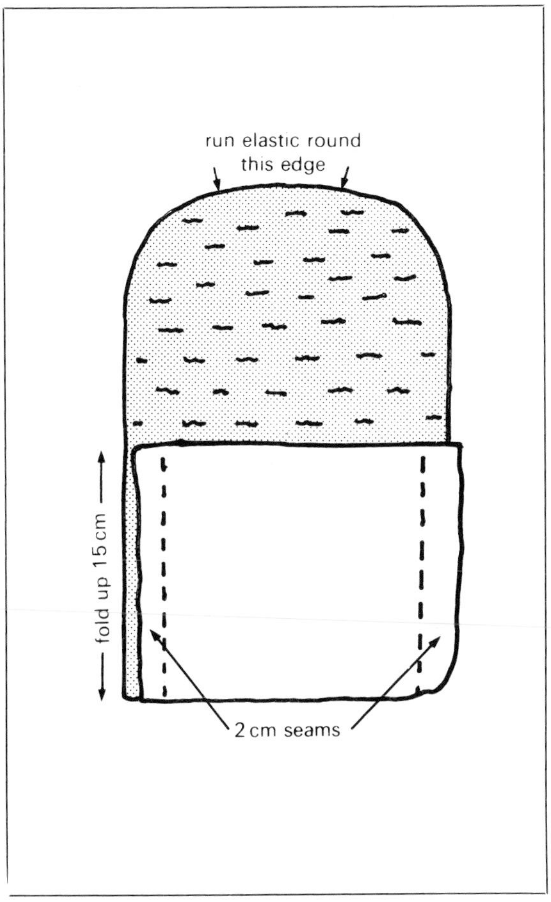

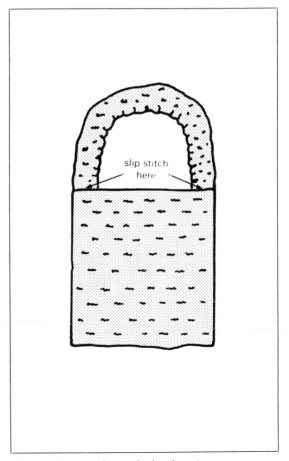

Diagram 1 How to sew up the sleeping bag

Diagram 2 Completing the hood section

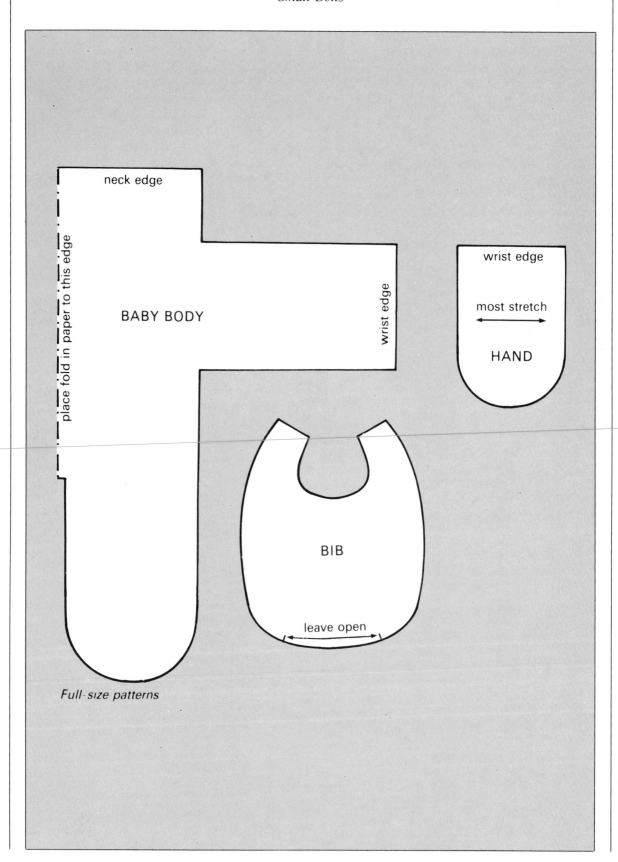

neck edge

place fold in paper to this edge

BABY BODY

wrist edge

wrist edge

most stretch

HAND

BIB

leave open

Full-size patterns

Snowbabies

These little snowbabies, about 15 cm (6 in) tall, can be made as Christmas tree decorations, or as last-minute stocking-fillers for the children.

You will need: Oddments of white fleecy fabric, stuffing, printed fabric, felt, narrow sparkly braid, narrow ribbon, white double knitting yarn, red thread, red pencil, adhesive.

Notes: The pattern outlines are the actual stitching lines. Trace all patterns off the page on to thin paper. When tracing the body pattern, use folded paper and place the fold to the dot-and-dash line as shown; then cut out and open up the folded paper to give you the full-size pattern.

5 mm ($\frac{1}{4}$ in) seams are allowed on clothes.

Basic doll

Pin the pattern to two layers of fleece, with right sides of fabric facing. Machine stitch all round close to the edge of the pattern, leaving a gap in stitching at top of head as shown on the pattern. Mark a pencil line on the fabric, level with edge of pattern at top of head, to denote the seamline. Now remove the pattern and cut out close to seamline all round doll.

Turn doll right side out. Stuff legs and arms, then body and head. Ladderstitch open edges at top of head. Tie doubled sewing thread tightly around neck to shape it.

Cut two 5 mm ($\frac{1}{4}$ in) diameter circles of black felt for eyes (use a leather punch if possible). Glue eyes in place halfway down face, about 1·5 cm ($\frac{5}{8}$ in) apart. When working mouth stitches, take threads through from top of head and fasten off there also. Work a short line for mouth, 1 cm ($\frac{3}{8}$ in) below eyes, using four strands of red sewing thread. Work a tiny vertical stitch at centre of mouth, to pull first stitch into a V-shape.

Sew a few loops of double knitting yarn to forehead above eyes. Mark nose and colour cheeks with moistened tip of red pencil.

Boy snowbaby

Make the basic doll. For pants, cut a 3·5 by 15 cm ($1\frac{3}{8}$ by 6 in) strip of felt. Join ends then put pants on doll, with top edge just under arms. Cut two lengths of braid for braces, one to go over each shoulder. Cross braces over at back and tuck ends inside top of pants. Now sew waist edge of pants to doll, catching ends of braces in as you go. Catch lower edge of pants together at centre front and back, between doll's legs. Glue braid round top edge of pants.

For cap, cut a strip of fabric 5 by 18 cm (2 by 7 in). Join ends of strip. Gather up one remaining raw edge tightly and fasten off. Turn cap right side out. For bobble, cut, gather and stuff a 4 cm ($1\frac{1}{2}$ in) diameter circle of white fleecy fabric. Sew this to top of cap. Put cap on doll as shown in illustration on page 59 and sew the lower edge to head. Glue braid round to cover raw edge.

For scarf, tie a 17 cm ($6\frac{3}{4}$ in) length of ribbon round neck and cut ends at an angle. If the doll is to be hung on the tree, sew a thread loop through top of head and knot the ends.

Girl snowbaby

Make the basic doll. For long hair, cut ten 20 cm (8 in) lengths of yarn and sew centres to top of head. Gather strands to each side of face and sew them there. Tease out ends of yarn and trim them to even lengths. Make hat and scarf as for boy doll.

For skirt, cut a strip of fabric 3·5 by 28 cm ($1\frac{3}{8}$ by 11 in). Join ends then hem one long edge. Gather remaining raw edge and pull it up round doll below arms, then fasten off. Glue braid round waist to cover gathered raw edge.

The hand-held accessories

Christmas tree: Pin the pattern to two layers of green felt and trim felt level with lower edge of pattern. Stitch round, close to remaining edges of pattern. Remove the pattern and cut out tree. Stuff lightly then make trunk as for tree, stitching round pattern pinned to brown felt. Push the trunk inside lower edge of tree and stitch across.

Broom: Cut a 5 by 8 cm (2 by 3¼ in) strip of brown felt. Make 3 cm (1¼ in) long cuts along one short edge, to form the bristles. Roll up the strip across its width and wind sewing thread tightly round handle above the bristles.

Stocking: Make as for tree, using red felt,

trimming felt level with upper edge of pattern before stitching. Glue braid round upper edge.

Parcel: Pin pattern to two layers of felt. Stitch all round, then remove pattern and cut out. Tie braid round parcel.

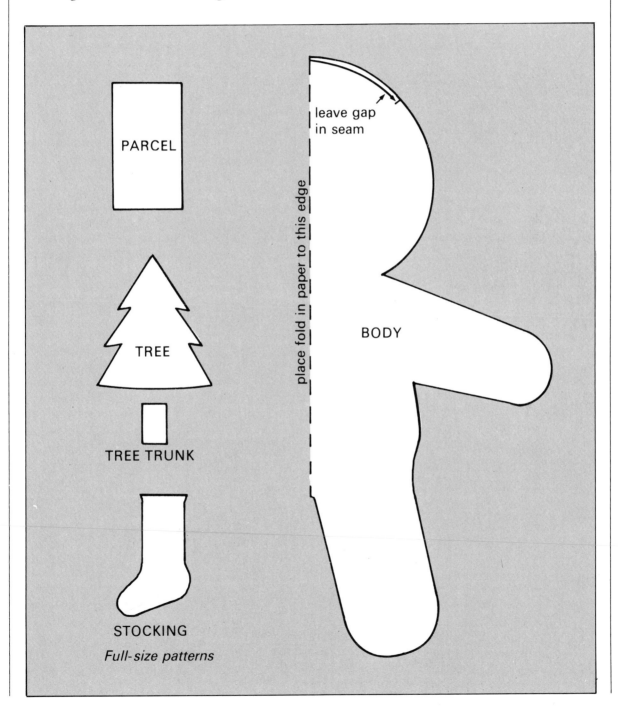

PARCEL

leave gap
in seam

place fold in paper to this edge

BODY

TREE

TREE TRUNK

STOCKING

Full-size patterns

The Well-dressed Doll

This charming rag doll stands just 25 cm (10 in) tall and has a wardrobe of five pretty outfits. She would make a perfect playmate for any little girl who loves clothes

For the doll you will need: Small pieces of pink cotton fabric; fur fabric for hair; white and black felt; pink and red thread; red pencil; a small amount of stuffing; adhesive.

For the clothes: Scraps of fabrics and trimmings; narrow elastic; lace edging; felt; small snap fasteners.

Notes: Trace off all the pattern pieces onto paper. Where patterns have a dot and dash edge, fold the paper in half and place the fold over this line. Trace off the outline then cut out through both layers of paper. Open up to give full-size patterns.

Cut out all pieces following the directions on the patterns.

Join all pieces with right sides facing; take 5 mm ($\frac{1}{4}$ in) seams unless otherwise stated.

The doll

To make head and body: Cut two body pieces from pink fabric. Mark the face on the right side of one piece then make neck darts on wrong side of both pieces. Join body pieces round edges leaving a gap in the seam at the lower edge as indicated on the pattern. Trim seam and turn body right side out. Stuff head firmly then stuff body. Ladder stitch gap in seam. Work nose in pink satin stitch. Work mouth in small back stitches using red thread, then work back, oversewing through each stitch. Cut eyes from black felt and stick in place. Colour cheeks by rubbing with red pencil.

Cut two hair pieces from fur fabric with smooth stroke of fur in direction shown on pattern. Join pieces round outer edges then turn in remaining raw edges a little and slip stitch. Pull hair on head to fit neatly then slip stitch to head all round. Sew small ribbon bow to hair.

To make legs: For legs cut two 8 by 9 cm ($3\frac{1}{8}$ by $3\frac{1}{2}$ in) pieces of pink fabric. Cut two pairs of sock pieces from white felt. Join sock pieces in pairs for about 2 cm ($\frac{3}{4}$ in) down front seam, press seam open then join upper edges of sock pieces to one short edge of each leg piece. Trim seam then join remainder of sock pieces round outer edges and join 9 cm ($3\frac{1}{2}$ in) edges of leg pieces. Trim seams round socks then turn legs right side out and stuff. Turn in upper edges of legs and slip stitch then sew to front of body about 1 cm ($\frac{3}{8}$ in) away from lower body seam.

Cut two pairs of shoe pieces from felt as directed on pattern and cut two 5 mm by 4 cm ($\frac{1}{4}$ by $1\frac{1}{2}$ in) strips of felt for shoe straps. Join shoe pieces in pairs round outer edges. Trim seams and turn right side out. Put shoes on feet and place straps in position as illustrated tucking ends of straps in shoes at each side, then sew shoes and straps to feet.

To make arms: Cut two pairs of arm pieces from pink fabric. Join them in pairs round edges leaving top edges open. Trim seams round hands, turn right side out and stuff to within 3 cm ($1\frac{1}{4}$ in) of top. Turn in top edges, bring seams together then make small inverted pleats as shown in diagram 1. Oversew all edges together then sew an arm to each side of body 5 mm ($\frac{1}{4}$ in) down from neck.

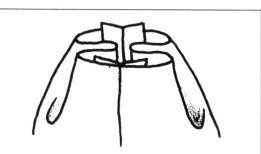

Diagram 1 Make one inverted pleat at either side of each arm

The clothes

Panties

Cut out two panty pieces and hem lower edges taking 5 mm ($\frac{1}{4}$ in) turnings twice to form casings for elastic. Sew narrow lace trimming to lower edges. Thread elastic through casings to fit legs and secure at each end with a stitch or two. Join pieces at centre front and back edges clipping curves in seams. Join at inside leg edges. Hem waist edge as for lower edges and thread through elastic to fit waist.

Nightdress

Cut out one pair of back bodice pieces and one front bodice cutting lower edges of pieces by dotted line indicated. Cut two long sleeves as shown on sleeve pattern. Cut a 2 by 14 cm ($\frac{3}{4}$ by $5\frac{1}{2}$ in) bias strip of fabric for binding neck edge. Sew ric-rac or trimming to bodice front as illustrated. Join front bodice to backs at shoulders. Run gathering threads along tops of sleeves as shown on pattern. Tack armhole edges of sleeves to armhole edges of bodice matching points A to shoulder seams and pulling up gathering threads on sleeves to fit. Sew seams as tacked then clip curves. Turn in lower edges of sleeves 5 mm ($\frac{1}{4}$ in) twice and stitch, forming casings, for elastic. Thread elastic through to fit wrists and secure at each end of casings with a stitch or two. Turn in back edges of bodice 5 mm ($\frac{1}{4}$ in) twice and stitch. Bind neck edge with bias strip, clipping curves. Now join side edges of bodice and underarm edges of sleeves to complete top of nightdress.

For skirt, cut a 16 by 30 cm ($6\frac{1}{4}$ by 12 in) strip of fabric. Sew trimming parallel to and 3 cm ($1\frac{1}{4}$ in) away from one long edge – this will be the hem edge. Join the short edges from hem taking 1 cm ($\frac{3}{8}$ in) seam and leaving 4 cm ($1\frac{1}{2}$ in) open at top of seam. Press seam to one side then turn in raw edges of seam and stitch to neaten. Hem lower edge of skirt then gather upper edge to fit lower edge of bodice. Sew gathered edge of skirt to bodice. To finish off the nightdress, sew ribbon bow to the front and three snap fasteners to back edges.

Short red dress

Make as for nightdress cutting short sleeves as indicated on pattern. Make short skirt as for nightdress using a 9 by 34 cm ($3\frac{1}{2}$ by $13\frac{1}{2}$ in) strip of fabric. To complete the dress, sew lace edging to the hem edge.

Frilled pop-over

Cut one pair of back pieces and one front piece as directed on pattern. Join front to backs at side edges then turn in shoulder edges 5 mm ($\frac{1}{4}$ in) and press. Cut a 45 cm ($17\frac{3}{4}$ in) length of 4 cm ($1\frac{1}{2}$ in) wide lace edging for frill. Gather lace to fit round lower edge of pop-over between points A on the back pieces. Sew gathered edge of lace in position with right sides facing and raw edges level. Cut out and make lining in the same way as for pop-over omitting frill. Place lining and pop-over together and join round front neck and back neck edges, armholes and centre back edges. Clip curves in seams and turn pop-over right side out pushing shoulder edges through with a knitting needle. Slip stitch front shoulder edges of pop-over and lining to back shoulder edges. Turn in and slip stitch lower edge of lining over frill seam. Sew narrow lace edging round neck edge and round frill seam then sew a snap fastener to back neck edges.

Flowery blouse

Make bodice as for nightdress bodice cutting lower edges by line indicated on pattern and using short sleeve pattern. Hem lower edges of sleeves and omit elastic.

Felt pop-over

Cut two backs and one front as directed on pattern trimming away side edges as indicated. Trim 5 mm ($\frac{1}{4}$ in) off all neck and armhole edges. Cut two pockets using pocket pattern. Stitch pockets to front as shown on pattern. Join front to backs at shoulders then trim seams. On right side of pop-over, top-stitch all round neck and armhole edges as illustrated. Join side seams then top-stitch all round back and lower edges. Sew snap fasteners to back edges.

Nurse's outfit

Use pale blue fabric for the dress. Cut bodice front and backs using bodice pattern and cutting lower edges by line indicated. Cut two sleeves using nurse's sleeve pattern. For skirt, cut a 9 by 26 cm (3½ by 10¼ in) strip of fabric. Make as for nightdress but instead of gathering sleeve tops, ease them into armholes. Omit elastic in lower edges of sleeves and, instead, bind with a 2 cm (¾ in) wide bias strip of white fabric. Bind neck edge.

For apron skirt cut a 7 by 24 cm (2¾ by 9½ in) strip of white fabric. Take narrow hems on all edges except for one long edge. Gather this edge to measure 16 cm (6¼ in); then bind this edge with a 3 by 20 cm (1¼ by 8 in) bias strip of white fabric, with the skirt placed centrally so an equal portion of band extends at each side for the back overlap. For apron bib, cut a 6 cm (2⅜ in) square of fabric. Narrowly hem all raw edges then slip one edge behind waistband at front and slip stitch in position. Sew a snap fastener to back waistband overlap and halves of two snaps to top corners of bib. Sew other halves of snaps to dress front to hold bib in position. Use ball point pen to mark red cross on bib.

Cut cap as directed on pattern. Join raw edges leaving one short straight edge open. Turn cap right side out then turn in and slip stitch opening. Top-stitch cap round edges and sew a 10 cm (4 in) strip of narrow elastic to short edges. Mark on red cross.

Scottish dance dress

Note that the skirt and blouse are sewn together for ease in dressing the doll. Make bodice as for short dress with puffed sleeves, using white fabric and trimming neck and sleeve edges with narrow lace edging. Make a pattern for circular skirt as follows: draw and cut out a 20 cm (8 in) diameter circle of paper then draw and cut a 6 cm (2⅜ in) diameter circle from the centre and discard it. The inner edge of the pattern is the waist edge and the outer edge is the hem. Cut one skirt piece from checked fabric then make a cut from hem to waist edge for back opening. Join these edges from hem to waist taking a 1 cm (⅜ in) seam and leaving a 4 cm (1½ in) gap at the top of the seam. Finish this opening as for the short dress. Run a gathering thread round the waist edge and pull up gathers to fit lower edge of bodice then sew in place. Hem lower edge of skirt then sew snap fasteners to back edges.

For black felt bodice, cut one pair of fronts and one pair of backs as directed on felt bodice pattern. Join fronts to backs at shoulders and sides oversewing edges together neatly. Turn right side out and use needle and thin cord to lace front edges together as illustrated, tying cord in a bow at top. Sew snap fasteners to back.

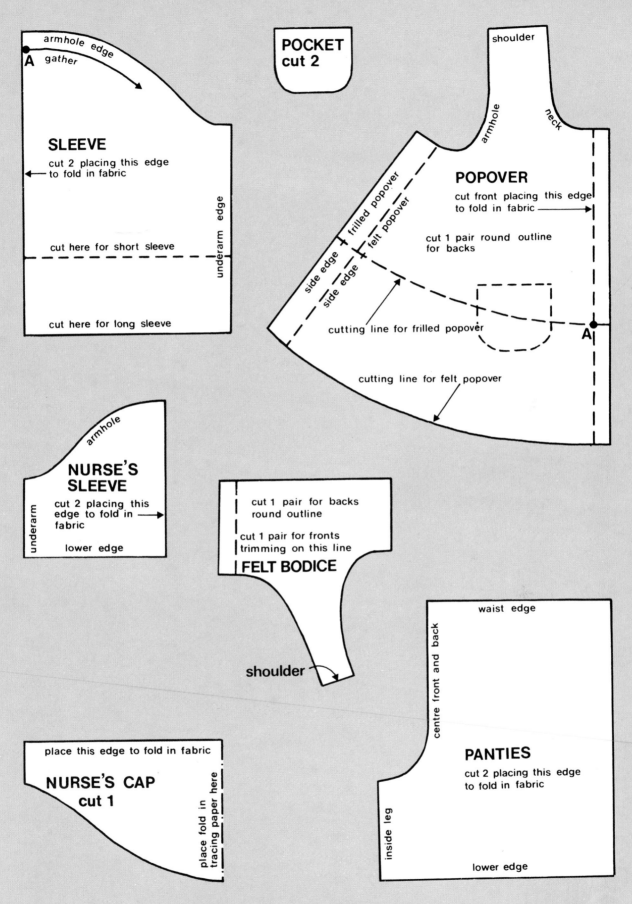

SLEEVE

cut 2 placing this edge to fold in fabric

armhole edge

gather

A

underarm edge

cut here for short sleeve

cut here for long sleeve

**POCKET
cut 2**

shoulder

armhole

neck

POPOVER

cut front placing this edge to fold in fabric

cut 1 pair round outline for backs

frilled popover

felt popover

side edge

side edge

cutting line for frilled popover

A

cutting line for felt popover

armhole

**NURSE'S
SLEEVE**

cut 2 placing this edge to fold in fabric

underarm

lower edge

cut 1 pair for backs round outline

cut 1 pair for fronts trimming on this line

FELT BODICE

shoulder

waist edge

centre front and back

PANTIES

cut 2 placing this edge to fold in fabric

inside leg

lower edge

place this edge to fold in fabric

**NURSE'S CAP
cut 1**

place fold in tracing paper here

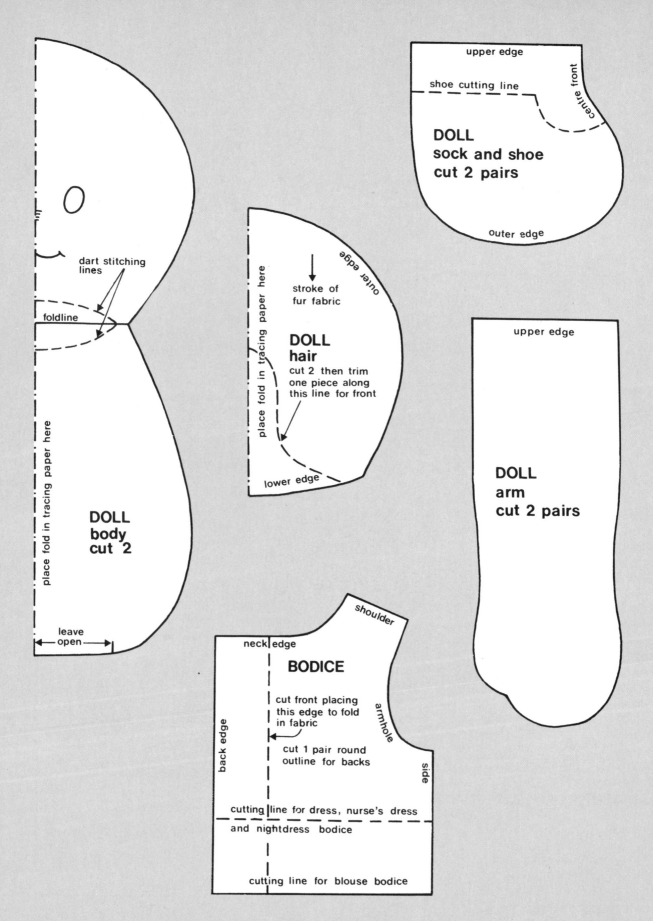

DOLL
sock and shoe
cut 2 pairs

upper edge

shoe cutting line

centre front

outer edge

DOLL
hair
cut 2 then trim
one piece along
this line for front

stroke of
fur fabric

outer edge

place fold in tracing paper here

lower edge

dart stitching
lines

foldline

place fold in tracing paper here

DOLL
body
cut 2

leave
open

DOLL
arm
cut 2 pairs

upper edge

BODICE

shoulder

neck edge

cut front placing
this edge to fold
in fabric

cut 1 pair round
outline for backs

back edge

armhole

side

cutting line for dress, nurse's dress
and nightdress bodice

cutting line for blouse bodice

Knit a Nursery Rhyme

Three popular nursery rhymes, all knitted in 4 ply yarn. Each measure about 11.5 cm [4½ in] in height. Sew the dolls in place to make decorations, or leave them free.

You will need: Oddments of 4 ply yarn in assorted colours as shown in the illustrations; a pair of 3 mm [No 11] knitting needles; small amount of stuffing; tiny guipure flower trimming; a short length of silver gift cord for Miss Muffet's spoon; a red pencil.

Abbreviations: See page 17.

Notes: Use the illustrations as a guide to the colours used. Particular colours of yarn are only mentioned in the instructions when necessary, e.g. white for Mary's lamb, green for the grassy banks.

When sewing up the items, split the yarn into two 2 ply strands and use one strand only. Join all the seams by oversewing the edges together instead of back stitching.

The looped pattern: The hedgerows around each scene and the haycock are all knitted in a two row looped pattern which is given here to avoid repetition throughout the instructions.

Cast on the required number of sts as stated in the individual instructions.

1st row: K 1; * insert right hand needle K wise into next st, place first finger of left hand at back of st, wind yarn anti-clockwise round needle and finger 4 times then round tip of right hand needle only, draw through the 5 loops; repeat from * until 1 st remains; K 1.

2nd row: K 1; * K 5 tog, pulling the loops down firmly as you go; repeat from * until 1 st remains; K 1.

Little Miss Muffet

Grassy bank

Using two strands of green in different shades, cast on 14 sts.

1st row: Inc K wise into every st – 28 sts.
Work in g-st until work measures 10 cm [4 in].

Next row: (K 2 tog) to end – 14 sts. Cast off.

Fold 4 cm [1½ in] under at one side edge of the work and sew it in place while at the same time pushing in stuffing to make the raised 'tuffet' at the back of the bank.

Side hedgerows

Make two pieces alike one for each side of the grassy bank, as follows.

Using green cast on 16 sts and work the two row looped pattern 4 times. Cast off.

Back hedgerow

For the piece at the back of the grassy bank, cast on 16 sts and work the two row looped pattern 6 times. Cast off.

Oversew the cast on and cast off edges of each hedgerow piece together then sew hedgerows to sides and back of bank, catching the row ends together at the corners where they meet each other.

Legs and body

Begin at the ankle edge of one leg and using white or other suitable colour for stockings cast on 4 sts.

1st row: Inc K wise into every st – 8 sts.

Now beginning with a P row, work 15 rows in st-st. Leave sts on a safety pin. Work second leg in the same way, then with right side of work facing, K across 8 sts of second leg then 8 sts of first leg – 16 sts.

St-st 7 rows. Break off yarn and join on colour for top of body. St-st 8 rows. Break off yarn and join on pink for the head then st-st 10 rows.

Next row: (K 2 tog) to end – 8 sts.

Break off yarn leaving a long end then thread it loosely through remaining sts.

Join row ends of each leg then join body and head seam leaving top of head open.

Turn right side out. Stuff legs leaving a small gap in stuffing at tops of legs so that they will bend, then stuff body and head. Pull up yarn tightly at top of head and fasten off. Tie a strand of yarn tightly round neck then sew ends of yarn into body.

Arms [make two alike]

Begin at hand and using pink cast on 3 sts.

1st row: Inc K wise into every st – 6 sts.

Beginning with a P row, st-st 3 rows. Break off pink and join on yarn to match top of body. St-st 14 rows then cast off loosely.

Join row ends leaving cast off edges open. Turn right side out and stuff, then tie a strand of yarn round each wrist as for neck.

Sew the open top edges of arms to each side of body 2 rows below neck. Bend arms at the elbows as shown in the illustration and catch in place at the bends.

Shoes [make two alike]

Begin at top edge of shoe and cast on 13 sts.

1st row: K 5, inc in next 3 sts, K 5 – 16 sts.

Next row: P. Break off yarn and join on contrast colour for shoe sole.

Next row: K 5, (K 2 tog) 3 times, K 5 – 13 sts. Cast off.

Join row ends and cast off edges of shoes leaving cast on edges open. Turn right side out, stuff toes of shoes, then push shoes onto ends of legs and sew top edges to legs.

Face and hair

Work the facial features slightly to one side of the head so that Miss Muffet will appear to be turning to look at the spider.

Use double red yarn for the mouth and work a single vertical stitch 2 knitted rows above the neck. Work a small black stitch at centre of mouth. Use black yarn for the eyes and work a single chain stitch for each eye, 2 knitted stitches apart and 1 knitted row above the mouth. Colour cheeks with red pencil.

For the hair, split a few 15 cm [6 in] lengths of yellow yarn into single strands. Sew centre of strands to top of head then sew strands in bunches to each side of head. Trim ends of hair evenly. Remainder of the head will be covered by the hat.

Little Miss Muffet (page 69)

Hat

Cast on 44 sts and g-st 2 rows. Beginning with a K row, st-st 2 rows.

* *Next row:* (K 2 tog) to end – 22 sts. Join on contrast yarn for hat band and beginning with a P row st-st 2 rows. Break off contrast yarn and continue in hat colour, st-st 5 rows.

Next row: (K 2 tog) to end – 11 sts.

Break off yarn leaving a long end, thread through remaining sts, then pull up tightly and fasten off. Press the hat brim with a warm iron. Oversew row ends together. Place hat on head and sew it to head through the row knitted before the hat band rows.

Skirt and bodice

Begin at hem edge of skirt and cast on 36 sts. G-st 2 rows.

Beginning with a K row, st-st 10 rows.

Next row: (K 2 tog) to end – 18 sts. Break off skirt colour and join on contrast yarn for bodice.

Beginning with a P row st-st 6 rows. Cast off loosely.

Sew 3 small horizontal contrast colour stitches down centre front of bodice and take

Little Boy Blue (page 72)

Mary had a little lamb (page 73)

small running stitches round lower edge of skirt as shown in illustration. Join row ends of skirt and bodice and put on doll having cast off edge of bodice under the arms. Use double yarn in the bodice colour to work a stitch over each shoulder from front to back, for the shoulder straps.

Spoon

Cut a 10 cm [5 in] length of silver gift wrapping cord. Make it into a twisted cord and knot the ends together. Trim off the ends of cord close to the knot then press the knot to flatten it and form the bowl of the spoon. The spoon should be about 2 cm [¾ in] long. Use tweezers to pass the spoon through Miss Muffet's hand then catch it in place with sewing thread.

Bowl

Cast on 14 sts and st-st 4 rows. Break off yarn leaving a long end. Thread it through sts and pull up tightly then fasten off. Join row ends of work then turn bowl right side out. Tease out a strand of cream coloured yarn and sew

into bowl using sewing thread.
Sew the bowl to Miss Muffet's hand then sew it to her skirt where it touches.

Spider

Using dark brown cast on 4 sts for the body.
  1st row: Inc K wise into every st – 8 sts.
  Beginning with a P row, st-st 6 rows.
  Next row: (P 2 tog) to end – 4 sts.
  Cast off.
Gather round edge of knitting and pull up gathers tightly enclosing a little stuffing then fasten off. Work 2 small white stitches for eyes. Sew the centres of four 5 cm [2 in] lengths of dark brown yarn underneath body for the legs. If desired, put a dab of adhesive on the end of each leg and roll between your finger and thumb to prevent the yarn from fraying out. Trim the ends of the legs.

To assemble the scene

Place Miss Muffet in position on the grassy bank. Sew skirt and shoes in place where they touch the bank. Using yellow yarn sew a few guipure flowers to the bank taking stitches through their centres. Sew the spider in place if desired.

Little Boy Blue

The field

Begin at front edge and using one strand of yellow together with one strand of pale green, cast on 24 sts.

Work in g-st, inc 1 st at each end of every row until there are 36 sts. Continue in g-st until work measures 11 cm [4½ in] from the beginning. Cast off.

Hedgerow

Using green cast on 75 sts. Work the two row looped pattern once, then cast off. Oversew the cast off edge to the sides and back of the field. Spread out the loops and catch to field here and there where they touch.

Make another hedgerow piece in the same way and oversew the cast off edge to the cast off edge of the first piece.

Haycock

Using yellow cast on 28 sts. Work the two row looped pattern once.

Now continue working the two row pattern and at the same time dec 1 st at each end of the next and every alternate row until 10 sts remain. Break off yarn leaving a long end and thread it through remaining sts, pull up tightly and fasten off.

Join row ends of work, back stitching seam to bring loops together and pulling stitches tightly to shorten this edge slightly. Turn right side out and stuff, then sew lower edge of haycock to a corner of the field.

Legs, body and shoes

Make these as for Miss Muffet using shades of blue as shown in the illustration on page 34.

Jacket body

Begin at lower edge and using blue to match the legs cast on 26 sts.

G-st 2 rows.
Next row: K.
Next row: K 2, P to last 2 sts, K 2.
Repeat the last two rows 5 more times.
Next row: K.2, (K 2 tog) to last 2 sts, K 2 – 15 sts.

Break off yarn leaving a long end and thread it through remaining sts. Place this edge round doll's neck and pull up yarn length tightly, catching row end sts together at centre front. Sew a small yarn bow to neck at front.

Arms

Make as for Miss Muffet using blue to match jacket body. Sew tops of arms to each side of jacket taking stitches through jacket and into body.

Face and hair

Work a small red stitch for mouth and small V-shapes for the eyes in black and referring to Miss Muffet instructions on page 34 for placing the features etc. For the ears thread a darning needle with double pink yarn and work a small loop at each side of the head. For the hair thread a darning needle with brown yarn and work long vertical stitches above the forehead, in front of the ears and above the neck at back. Remainder of the head will be covered by the hat.

Hat

Using blue to match the jacket cast on 44 sts and g-st 2 rows. Now work as for Miss Muffet's hat from * to the end.

The horn

Using brown yarn cast on 4 sts. Beginning with a K row st-st 4 rows.
Next row: K, inc in first and last st – 6 sts.
St-st 6 rows then cast off.

Oversew row ends of work together pulling stitches tightly to make the horn curve. Turn right side out and stuff.

To assemble the scene

Sew Boy Blue and horn in position on the field as shown in the illustration, catching pants, shoes and hands to the field where they touch. Sew the hat to the haycock also.

Mary had a little lamb

Grassy bank and Mary

Make in the same way as for Miss Muffet using different colours of yarn as illustrated and making the mouth stitch as for Boy Blue.

Lamb's body

Begin at front end of the body and using white cast on 8 sts.
    1st row: Inc K wise into every st – 16 sts.
    Work 16 rows in g-st.
    Next row: (K 2 tog) to end – 8 sts. Cast off.
    Oversew row ends of work together then across cast off edge. Turn right side out and stuff, then oversew the opening.

Head

Using white cast on 12 sts and work 10 rows g-st.
    Next row: (K 2 tog) to end – 6 sts.
    Next row: (K 2 tog) to end – 3 sts.
    Break off yarn leaving a long end, thread it through remaining sts then pull up tightly and fasten off. Oversew row ends of work together then turn right side out. Bring seam to centre back of head then stuff head and oversew cast on edges to close. Sew back of head to front of body, turning it slightly to one side. Work the eyes as for Miss Muffet, then work a small black stitch for the mouth and a pink stitch for the nose as illustrated on page 71.

Ears [make two alike]

Using black cast on 4 sts and K 1 row.
    Next row: (P 2 tog) twice – 2 sts.
    Next row: K 2 tog and fasten off.
    Sew cast on edges of ears to sides of head as illustrated on page 71.

Legs [make four alike]

Note that P side of the white portion of the legs is the right side. Begin at top of leg and using white cast on 5 sts.
    Beginning with a K row, st-st 4 rows.
Break off white and join on black.
    Next row: P.
    Next row: K. Break off yarn leaving a long end. Thread it through sts, pull up tightly and fasten off then oversew row ends of work together. Turn right side out and stuff, then sew open ends of legs underneath body at the front and back.

Tail

Note that P side of work is the right side. Using white cast on 4 sts and beginning with a K row, st-st 10 rows. Break off yarn leaving a long end. Thread it through sts, pull up tightly and fasten off. Oversew row ends of work together having right side outside, then sew cast on edge of tail to back of lamb.
Make a twisted cord from a single strand of yarn and tie in a bow round lamb's neck.

To assemble the scene

Sew Mary and lamb to the grassy bank as for Miss Muffet.

3
ROSETTE DOLLS

Dutch Dolls

These traditionally dressed Dutch boy and girl are about 36 cm (14 in) tall. They are both rosette dolls and so are very simple to make as their bodies, arms and legs are gathered circles slipped on to elastic

You will need: Oddments of fabrics and felt for gathered circles and clothes; small pieces of stockinette (or cuttings off an old T-shirt) for heads and hands; 2·10 m (2¼ yd) of thin elastic cord; cotton curtain lace and iron-on interlining for girl's bonnet; 25 g of double knitting yarn for hair; stuffing; thin card for circle templates; adhesive; red pencil.

Notes: The seam allowance is 5 mm (¼ in) on stuffed pieces unless otherwise stated.

For fairly authentic costumes, use photographs as a guide to correct colours, noting the following – red and white striped fabric for boy's jacket; multi-coloured striped fabric for girl's skirt, or plain blue instead; flower-patterned fabric for top two circles of girl's bodice.

Make the gathered fabric circles as described on pages 12–13.

Circle diameters

A = 8 cm (3 in)	B = 9 cm (3½ in)
C = 10 cm (4 in)	D = 11 cm (4¼ in)
E = 12 cm (4¾ in)	F = 13 cm (5¼ in)
G = 16 cm (6¼ in)	H = 17 cm (6¾ in)

Dutch boy

Cut out and gather circles as follows: for bodice, six G; for collar, two D; for each sleeve, eight C, six B, and four A; for trouser top five H; for each leg, four F, four E and twelve D.

Head: Cut a 13 by 15 cm (5¼ by 6 in) piece of stockinette with most stretch in the fabric going across the short edge. Join the long edges then gather round one short edge. Pull up gathers tightly and then fasten off. Stuff head firmly and run a gathering thread round

remaining raw edge. Cut a 70 cm (27½ in) length of elastic, fold it in half and make a knot in the folded end. Pull up head gathers, turning in raw edges and enclosing knotted end of elastic. Fasten off, oversewing through elastic to secure.

Body and legs: Thread two collar circles on to the double body elastic, then two bodice circles. Cut a 35 cm (13¾ in) length of elastic for the arms and pass it between the body elastics. Thread remaining four bodice circles on to body elastics, then the five trouser top circles.

On to each body elastic, thread leg circles as follows: four F, four E and twelve D. Securely knot each elastic close to last circle, trimming off any excess.

Clogs: Cut four felt clog pieces from pattern. Join them in pairs, stitching close to edges and leaving top edges open. Turn right side out and stuff very firmly. Run gathering threads round top edges and pull up gathers tightly, enclosing knots in leg elastics. Oversew through elastic.

Arms: On to each end of arm elastic, thread sleeve circles as follows: eight C, six B and four A. Knot ends of elastic as for legs. Use the pattern to cut two pairs of hand pieces from stockinette with most stretch in fabric in direction shown on pattern. Join hands in pairs, leaving wrist edges open. Trim seams, turn and stuff, then gather wrist edges and sew to knots as for legs, turning in raw edges of fabric.

Face and hair: Cut eyes from black felt using pattern. Stick them half-way down face and 2·5 cm (1 in) apart. Work a small U-shape for mouth in red thread, 1·5 cm (⅝ in) below eyes. Colour cheeks and nose with red pencil.

For hair, wind yarn four times round two

fingers then slip it off fingers and machine stitch through one end of loops. Continue making loops until a 26 cm (10¼ in) continuous length is formed. Pin and sew this across forehead, round sides and back of head above neck.

Cap: For cap side, cut a 4 by 28 cm (1½ by 11 in) strip of felt. Join short edges then turn in one long edge and stitch down. Run a gathering thread round remaining edge. Cut an 8 cm (3 in) circle of felt for top of cap and oversew it to gathered edge of cap, pulling up gathering thread slightly to ease side of cap to fit top. Turn right side out. Cut two cap peak pieces from felt, placing pattern to fold in felt. Oversew outer edges together then turn right side out. Top-stitch round outer edge. Oversew inner edges of peak to cap front at lower edge. Put a little stuffing inside cap and sew it to head to cover top of hair.

Dutch girl

Cut out and gather fabric circles as for boy, making top two bodice circles from flower patterned fabric. Omit the A sleeve circles.

Head: Make the girl's head exactly in the same way as before.

Skirt and apron: Cut a 20 by 65 cm (8 by 25½ in) strip of fabric. Join short edges and take a narrow hem on one remaining raw edge.

For apron top cut a 7 by 22 cm (2¾ by 8¾ in) strip of striped fabric and a 12 by 22 cm (4¾ by 8¾ in) strip for lower portion. Join them at one long edge. Take a narrow hem round apron except striped edge. Tack this raw edge level with top raw edge of skirt at front. Gather round top raw edge of skirt, pull up gathers until raw edges meet then fasten off.

Body and legs: Make as for boy, threading skirt on to elastics between bodice and pants top circles.

Clogs: Make clogs for the girl in the same way as for boy.

Arms: On to each arm elastic thread arm circles as follows: eight C, and six B circles. Extend wrist edge of hand pattern by 5 cm (2 in) as shown on pattern to form lower portion of arms. Cut out, make and attach as for boy. Tie sewing thread tightly round at position of wrists then sew thread ends into hands. Now sew upper ends of arms to fabric circles where they touch.

Face and hair: Make face as for boy. Cut about forty 50 cm (19½ in) lengths of yarn and tie at centre with a strand of yarn. Sew this centre to forehead 4 cm (1½ in) above eyes. Tie strands again at each side of head, level with mouth, then sew to head. Plait hair. Tie yarn round ends and trim to even lengths.

Lace bonnet: Iron the interlining to wrong side of lace fabric before cutting out pieces from pattern. Cut one pair of bonnet pieces and sew the darts as shown on pattern. Trim darts. Join pieces along top and centre back edges. Make bonnet lining in same way but do not stitch darts. Join bonnet and lining pieces round face and neck edges, leaving a gap in neck edge at back. Turn right side out and slip stitch gap. Stitch all round close to edge of bonnet. Run a gathering thread along neck edge as shown on pattern put bonnet on doll and pull up gathers to fit at back of neck. Fasten off. Stuff top of bonnet then sew to head at each side at position of dotted line shown on pattern.

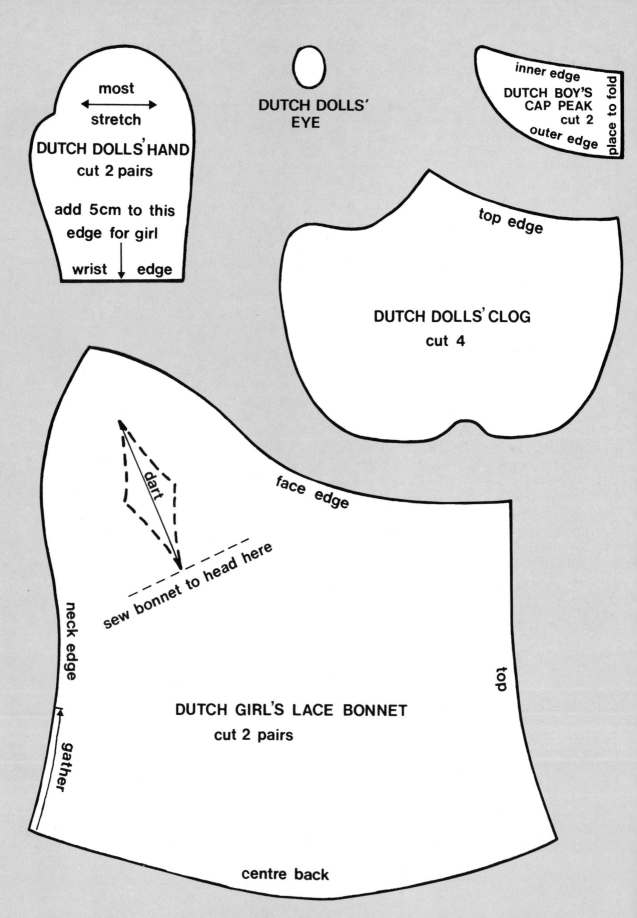

most
stretch

DUTCH DOLLS' HAND
cut 2 pairs

add 5cm to this
edge for girl

wrist ↓ edge

DUTCH DOLLS'
EYE

inner edge
DUTCH BOY'S
CAP PEAK
cut 2
outer edge

place to fold

top edge

DUTCH DOLLS' CLOG
cut 4

face edge

dart
sew bonnet to head here

neck edge

gather

top

DUTCH GIRL'S LACE BONNET
cut 2 pairs

centre back

Six Stretchy Dolls

A half-dozen colourful stretchy dolls about 26·5 cm (10½ in) in height, which are so easy to make from oddments of fabric. Their bodies, arms and legs are made from gathered circles, lightly stuffed, before threading on to elastic.

You will need: Oddments of fabrics (dress-weight cottons, etc. – which must be thin and soft enough to gather up tightly); 80 cm (32 in) of cord elastic, about 2 mm ($\frac{1}{16}$ in) in diameter, for each doll; pink or white cotton stockinette for heads and hands (or cuttings off an old plain T-shirt); small pieces of felt; small pieces of fur fabric for hair; oddments of braid and ribbon; stuffing; thin card for circle templates (cuttings off cereal packets, etc.); a red pencil for colouring cheeks; a bodkin with a large eye; adhesive.

Notes: 5 mm ($\frac{1}{4}$ in) seams and turnings are allowed unless otherwise stated. Follow basic instructions when making each doll, but refer to individual doll instructions before starting.

Basic doll

To make the gathered circles

Cut card templates in the following diameters: 10 cm (4 in), 11 cm ($4\frac{1}{4}$ in), 13 cm (5 in), 14 cm ($5\frac{1}{2}$ in), and 15 cm (6 in). Now referring to the table, cut out the number of circles stated in each size, by drawing round the templates on to fabric. Several circles can be cut at one time by pinning a few layers of fabric together. Cut bodice or shirt circles from one fabric and pants circles from another fabric, as shown in table and diagram, if the individual instructions say so.

Fold each circle into quarters and snip off the corner at the circle centre to form a tiny hole. Now turn in the raw edge of each circle 3 mm ($\frac{1}{8}$ in) and gather, taking 5 mm ($\frac{1}{4}$ in) long running stitches. Pull up gathers, stuffing the circle lightly, then pull up gathers as tightly as possible and fasten off.

To make the doll

For the head, cut a piece of stockinette 13 by 14 cm (5 by 5½ in), with the most stretch in stockinette going across the 14 cm (5½ in) measurement. Join short edges of fabric, then gather round one remaining raw edge, pull up gathers tightly and fasten off. Turn the head right side out.

For the body, cut a 50 cm (20 in) length of elastic. Fold it in half and knot the folded

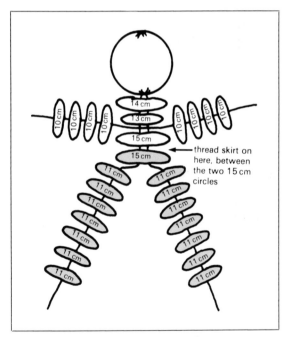

How to thread gathered circles on to elastics

TABLE
giving number of circles required
Cut these circles for bodice or shirt:—
EIGHT × 10 cm diameter
ONE × 13 cm diameter
ONE × 14 cm diameter
ONE × 15 cm diameter
Cut these circles for pants:—
ONE × 15 cm diameter
FOURTEEN × 11 cm diameter.

end. Stuff head to measure about 23 cm (9 in) around, then run a gathering thread round, 1 cm ($\frac{3}{8}$ in) away from remaining raw edge. Pull up gathers, turn in raw edges and enclose the knotted end of elastic. Fasten off gathers tightly, then oversew through elastic.

Now, referring to the diagram for the correct sizes, thread the first two gathered circles on to the doubled body elastic and push them up against the head. Cut a 30 cm ($11\frac{3}{4}$ in) length of elastic for the arms and pass this between the two body elastics. Continue threading circles on to the body elastics as shown in the diagram, noting position for threading on skirt for girl doll. Finally, thread arm circles on arm elastic.

Push all circles firmly together along each elastic, knot elastic and trim off excess.

Hands: Trace hand pattern off the page on to thin paper, then cut out. Pin the pattern on to two layers of stockinette, with most stretch in fabric in the direction shown on pattern. Trim fabric level with wrist edge of pattern. Now stitch all round, close to edge of pattern, leaving wrist edges open.

Remove pattern and cut out hand close to stitching line. Turn right side out and stuff. Gather wrist edge and insert knot at end of arm elastic, in same way as for head.

Shoes: Trace shoe pattern off the page as for hand. Pin pattern on to two layers of felt, then stitch all round close to edge of pattern. Mark the slit on to felt before removing pattern. Cut slit in this layer of felt only. Turn shoe right side out through slit, then stuff firmly.

Push knotted end of leg elastic inside the shoe at position of dot on pattern. Now ladderstitch edges of slit together, taking care to sew elastic securely to each shoe.

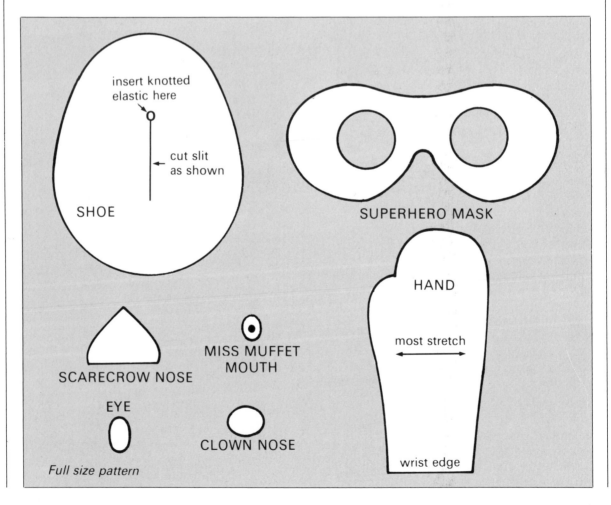

insert knotted elastic here

cut slit as shown

SHOE

SUPERHERO MASK

SCARECROW NOSE

MISS MUFFET MOUTH

EYE

CLOWN NOSE

HAND

most stretch

wrist edge

Full size pattern

For face: Cut eyes from black felt and stick them in place half-way down face and 2 cm ($\frac{3}{4}$ in) apart. Work a V-shaped mouth, using four strands of red sewing thread, 1·5 cm ($\frac{5}{8}$ in) below eyes.

Colour the cheeks by rubbing them with red pencil.

For the nose, mark a red dot between the eyes of the doll.

The clown

Make the basic doll, using same fabric for all circles except for neck, wrist and ankle circles. Make these in a contrast colour.

Cut nose from red felt and glue it in place. Work a small black stitch above each eye for eyebrows.

For hair cut a strip of fur fabric 2·5 by 23 cm (1 by 9 in), with smooth stroke of fur pile going towards one long edge (this will be the face edge of hair). Oversew short edges of strip together. Turn in face edge of strip and catch it down. Place hair on head as shown in illustration (*right*) and sew both long edges to head.

For cap, cut a strip of fabric 12 by 26 cm ($4\frac{3}{4}$ by $10\frac{1}{4}$ in), to match body circles. Join short edges of strip. Turn in one long edge and press. Gather the remaining raw edge up tightly and fasten off. Turn cap right side out. Stuff top of cap lightly and sew turned-in edge to head, just overlapping hair. Gather and stuff a 6 cm ($2\frac{3}{8}$ in) diameter circle of contrast fabric, sew it to top of cap.

Make three more bobbles in the same way, using 3 cm ($1\frac{1}{4}$ in) diameter circles of fabric. Sew them to body circles at front of doll. Pull cap to one side and catch it to head.

The super hero

The super hero's suit looks most realistic made from ciré nylon fabric – silver for the main part of his body, contrasted with bright red for the details.

Make the basic doll, using same fabric for all circles except for neck and wrist circles

and the two circles at end of each leg. Make these in contrast colour. Make shoes to match these circles.

For hair, cut a 15 cm (6 in) diameter circle of fur fabric. Gather round edge and put hair on doll's head as shown in illustration (*below*) with smooth stroke of fur fabric going from back of neck towards forehead. Pull up gathers to fit head and fasten off. Sew gathered edge to head.

For the cape, cut two pieces of fabric 14 by 20 cm ($5\frac{1}{2}$ by 8 in), to match contrast circles. Join them, leaving a gap in seam for turning. Turn right side out and slipstitch gap. Gather one long edge and secure gathering thread round the elastic below the head.

Cut mask from felt and glue it to face.

The cowboy

Make the basic doll, using checked fabric for shirt circles and blue fabric for pants circles. Make hair as for super hero.

For the neckerchief, cut a 17 cm ($6\frac{3}{4}$ in) square of fabric. Fray out edges then fold into a triangle and tie round elastic below head.

For hat brim, cut a 15 cm (6 in) diameter circle of paper, then cut a 9 cm ($3\frac{1}{2}$ in) diameter circle from the centre. Pin brim pattern on to two layers of felt. Stitch all round, close to outer and inner edges of pattern. Remove pattern and cut out brim close to stitching lines.

For hat crown, cut two pieces of felt 8 by 14 cm (3 by $5\frac{1}{2}$ in), to match brim. Round off one long edge of each piece to form a semi-circle. Stitch pieces together round curve. Trim seam and turn right side out. Oversew straight edges of crown to inner edge of brim.

Stuff top of hat, place it on head and sew it to head round lower edge of crown. Glue braid round for hatband. Indent crown at top and sides, then catch it to head at these positions. Turn up brim at front and back and catch to crown.

The scarecrow

Make the basic doll, using one fabric for shirt circles and another for pants circles. Before threading circles on to elastic, sew on a few coloured fabric patches. Patch the shoes and darn hands also.

Cut nose from orange felt and oversew side edges together. Stuff nose and sew it to face. For hair, cut a strip of coarsely woven yellow fabric, 10 by 24 cm (4 by $9\frac{1}{2}$ in). Fray out both long edges, leaving a 2 cm ($\frac{3}{4}$ in) portion at centre of strip unfrayed. (*Note:* keep the frayed-out strands until later on.) Fold hair strip, bringing long frayed-out edges together, and sew the folded edge round head. Trim strands short above eyes.

Now, using the frayed-out strands, knot a few here and there round body and leg elastics between the circles, and trim ends.

Make hat and sew it in place as for cowboy hat, using tweedy fabric and the following sizes: For brim, a 12 cm ($4\frac{3}{4}$ in) diameter circle with a 7 cm ($2\frac{3}{4}$ in) circle at centre; for crown, two 7 by 13 cm ($2\frac{3}{4}$ by 5 in) pieces, rounding off one long edge of each. For scarf, cut a strip of fabric 6 by 24 cm ($2\frac{1}{4}$ by $9\frac{1}{2}$ in). Fray out edges and knot scarf round elastic below head.

Miss Muffet

Make skirt first. Cut a strip of fabric 14 by 50 cm ($5\frac{1}{2}$ by 20 in), and join short edges. Narrowly hem one long raw edge and sew on braid above hem. Gather remaining long raw edge up tightly and fasten off.

Now make basic doll, using same fabric as skirt for bodice, except for neck and wrist circles. Make these in contrast colour.

Make pants circles in a different fabric. Thread on skirt at position shown on diagram.

Cut mouth from red felt and mark black dot at centre. Stick mouth in place. Make hair and sew it in place as for super hero, but use a 16 cm ($6\frac{1}{4}$ in) diameter circle of fur fabric. Sew ribbon bow to hair.

For the spider, gather and stuff a 4 cm ($1\frac{1}{2}$ in) diameter circle of black fabric. To make the legs, use double black thread and sew four short loops at each side of spider. Spread loops with a little glue and smooth the strands of thread together. Trim legs to even lengths. Work two white stitches for eyes. Sew spider to the skirt.

Cinderella

Make skirt first as for Miss Muffet, and sew on patches of fabric as shown in illustration. Make basic doll and hair as for Miss Muffet but work a small inverted V-shape for mouth.

For the broom, cut a strip of brown tweedy fabric 9 by 16 cm ($3\frac{1}{2}$ by $6\frac{1}{4}$ in) and fray out 5 cm (2 in) at one short edge. Now roll up fabric strip very tightly across the width, then wind strong thread tightly round and round to make a firm handle, leaving frayed-out strands unbound. Sew the thread ends into the handle, then sew the broom handle to Cinderella's right hand.

Home on the Range

Three colourful characters from the Wild West – a cheery cowboy, his pretty partner and, of course, his horse. They are all stretchy toys made of gathered circles of fabric threaded on elastic. The finished dolls are about 55 cm (21½ in) high and the horse is about 27 cm (10¾ in) tall

The cowboy

You will need: Oddments of fabric; for head and hands – a pair of stretchy nylon tights or stockings (one leg makes one doll); for hair – a small ball of thick-knit yarn and 34 cm (13½ in) of tape or bias binding; felt for hat, waistcoat and shoe soles; a little stuffing; 60 cm (23½ in) of narrow braid for trimming boots; thin card for circle templates; 120 cm (47¼ in) of thin elastic cord; black felt, red pencil, black and white thread for features; adhesive.

Notes: Seams as stated in instructions. Make the gathered fabric circles as described on pages 12–13.

Circle diameters
A = 20 cm (8 in)   B = 18 cm (7 in)
C = 14 cm (5½ in)   D = 12 cm (4¾ in)
E = 10 cm (4 in)   F = 8 cm (3 in)

Cut out and gather circles as follows.

For each trouser leg cut twenty C circles, four D and two E circles.

For top of trousers cut four A circles. For belt cut two A circles. For shirt cut six A circles. For top of shirt cut three B circles. For collar cut two C circles.

For each sleeve cut sixteen D circles, four E circles and two F circles.

To assemble the circles: Cut a 76 cm (30 in) length of elastic, fold it in half and push looped end through centres of trouser top circles, then through the belt, shirt, shirt top and lastly collar circles. Knot looped end of elastic and push a needle through knot to stop circles slipping off.

Now thread circles for one leg on to one free end of elastic as follows – ten C circles,

two D, two E, two D, and lastly ten C circles. Make a large knot in end of elastic and push a needle through as before. Thread on other leg circles in same way.

For arms cut a 44 cm (17½ in) length of elastic. Make a large knot in one end and push a needle through knot. Thread circles on to elastic for one sleeve as follows – eight D circles, two E, two F, two E, and lastly eight D circles. Thread unknotted end of elastic through doubled body elastic below the five shirt top and collar circles. Thread on remaining circles for other sleeve as for first sleeve. Knot end of elastic and push a needle through to hold circles.

Head: Cut across one leg of tights or stockings close to ankle, then cut leg above ankle into three sections 12 cm (4¾ in) long. Place these inside each other to make a triple-thickness tube, with raw edges level. Run a gathering thread round 1 cm (⅜ in) from one end of tube through all thicknesses, pull up gathers tightly and fasten off. Turn tube right side out, tack the three layers together at raw edges. Stuff head to measure about 33 cm (13 in) around, and 30 cm (12 in) measuring from neck edge at front, over gathered top of head to neck edge at back. Fasten a rubber band round neck end, about 4 cm (1½ in) up from raw edges.

For eyes cut two 1·5 cm (⅝ in) diameter circles of black felt. Using white thread work a few small straight stitches on each eye as shown in our picture. Glue eyes to head half-way down face, 3·5 cm (1⅜ in) apart. Colour cheeks with moistened red pencil.

Work eyelashes and nose with straight stitches. Work mouth in back stitch, then oversew, working back through each stitch.

For hair cut yarn into 8 cm (3 in) lengths and stitch centre of lengths down centre of tape or binding until it is covered. Fold yarn strands in half round tape (folding tape along its length) and stitch through looped ends of yarn and folded tape, to form a fringe. Over-sew top of fringe to head above eyes and round back of head.

For hat brim cut a 22 cm (8¾ in) diameter circle of felt with a 10 cm (4 in) diameter circle cut out of centre.

For hat crown cut two felt pieces 16 by 12 cm (6¼ by 4¾ in). Join crown pieces round edges taking 5 mm (¼ in) seam, leaving one pair of long edges open and rounding off other corners for top of hat. Trim seam and press. Turn crown right side out and sew lower edge of crown to inner edge of brim, taking a tiny seam.

Put a little stuffing in crown to shape it and make a dent in crown centre. Place hat on head, with lower edge of crown resting on top of hair. Sew hat to head through lower edge of crown. Catch brim to crown at centre front and back.

Run a gathering thread round neck near rubber band, remove band and trim off nylon fabric about 1 cm (⅜ in) below gathering thread. Turn in cut edges of neck and place knotted end of body elastic into opening. Pull up gathers and oversew neck edges securely, sewing through elastic.

Hands: For each hand pin pattern on to three layers of nylon fabric folded in half, with edge of pattern marked fold against fold in fabric. Stitch round hand close to pattern, leaving lower straight edges open. Cut out hand close to stitching. Turn right side out and stuff. Make thumb by taking a large stitch round hand at one side, pulling stitch up tight.

Gather round raw edges of hands 1 cm (⅜ in) from edges and sew to knotted ends of arm elastic as for head.

Boots: Cut two soles from card. Cut two pairs of uppers from fabric and join them in pairs at centre front and back edges, taking narrow seams. Turn right side out and place a card sole inside lower edge of each boot, matching centre front and back points. Glue lower edges of uppers 5 mm (¼ in) on to card soles.

Cut two felt soles and glue them in place to cover card soles and raw fabric edges. Stuff

boots to within 2 cm (¾ in) of top edges. Glue braid round boots at lower edges. Gather boot tops and sew to knotted ends of leg elastic as for head.

Waistcoat: Cut two fronts and one back from felt, as directed on pattern. Join fronts to back at sides, oversewing edges together. Fold back lapels on fronts and press.

Machine round edges of waistcoat and lapels. Join shoulder seams, oversewing edges together. Press seams.

Neckerchief: Cut a triangle of fabric, 50 cm (19½ in) across the base by 20 cm (8 in) high. Hem edges and knot round doll's neck.

The cowgirl

You will need: Materials as for boy (omitting tape for hair, braid, felt for hat and waistcoat). Also 3 m (3⅜ yd) lace edging, 4 cm (1½ in) wide; quilted fabric for bonnet; 30 by 91 cm (11¾ by 36 in) of printed fabric for skirt; same amount of plain fabric for underskirt; 1·5 m (1⅝ yd) of ribbon for trimming bonnet and shoes; 10 cm (4 in) of narrow elastic.

To make circles: Work as for Cowboy, but make the two belt circles from same fabric as used for legs.

The lace frills: For each cuff frill cut a 30 cm (12 in) length of lace edging. Join short edges, gather up one long edge tightly and fasten off. For neck frill cut a 40 cm (15¾ in) length, make in same way.

The skirt: Join short edges of fabric. Make a 4 cm (1½ in) hem on one long raw edge, then sew on lace edging. Gather round other remaining raw edge tightly, fasten off.

The underskirt: Make as for skirt, taking a slightly larger hem and sewing on lace edging so it hangs slightly below skirt hem.

To assemble the circles: Work as for Cowboy, threading on lace frills at neck and wrist edges. Thread underskirt and skirt on to elastic between top of belt and shirt circles.

The head: Make as for Cowboy except for hair. Wind yarn into a hank measuring about 50 cm (19½ in). Back stitch strands of yarn at centre of hank to centre top of head. Take yarn loops to each side of head and sew in place in a bunch. Cut through yarn loops to separate strands, then trim ends evenly.

For bonnet brim cut two fabric strips 27 by 7 cm (10⅝ by 2¾ in). Join edges taking a 5 mm (¼ in) seam, leaving one pair of long edges open and rounding off other corners. Trim seam and turn right side out. Top stitch through brim close to seam edge, then tack raw edges together.

For back of bonnet cut a 40 cm (15¾ in) diameter semi-circle. Turn in straight edge

1 cm ($\frac{3}{8}$ in) and hem. Thread narrow elastic through hem, securing elastic each end with a few stitches. Gather curved edge of semi-circle to fit raw edges of brim; join them taking a 5 mm ($\frac{1}{4}$ in) seam.

Decorate bonnet by sewing a strip of ribbon across brim, and a ribbon rosette to each side. Place bonnet on head behind hair and catch it to head with stitches at each side, lower back edge and top of brim. Sew head to elastic as for Cowboy.

The hands: Make as for Cowboy.

The boots: Make and sew to leg elastics as before, cutting upper edges of boot uppers along dotted line shown on pattern. Omit braid, and sew a ribbon bow to front of each boot.

The horse

You will need: Oddments of fabric; for head, ears and hooves – a pair of men's plain socks (such as stretchy towelling ones); a small ball of thick-knit yarn for mane and tail; a little stuffing; thin card for soles of hooves and for circle templates; 170 cm (67 in) of thin elastic cord; scraps of felt for soles of hooves, eyes and nostrils; thin yarn for mouth; 1 m (39$\frac{1}{2}$ in) of braid for reins; adhesive.

Circle diameters

A = 24 cm (9$\frac{1}{2}$ in)	B = 22 cm (8$\frac{3}{4}$ in)
C = 20 cm (8 in)	D = 18 cm (7 in)
E = 16 cm (6$\frac{1}{4}$ in)	F = 14 cm (5$\frac{1}{2}$ in)
G = 12 cm (4$\frac{3}{4}$ in)	H = 10 cm (4 in)
I = 8 cm (3 in)	

Cut out and gather circles as follows.

For neck cut fourteen E size circles and two D circles.

For body cut two D circles, four C, four B, and six A circles.

For rear end of body cut two B circles, one D, one E, one F and one G circle.

For each front leg cut two E circles, twelve F, ten G, four H and two I circles.

For each back leg cut two D circles, two E, ten F, ten G, four H and two I circles.

To assemble the circles: Cut two 45 cm (17$\frac{3}{4}$ in) lengths of elastic for legs and put them aside.

For body cut 80 cm (31$\frac{1}{2}$ in) of elastic, fold it in half and knot ends together, slipping a needle through knot. Push opposite looped end of elastic through body circles as follows (starting at rear of body) – one G, one F, one E, one D, two B circles. Now thread one length of leg elastic through the doubled body elastic.

Continue threading on body circles – six A, four B, four C, two D circles. Now thread remaining length of leg elastic through the doubled body elastic.

Thread on neck circles – two D and fourteen E circles. Knot looped end of elastic and push a needle through knot.

Thread front leg circles for each leg on to each appropriate end of elastic as follows – two E, twelve F, two G, two H, two I, two H, and eight G circles. Knot elastic ends and push needles through knots.

Thread back leg circles on to each end of leg elastic as follows – two D, two E, ten F, two G, two H, two I, two H, and eight G circles. Knot elastic ends and push needles through knots to hold circles.

Head: Stuff the foot of one sock into a slightly tapered shape, about 20 cm (8 in) long by about 28 cm (11 in) around widest part. Cut off sock foot at an angle (see diagram 1), for neck edge of head. Gather round this cut edge about 1 cm ($\frac{3}{8}$ in) from edge. Turn in raw edge and pull up gathering thread, pushing knotted neck end of body elastic inside head. Pull up gathers and oversew securely through elastic to hold it in place.

From blue felt cut two oval shapes from eye pattern. Cut two circles of black felt, and glue them to blue pieces as shown on pattern. Work a few small straight stitches in white thread at top of each eye, as shown in illustration. Glue eyes to head.

Cut two 2 cm ($\frac{3}{4}$ in) diameter circles of pink felt for nostrils and two slightly smaller black felt circles. Glue black circles to centres of pink ones, then glue nostrils in place.

Using doubled thin yarn, work mouth round end of face, taking a large stitch round from one side to the other.

Make a triangular pattern for ears, 8 cm

(3 in) across the base by 9 cm (3½ in) high. Cut two ear pieces from remaining piece of sock, and also two from fabric. Join pieces in pairs, taking 5 mm (¼ in) seam, leaving base edges open and rounding off points at tops. Trim off points and turn ears right side out. Turn in remaining raw edges 5 mm (¼ in) and oversew pulling stitches to gather slightly. Fold ears and sew folded lower edges to head.

Mane: Cut about twenty 30 cm (12 in) lengths of yarn. Fold them in half and tie a yarn strand round, about 7·5 cm (3 in) from folded ends. Sew this tied point to top of head just behind ears, so looped ends hang over forehead.

Tail: Cut yarn lengths as for mane. Thread lengths through knotted elastic at end of body, and fold in half to hang down evenly. Tie a yarn strand round close to folded ends, enclosing elastic knot.

Hooves: Cut four 7 cm (2¾ in) diameter circles of card. From the remaining sock cut four tubular sections, each 6 cm (2⅜ in) long, cutting right across leg and foot of sock as shown in diagram 2. Place a card circle 1 cm (⅜ in) inside one raw edge of each tube, and stick fabric edges on to card.

Stuff each hoof and gather all round close to remaining raw edge. Turn in raw edge, pull up gathers and enclose knotted end of leg elastic, oversewing securely through elastic to hold knot in place.

Glue a 7 cm (2¾ in) diameter circle of felt to sole of each hoof to cover raw edges.

Reins: Cut a 25 cm (9¾ in) length of braid, overlap short ends 1 cm (⅜ in) and sew in place. Slip this circle over horse's nose and pin ends of remaining braid to it each side. Take reins off horse and sew ends of braid in place.

For rosettes make two 8 cm (3 in) diameter gathered circles, turning in edges when gathering. Sew one each side of reins to complete the horse.

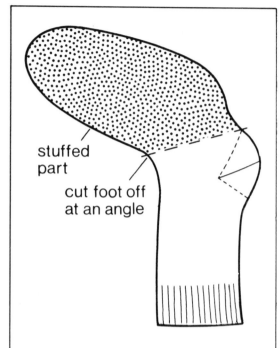

stuffed part

cut foot off at an angle

Diagram 1 How to make horse's head

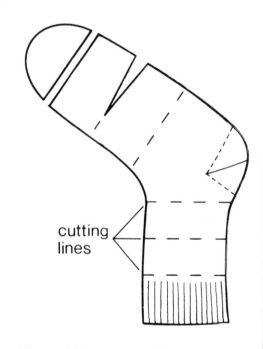

cutting lines

Diagram 2 Cutting the 6 cm (2⅜ in) sections for horse's hooves

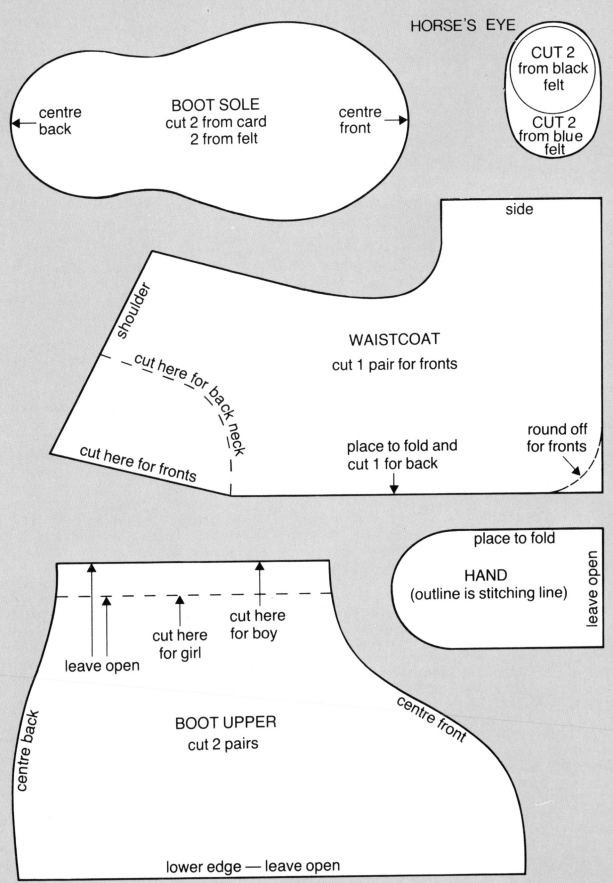

HORSE'S EYE

CUT 2
from black
felt

CUT 2
from blue
felt

BOOT SOLE
cut 2 from card
2 from felt

centre
back

centre
front

side

WAISTCOAT

cut 1 pair for fronts

shoulder

cut here for back neck

cut here for fronts

place to fold and
cut 1 for back

round off
for fronts

place to fold

HAND
(outline is stitching line)

leave open

leave open

cut here
for boy

cut here
for girl

leave open

centre back

centre front

BOOT UPPER

cut 2 pairs

lower edge — leave open

Turnabout Dolly

This 43 cm (17 in) double-ended doll has a dual personality. At one end she's a smiling brunette; turn her upside down and she's a beautiful blonde with a tearful face. Easy and inexpensive to make from gathered fabric circles with a pair of socks used for the heads and hands.

You will need: One pair of size 9 ankle socks (preferably with a plain-knit sole) in pink or white; about half a ball each of black and yellow 4-ply knitting yarn; scraps of black and blue felt; 2·5 m (2¾ yd) of 4 cm (1½ in) wide broderie Anglaise edging; stuffing; 1 m (1 yd) of thin elastic cord; adhesive; red pencil.

For each doll's dress; 1·2 m (1¼ yd) of 91 cm (36 in) wide gingham; scraps of contrast coloured fabric for collar and cuffs; 2 m (2 yd) ric-rac braid to match contrasting fabrics; scraps of ribbon; thin card for circle templates.

Notes: Seams as stated in instructions. Make the gathered fabric circles as described on pages 12–13. Before cutting out the gingham circles, first cut a 30 by 91 cm (12 by 36 in) strip from each piece of gingham for each doll's skirt.

Circle diameters

A = 18 cm (7 in) B = 15 cm (6 in)
C = 10 cm (4 in)

Cut out and gather circles as follows.

For each doll's bodice, cut five A circles from gingham, then cut two B circles from contrast fabric for each doll's collar. For each sleeve cut seventeen C circles from gingham then cut one C circle from contrast fabric.

Broderie Anglaise frills: For frills at neck and wrists of both dolls cut six 25 cm (10 in) lengths of broderie Anglaise. Join short edges of each strip taking tiny seams then run a gathering thread along raw edge, pull up gathers tightly and fasten off. (Trim a little off long raw edges of four of the strips before gathering up, to make narrower frills for the wrists.)

Skirt: Stitch two rows of ric-rac braid near one long edge of each gingham strip spaced as shown in the illustrations, this will be the hem edge. With right sides facing, join short edges of each skirt strip taking a 1 cm (⅜ in) seam. With raw edges level sew broderie Anglaise trimming to hem edge of one skirt piece on right side. Having right sides together join both skirt pieces at hem edges taking a 1 cm (⅜ in) seam. Turn right side out bringing raw edges together then press. Using strong thread, run a gathering thread round

1 cm (⅜ in) from raw edges through both thicknesses of fabric. Pull up gathers tightly and fasten off.

To assemble the body pieces: Cut a 25 cm (10 in) length of elastic, fold it in half and knot ends together. Push looped end of elastic through circles and other pieces as follows: thread on one broderie Anglaise collar frill, two B contrast colour collar circles, five A gingham bodice circles, then the skirt (taking care to have correct fabric against matching bodice circles), remaining five A gingham bodice circles, two other B contrast colour collar circles and lastly one broderie Anglaise collar frill. Slip a pencil through knotted and looped ends of elastic to prevent circles slipping off.

To assemble the arm pieces: Cut a 33 cm (13 in) length of elastic and knot one end then push a darning needle through knot to prevent circles slipping off. Thread on one broderie Anglaise wrist frill, one C contrast colour circle, then seventeen sleeve circles. Thread the un-knotted end of the elastic through doubled body elastic below top four collar and bodice circles at one end of body. Now thread on the remaining sleeve circles and lastly the C contrast colour circle and the broderie Anglaise frill. Knot end of elastic and push a darning needle through knot.

Make up the other pair of arms in the same way threading elastic through doubled body elastic at other end of doll.

Head with crying face: Stuff the toe of one sock firmly to form a ball about 28 cm (11 in) in circumference. Secure sock at neck end with a rubber band and use plainest part of sock for face. For eyes cut two 1·5 cm (½ in) diameter circles of blue felt and two of black felt. Trim a little off one side of each black circle and glue to blue circles as shown in illustration. Glue eyes to head about 6·5 cm (2½ in) up from rubber band having them about 2·5 cm (1 in) apart. Work straight stitches for eyelashes using black thread. Colour cheeks with moistened red pencil then work tears in single large chain stitches using black thread. Using white thread work a few tiny satin stitches at base of each tear for a highlight. Work nose and mouth with red

thread as illustrated. For hair, wind most of
the yellow yarn into a hank 20 cm (8 in) long.
Tie a length of matching yarn round centre of
hank. Place this tied centre at top of head so
that looped ends will hang down further at
back of head than front. Sew tied centre of
yarn in position. Spread out loops evenly all
round head and sew ends of loops to head as
illustrated taking care to make stitches as
small as possible. Make a small bunch of yarn
from remainder and twist and sew it to top of
head for a top knot of hair. Sew small ribbon
bow to front of top knot.

Run a gathering thread round neck near
rubber band, remove band, pull up gathers
then cut off remainder of sock 1 cm ($\frac{3}{8}$ in)
below thread. Turn in cut edges of neck and
place looped or knotted end of body elastic
into neck opening. Pull up gathers and oversew edges firmly, enclosing elastic in stitching.

Head with smiling face: Stuff head and
make eyes, eyelashes and nose as for other
head. Work smiling mouth as illustrated. For
hair, make a 25 cm (10 in) hank of yarn using
most of the yarn. Tie hank at centre and sew
to top of head as given for other head. Divide
looped ends to either side of face. Sew ends of
loops evenly in place all round head as for
other head then back stitch through yarn
strands all round head about 2·5 cm (1 in) up
from looped ends. Sew a few short loops of
yarn to forehead above face for a fringe then
sew ribbon bow above fringe. Attach head to
other end of body elastic in same way as
given for other head.

Hands: Using remaining pieces of socks, cut
out four hand pieces using pattern and placing
edge indicated against a fold for each one.
Stitch a narrow seam on each hand as shown
on pattern leaving straight edges open. Turn
hands right side out and stuff. Gather open
raw edges of each hand 1 cm ($\frac{3}{8}$ in) from edge,
turn in raw edges and place knotted end of
arm elastic inside each opening. Pull up
gathers and oversew, enclosing elastic in
stitching.

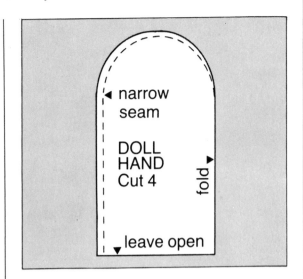

4
LARGE TOYS

Cuddly Koalas

The koala twins measure about 40 cm (16 in) tall. You can make them from pale fawn fur fabric using white fur fabric for their chests and shaggy white fur fabric to line their ears. They each have three outfits of clothes – cosy sleeping suits (the same style for both bears), swimsuits, and playclothes (dungarees and sundress).

The Koalas

You will need: 60 cm ($\frac{3}{4}$ yd) of 138 cm (54 in) wide fawn fur fabric; 600 g (1 lb 5 oz) of stuffing; oddments of long- and short-pile white fur fabric for fronts of ears and chest pieces; scraps of black felt; metric graph paper; adhesive.

Notes: Copy the patterns on to graph paper, square by square; each square on diagram = 5 cm. See page 100.

Mark points A and B on body pieces and points C and D on arm pieces. Mark mouth line on wrong side of each front head piece and also mark centre of each eye with a length of coloured thread taken through to right side of fabric.

5 mm ($\frac{1}{4}$ in) seams are allowed on fur fabric pieces unless otherwise stated.

Body and head

Take the front head pieces and, on the wrong side of each one, machine stitch over the mouth line about six times using black thread, to make a thick line. Join them at centre front edges.

Join the body front pieces at centre front edges, from point A to neck edge, leaving a gap in the seam as shown on pattern. Gather neck edge of head front to fit neck edge of body front, then join neck edges matching centre front seams.

Join back head pieces at centre back edges. Join back body pieces at centre back from point B to neck edge. Now join neck edges of these pieces matching centre back seams.

Join entire front of koala to back, round sides of head and body, then round legs, matching points A and B. Turn right side out through front opening. Stuff head firmly, taking care to push stuffing in well at sides, above gathers at neck front and at nose. Stuff legs, then body, then ladderstitch gap in seam.

Chest piece: Cut one pair of chest pieces from short-pile white fur fabric, using the cutting line shown on body front pattern. Join pieces at centre front edges. Pin chest piece to front of koala, matching centre front seams and neck edges. Sew raw edges to koala.

Face: Cut nose from black felt then pin it to face, with lower edge about 1·5 cm ($\frac{5}{8}$ in) above centre of mouth. Sew nose in place.

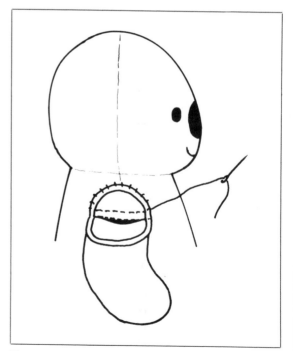

How to sew on the arms

Cut eyes from black felt. Trim off fur pile in a small circle around the marked centre of each eye. Glue eyes in position, pressing them firmly in place until glue dries. Trim fur pile slightly shorter below nose and above mouth.

Arms: Join arm pieces in pairs, leaving upper edges open between points C. Turn in seam allowance at open upper edges and tack. Turn arms right side out and stuff lower halves. Place an arm at each side of koala, with points D 2 cm ($\frac{3}{4}$ in) down from neck at side seams. Pin arm pieces which are nearest to body in place, then sew arms to body round upper edges and also backstitch them to body along the upper stitching line shown on arm pattern (*see diagram, opposite*). Stuff tops of arms very lightly then join upper edges.

Ears: Place ear pieces together in pairs then oversew raw edges together, leaving lower edges open. Turn right side out and oversew lower edges of each ear together, pulling stitches tightly to gather. If white fur pile is very long, trim it slightly. Sew ears to head front (see pattern on page 100 for position).

The clothes

Notes: 1 cm ($\frac{3}{8}$ in) turnings are allowed on all pieces unless otherwise stated. Draw patterns on to graph paper as for the koala patterns, marking on all details. Cut out fabric pieces as stated on patterns, noting any alterations in individual garment instructions.

Boy's dungarees

You will need: 30 cm ($\frac{3}{8}$ yd) of 91 cm (36 in) wide fabric; oddment of contrast fabric for pockets and binding; short lengths of narrow elastic; four small buttons; two snap fasteners.

To make dungarees: Join back pieces at centre back edges, stitching curve in seam twice to reinforce. Clip and trim seam at curve. Turn in waist edge 5 mm ($\frac{1}{4}$ in) then 1·3 cm ($\frac{1}{2}$ in) and stitch. Thread an 18 cm (7 in) length of elastic through this casing and secure it at each end.

Cut four pocket pieces from contrast fabric and join them in pairs, leaving a gap for turning. Trim seams and corners, then turn pockets right side out and slipstitch gaps. Sew pockets to positions shown on dungarees fronts. Join centre front edges of front pieces as for back pieces. Cut a 3 cm ($1\frac{1}{4}$ in) wide bias strip of contrast fabric. Sew one long edge to waist and bib edges of front on right side, taking a 5 mm ($\frac{1}{4}$ in) seam. Turn binding to wrong side, turn in raw edge 5 mm ($\frac{1}{4}$ in) and slipstitch to seam line.

Join front of dungarees to back at side edges. Hem ankle edges as for back waist edge and thread through elastic to fit ankles. Now bring centre front and back seams together and join inside leg edges of each leg, then clip seams.

For each shoulder strap cut a 4 by 24 cm ($1\frac{1}{2}$ by $9\frac{1}{2}$ in) strip of fabric. Join long edges and across one short edge of each strap, taking a 5 mm ($\frac{1}{4}$ in) seam. Trim seams and corners and turn straps right side out. Sew short raw edges of straps to inside waist edge at back of dungarees as shown on pattern. Sew snap fasteners to other ends of straps and inside top corners of bib. Sew buttons to pockets and to right side of bib at corners.

Girl's dress and panties

You will need: 40 cm ($\frac{1}{2}$ yd) of 91 cm (36 in) wide fabric; 1·60 m ($1\frac{3}{4}$ yd) of ric-rac braid; two snap fasteners; short lengths of narrow elastic.

To make the dress: Join dress bodice pieces round edges, leaving waist edges open. Trim seam and corners and turn bodice right side out.

For dress skirt cut a 12 by 91 cm ($4\frac{3}{4}$ by 36 in) strip of fabric. Sew on ric-rac 2·5 cm (1 in) away from one long edge (this will be hem edge of skirt). Join short edges of strip, taking a 2 cm ($\frac{3}{4}$ in) seam and leaving 7 cm ($2\frac{3}{4}$ in) open at waist end of seam, for back waist opening. Press seam to one side. Narrowly hem lower edge of skirt. Gather waist edge to fit lower edge of bodice and

wide Acrilan or Courtelle fleece (this will make two suits); oddment of contrast fabric for binding neck and sleeve edges; a 15 cm zip fastener for each; short lengths of narrow elastic.

Notes: Take care to cut the suit pieces having the 'most stretch' (usually across the width of the fabric) in the direction shown on pattern pieces. After cutting one pair of body pieces to pattern outline, trim off neck edge at dotted line on next pair for front pieces.

To make cosy suit: Cut four 11 cm ($4\frac{1}{4}$ in) lengths of elastic. Stitch elastic to wrong side of leg of each suit piece at dotted line shown on pattern, stretching elastic to fit as it is sewn.

Join the two front pieces at front edges between points E and F as shown on pattern. Turn in remainder of centre front edges and tack, then sew zip fastener to these edges, letting excess length of fastener extend above neck edges. Open zip fastener, then trim off excess length of zip level with neck edge of suit pieces. *Do not* close zip until suit is completed, to prevent the slide fastener slipping off.

Make a pocket from contrast fabric, in the same way as given for dungarees pockets. Sew pocket to left front at position shown on pattern. Join suit back pieces at centre back edges, from point E to neck edge. Now join front to back at shoulder edges. Join side edges and around lower leg edges as far as point E. Trim seams around lower leg edges.

Cut two bias strips of contrast fabric 5 by 19 cm (2 by $7\frac{1}{2}$ in). Sew one long edge of each strip to wrist edges of sleeves, with right sides facing, raw edges level and stretching bias slightly to fit wrist edges. Join underarm edges of sleeves. Turn bias to inside, turn in raw edges and slipstitch over seam. Sew armhole edges of sleeves to armholes of suit, matching point G to shoulder seams and matching underarm seams to side seams. Stitch armhole seams again close to first line of stitching, then trim seams close to this stitching line.

For the neck binding cut a 6 by 34 cm ($2\frac{3}{8}$ by $13\frac{1}{2}$ in) bias strip of contrast fabric. Bind neck edge in same way as for sleeves, letting

sew it to one waist edge of bodice, with right sides facing, raw edges level and leaving other waist edge free. Turn in remaining waist edge and slipstitch it over seam.

For each shoulder strap cut a 4 by 13 cm ($1\frac{1}{2}$ by 5 in) strip of fabric. Make as for boy's dungarees straps. Put dress on koala and pin ends of straps at an angle, about 1 cm ($\frac{3}{8}$ in) inside top corners of bodice at front and back. Sew strap ends in place as pinned. Sew ric-rac round neck edges and over shoulder straps. Sew snap fasteners to back of bodice.

To make the panties: Use the dungarees back pattern for panties, cutting the lower edge along appropriate dotted line on pattern. Cut two pairs of pants pieces and join each pair at centre edges. Stitch curves in seams twice, then clip and trim the seams at the curves. Join the pairs to each other at side edges.

Hem waist and lower edges, taking 5 mm ($\frac{1}{4}$ in) then 1 cm ($\frac{3}{8}$ in) turnings to form casings for elastic. Thread elastic through to fit waist and legs, securing elastic at ends of casings. Bring centre seams together; join inside leg edges of each leg, then trim seam.

Cosy suits

You will need: 40 cm ($\frac{1}{2}$ yd) of 152 cm (60 in)

short ends of bias extend 1 cm ($\frac{3}{8}$ in) beyond centre front edges to allow for seaming. When turning bias to inside, turn in these short ends and slipstitch.

Boy's swimming shorts

You will need: Small piece of fabric; short lengths of bias binding and narrow elastic.

To make swimming shorts: Use the dungarees back pattern for the shorts, cutting the lower edge of pattern to the dotted line shown. Also trim 2 cm ($\frac{3}{4}$ in) off waist edge.

Join pairs of pieces at centre edges, stitching twice at curves to reinforce. Snip seam and trim at curves. Join the pairs to each other at side edges. Bind lower edges with bias. Hem waist edge and thread elastic through as for girl's panties. Now bring centre seams together and join inside leg edges of each leg, then trim seam.

Girl's bikini

You will need: 20 cm ($\frac{1}{4}$ yd) of 91 cm (36 in) wide fabric; 1·60 m ($1\frac{3}{4}$ yd) of narrow braid trimming; short lengths of narrow elastic; two snap fasteners.

To make panties: Make as for girl's panties, but trim 3 cm ($1\frac{1}{4}$ in) off waist edge of pattern before cutting out pieces. Sew trimming round waist edge stitching line.

To make top: Make top as for girl's dress bodice but join bodice pieces all round edges, leaving a gap for turning. Trim seams and corners, turn bodice right side out and slipstitch gap. Make and sew on straps as for girl's dress, using 4 by 11 cm ($1\frac{1}{2}$ by $4\frac{1}{4}$ in) strips of fabric. Sew trimming to lower edge, round top edges and over shoulders. Sew snap fasteners to back edges.

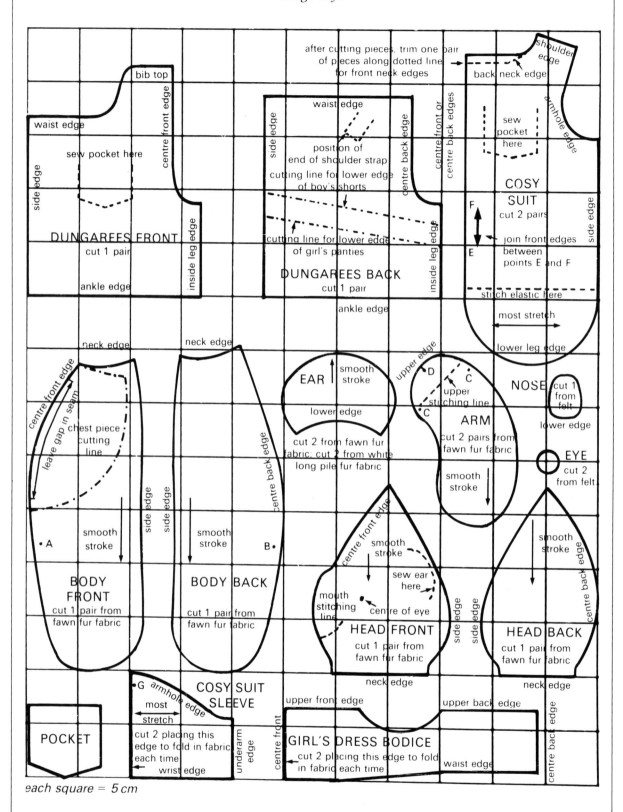

after cutting pieces, trim one pair
of pieces along dotted line →
for front neck edges

shoulder edge

back neck edge

bib top

waist edge

sew pocket here

COSY SUIT
cut 2 pairs
join front edges between points E and F

side edge

centre front edge

DUNGAREES FRONT
cut 1 pair

inside leg edge

ankle edge

waist edge

side edge

position of end of shoulder strap
cutting line for lower edge of boy's shorts
cutting line for lower edge of girl's panties

centre back edge

centre front or centre back edges

sew pocket here

F

E

DUNGAREES BACK
cut 1 pair

inside leg edge

ankle edge

stitch elastic here

most stretch

lower leg edge

neck edge

centre front edge

leave gap in seam

chest piece cutting line

neck edge

EAR smooth stroke

lower edge

cut 2 from fawn fur fabric; cut 2 from white long pile fur fabric

upper edge

D C

upper stitching line

C

NOSE cut 1 from felt

ARM
cut 2 pairs from fawn fur fabric

smooth stroke

lower edge

EYE cut 2 from felt

· A

smooth stroke

side edge

side edge

smooth stroke

B ·

centre back edge

smooth stroke

BODY FRONT
cut 1 pair from fawn fur fabric

BODY BACK
cut 1 pair from fawn fur fabric

centre front edge

smooth stroke

sew ear here

mouth stitching line

centre of eye

HEAD FRONT
cut 1 pair from fawn fur fabric

side edge

side edge

smooth stroke

HEAD BACK
cut 1 pair from fawn fur fabric

centre back edge

neck edge

neck edge

· G armhole edge

COSY SUIT SLEEVE

most stretch

POCKET

cut 2 placing this edge to fold in fabric each time

wrist edge

underarm edge

centre front

upper front edge

GIRL'S DRESS BODICE
cut 2 placing this edge to fold in fabric each time

upper back edge

waist edge

centre back edge

each square = 5 cm

Penguin

A cheery soft toy penguin, about 40 cm (16 in) high. He's clad for warmth in jacket and bobble-cap (both sewn on as part of the toy), and he's delightfully simple to sew from fur fabric pieces – no patterns needed except for eyes and beak.

You will need: 40 cm (16 in) of 138 cm (54 in) wide black fur fabric (this will make two penguins); 20 cm (8 in) of similar width red fur fabric; 10 cm (4 in) of similar width green fur fabric; oddments of white fur fabric, printed fabric, tape or string, yellow, black and white felt; 500 g (1 lb) of stuffing.

Notes: When making penguin and garments make sure the smooth stroke of all fur fabric pieces goes downwards on the toy. Take 1 cm ($\frac{3}{8}$ in) seams unless otherwise stated.

Bind the edges of garments as follows: Cut 5 cm (2 in) wide straight strips of green fur fabric long enough to bind the required edge. Sew one long edge of binding in place on right side of garment, with raw edges level. Turn binding to wrong side and slipstitch other raw edge of binding over the seam line.

The penguin

For the body: Cut a strip of black fur fabric 40 by 46 cm (16 by 18 in), with smooth stroke running parallel to the short edges. Join short edges and note that this seam will be at centre back of penguin.

For base of penguin: Cut a 15 cm (6 in) diameter circle of black fur fabric. Sew it to lower edge of body. Turn body right side out and stuff, keeping base as flat as possible. Using strong thread and large stitches, gather round remaining raw edge. Pull up tightly and fasten off, oversewing to close completely. To shape neck, tie a length of tape or string very tightly round the body, 22 cm ($8\frac{3}{4}$ in) down from gathered top of head.

For white chest piece at front of body: Cut a 20 cm (8 in) square of white fur fabric. Sew raw edges of square to penguin at front, with one edge at neck and opposite edge turned just underneath base.

For tail: Cut two triangles of black fur fabric, measuring 15 cm (6 in) across the base by 7 cm ($2\frac{3}{4}$ in) high at apex. Join pieces leaving base edges open. Trim corners then turn right side out and stuff. Sew open edges of tail to back of penguin, with lower raw edge tucked under base, and upper raw edge against body.

To make foot pattern: Cut a piece of paper 10 by 12 cm (4 by $4\frac{3}{4}$ in). Round off corners at one long edge to form a continuous curved shape for outer edge of foot. To shape inner edge of foot, place straight edge of pattern just under penguin at front and draw curved shape of base on foot pattern. Trim pattern along this line. Cut four foot pieces from yellow felt using this pattern. Join them in pairs leaving inner curved edges open. Trim seam, turn right side out and stuff lightly, then stitch inner edges of each foot together close to edges. Now sew inner edges of feet to body just under base, level with edge of white fur fabric.

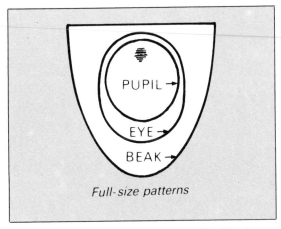

Full-size patterns

Full-size pattern for penguin's eye, pupil and beak

To make the face: Use the patterns on page 101 to cut two white felt eyes, two black felt pupils. Sew them together in pairs then work a highlight on each one with white stitches, as shown on pattern. Sew eyes in place, halfway down face and 2·5 cm (1 in) apart.

Use the pattern to cut two beak pieces in yellow felt; join them taking 3 mm ($\frac{1}{8}$ in) seam and leaving straight edges open. Turn right side out and stuff firmly, then sew beak to face below eyes as illustrated above.

The clothes

Jacket: Cut a strip of red fur fabric 15 by 50 cm (6 by 20 in). Round off the corners slightly at one long edge. Bind this edge and short edges with green fur fabric, easing binding round curves. Lay jacket aside for now.

For each sleeve cut a strip of red fur fabric 8 by 18 cm (3 by 7 in). Sew one edge of green fur fabric binding to one long edge of each

strip, then join short edges. Turn binding to inside and sew in place.

Make a paper pattern for wing by cutting an 8 cm (3 in) square and rounding off corners at one edge. Cut four wings from black fur fabric. Join them in pairs, leaving straight edges open; turn them right side out. Slip a wing inside green binding of each sleeve, with raw edges of wings level with binding seam. Sew lower edge of binding to wing. Put a little stuffing inside each sleeve then oversew top edges together. Sew tops of sleeves to jacket, 3 cm (1$\frac{1}{4}$ in) below neck edge and 8 cm (3 in) within each green fur-trimmed short edge.

Run a strong gathering thread round neck edge of jacket. Place it around penguin's neck and tie ends of gathering thread tightly together at centre front. Space out gathers evenly, then sew jacket to penguin through gathers.

The cap: Cut a strip of red fur fabric 16 by 50 cm (6$\frac{1}{4}$ by 20 in). Bind one long edge, join short edges and complete binding as for sleeves. Gather remaining raw edge of cap with large stitches, then pull up tightly and fasten off. Gather and stuff a 12 cm (4$\frac{3}{4}$ in) diameter circle of white fur fabric and sew it to gathers. Place cap on head as illustrated and sew lower edge in place. Pull top of cap to one side and catch it in place.

Scarf: Cut a strip of printed fabric 10 by 66 cm (4 by 26 in). Join long edges and turn right side out. For the bobbles, gather and stuff two 6 cm (2$\frac{1}{4}$ in) diameter circles of white fur fabric and push each raw end of scarf inside before fastening off securely and sewing bobbles to scarf. Tie scarf round neck.

Cuddly Kitten

This soft furry kitten, with jaunty knitted hat and scarf, is about 35·5 cm (14 in) long from head to curled-up tail.

The kitten

You will need: 40 cm (16 in) of 138 cm (54 in) wide white polished fur fabric (*note:* if you buy 60 cm (24 in), you will have enough to make two kittens); 250 g ($\frac{1}{2}$ lb) of stuffing; a scrap of pink fur fabric or felt for the ear linings; scraps of black and pink felt for features; white button thread; oddment of grey double knitting yarn for marking paws; adhesive; metric graph paper; invisible sewing thread for whiskers (optional).

Note: 5 mm ($\frac{1}{4}$ in) seams are allowed on fur fabric pieces.

Patterns: Draw out the patterns on to graph paper, following the outlines on the diagram square by square. Each square = 2 cm. Mark all details on to pattern pieces.

Body: Cut two body pieces from fur fabric. Cut away the underbody dart, as shown on the pattern, in one body piece only. Join the raw edges of this dart, leaving a gap in stitching at centre, for turning. Now join body pieces all round edges. Clip corners then turn the body right side out. Stuff, then ladderstitch the gap in the dart.

Using double strand of grey double knitting yarn, work three stitches round end of each paw.

Head: Cut one pair of head pieces from fur fabric. Mark the mouth line on the wrong side of each piece, and also mark the eye point on the right side of each piece with a coloured thread.

Now machine stitch twice along each mouth line, with wrong side of fabric uppermost and using black thread. Join the head pieces, leaving neck edges open. Turn right side out and stuff firmly. Using double

button thread, gather round neck edge. Pull up gathers to close neck edge completely, then fasten off. Trim fur pile above mouth lines, and at the end of the muzzle.

Glue two layers of pink felt together, then cut out nose using the full-sized pattern. Glue nose to end of muzzle.

Cut out eyes using the full-sized pattern. Use white thread to work a highlight on each eye as shown on the pattern. Place eyes on face, with top edges just below the coloured threads. Snip away the fur pile beneath each eye, then glue eyes in place. Snip off the coloured marking threads.

For whiskers, cut eight 25 cm (10 in) lengths of invisible sewing thread. Knot the lengths together at centre. Using a darning needle, take threads through the snout from one side to the other, pulling the threads until the knot catches. Knot threads at other side of snout, then trim whiskers to even lengths.

Place gathered edge of head on body at front, turning the head to one side. Hold the head in place with a couple of darning needles pushed into the head and body fabric. Ladderstitch head securely to body where they touch.

Cut one pair of ear pieces from white, and one pair from pink fur fabric. Oversew the ear pieces together in pairs, leaving lower edges open. Turn them right side out and oversew lower edges of each ear together, pulling stitches to gather slightly. Sew ears to head, setting them about 6 cm ($2\frac{3}{8}$ in) apart at top of head.

Cut one pair of tail pieces from fur fabric and oversew them together, leaving inner edges open. Turn tail right side out, using the knob of a knitting needle to push the end through, then stuff tail lightly. Sew inner edge of tail to centre back of underbody.

The hat and scarf

You will need: Two 20 g balls of double knitting yarn; a pair of $3\frac{3}{4}$ mm [No 9, USA 4] knitting needles; a cable needle.

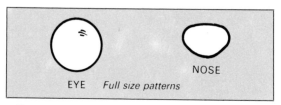

EYE   *Full size patterns*   NOSE

Full-size pattern for kitten's eyes and nose

Abbreviations: See page 17, as well as below – cable 6 (slip next 3 sts onto to cable needle and leave at front of work, K 3, then K 3 from cable needle).

Scarf

To make: Cast on 18 sts and work 6 rows in single rib. Work cable pattern as follows: *1st row:* (P 2, k 6) twice, p 2. *2nd row:* P. Repeat these 2 rows, twice more. *7th row:* (P 2, cable 6) twice, p 2. *8th row:* P. These 8 rows form the cable pattern. Work the 8 rows, 21 more times, then rows 1 to 4 again. Rib 5 rows, then cast off in rib.

Hat

To make: Cast on 80 sts and work 6 rows in single rib. Work cable pattern as follows: *1st row:* P 1, (K 6, P 2) to last 7 sts, K 6, P 1. *2nd row:* P. Repeat these 2 rows, twice more. *7th row:* P 1 (cable 6, P 2) to last 7 sts, cable 6, P 1). *8th row:* P. These 8 rows form the cable pattern. Work the 8 rows, 3 more times.
Next row: (K 2 tog) to end – 40 sts. Break off yarn leaving a long end. Thread yarn through sts, then pull up tightly and fasten off. Join row ends, then make a pompon and sew to top of hat.

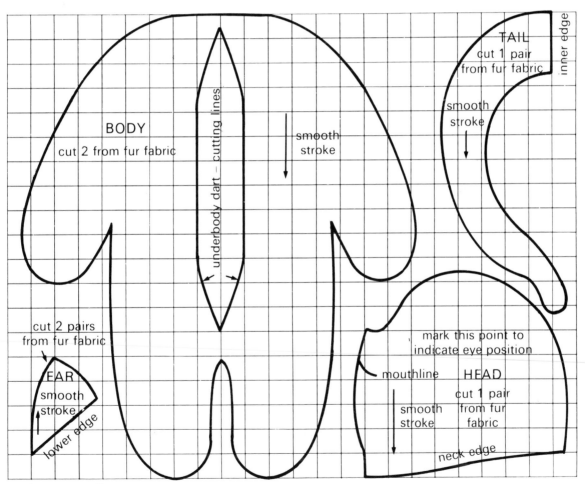

each square = 2 cm

Mother and Baby Panda

This lovable pair are both made from soft furry fabric. The eyes and noses are felt and are sewn in place so the toys are safe even for babies to play with. The pandas' legs are sewn in position to enable them to sit steadily. The mother measures about 34 cm (13½ in) and the baby about 21 cm (8¼ in) from top to tail

For the mother and baby panda you will need: 50 cm (½ yd) each of 138 cm (54 in) wide white and black fur fabric (the white is for the heads and bodies and the black is for the arms, legs, ears and eyes); scraps of black and brown felt; white thread; black double knitting yarn; 750 g (1½ lb) of stuffing; adhesive; metric graph paper; black and white button thread for sewing limbs and head in position.

Notes: 1 cm (⅜ in) seams are allowed on all pieces.

Cut pieces from either white or black fur fabric as stated in list of materials, following cutting directions on pattern pieces.

Mark darts, etc. on the wrong side of the fabric.

Copy all the pattern pieces square by square on to graph paper (each square on the diagram equals 5 cm). Mark all the details on to the pattern pieces.

Mother Panda

Sew dart in each side head piece as shown on the pattern then trim the dart. Join side head pieces from point A to neck edge down the centre front. Insert head gusset from point A along top of head to neck edge. Turn head right side out and stuff firmly pushing the stuffing well into 'snout' and above the darts. Run strong gathering thread round neck edge 1 cm (⅜ in) from the edge, pull up gathers turning in the raw edges then oversew to close completely.

Stitch darts on body pieces as shown on the pattern then trim darts. Join body pieces leaving the neck edge open. Turn, stuff and gather neck edge as for head. Place head on top of body matching the gathered portions,

centre front seams and taking care to keep back of head and back of body in line with each other. Turn head slightly to one side then push it down on to body and secure with darning needles. Ladder stitch head and body together securely all round twice using strong white thread.

Join each inner arm piece to outer arm piece as far as points A and B. Turn arms right side out and stuff. Slip stitch raw edges at tops of inner arms to the wrong side of outer arms piece to enclose stuffing. Turn in remaining raw edges of outer arms piece 1 cm (⅜ in) and tack. Place this portion around back of panda matching centre fold line to centre back seam of body and having top edge level with line where head joins body. Sew in place using strong black thread then continue ladder stitching tops of arms to body at each side where they touch.

On one pair of leg pieces, make darts as shown on the pattern. Join each of these pieces to the other leg pieces without darts, leaving a gap in the seam for turning as shown on the pattern. Turn and stuff legs then turn in raw edges and slip stitch gaps. Place legs in 'seated' position at each side of the body as illustrated with darted sides of the legs against the body. Secure legs with darning needles then ladder stitch to body where they touch using strong black thread.

Join ears in pairs leaving lower edges open. Turn right side out then oversew lower raw edges together pulling stitches to gather slightly. Sew ears to top of head as shown on head pattern. For mouth, work a shallow W using double black yarn about 2 cm (¾ in) below end of 'snout' as shown in illustration. Cut nose from black felt and stick to end of 'snout'. Cut one pair of eye patch pieces from black fur fabric. Clip fur pile short all over the pieces. Cut eyes from brown felt and pupils from black felt as shown on eye patch pattern.

Stick pupils to eyes then use white thread to work a small highlight on each one as shown in illustration. Stick felt eyes securely to eye patches then pin eyes in position as illustrated. Stick patches in position with a little glue spread under the felt eyes then sew patches in place all round the edges.

Baby Panda

Make baby in the same way as mother using the baby panda patterns and ignoring reference to darts on legs. Work mouth 1·5 cm ($\frac{5}{8}$ in) below end of 'snout' and trim seams on ears before turning right side out.

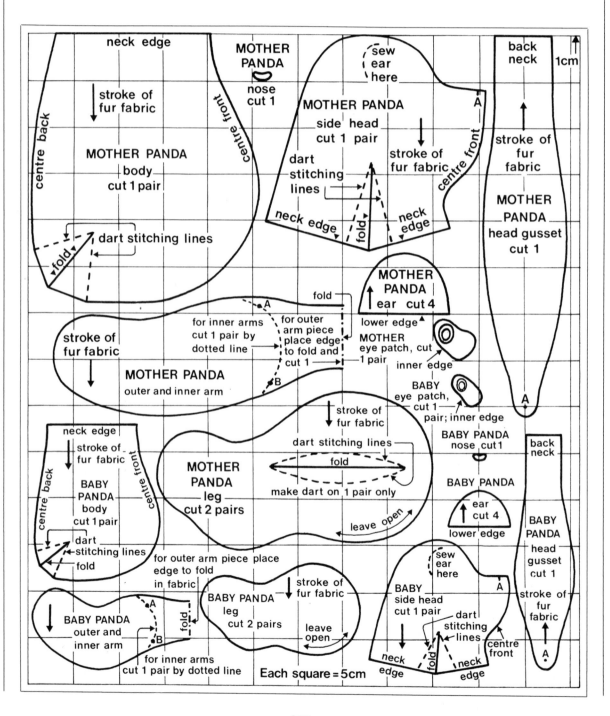

Teddy Bear

This traditional Teddy with his jointed arms and legs would make a super raffle prize for your local bazaar or, of course, the perfect gift for a favourite child. He measures 53 cm (21 in) tall

You will need: 50 cm ($\frac{5}{8}$ yd) of fur fabric 138 cm (54 in) wide; 500 g (about 1 lb) of stuffing; four 45 mm ($1\frac{3}{4}$ in) hardboard joints (see supplier's list on page 139); two 15 mm ($\frac{5}{8}$ in) diameter black buttons for eyes (optional); pieces of chamois leather or felt for foot and paw pads; scraps of thick felt, leathercloth or leather for masking the joints; scraps of black and brown felt and black yarn; small round-nosed pliers for bending the cotter pins on joints; metric graph paper; some wide ribbon.

Notes: The seam allowance is 5 mm ($\frac{1}{4}$ in) on all pieces except for paw pads – these are sewn round the edges to completed arms. Join pieces with right sides facing.

Copy the patterns onto metric graph paper, square by square (each square on diagram equals 2 cm).

From the patterns, cut out all pieces from fur fabric except for the foot and paw pads. Cut these from chamois or felt.

Mark the positions for the joints on wrong side of fur fabric.

To insert a joint: Each joint consists of two hardboard discs, two metal washers and a cotter pin. Also required are two circles of thick fabric such as felt or leathercloth cut out about 15 mm ($\frac{5}{8}$ in) larger in diameter than the discs. These are used to mask the hard edges of the joint against the fur fabric body and limbs.

Make up the limb as given in the instructions leaving the top edges open as indicated on the pattern. After stuffing the limb, take a joint set and on to the cotter pin thread a washer then a hardboard disc and lastly a circle of material. Push the cotter pin through the fabric at the marked point on the inside of the limb. Continue stuffing the limb around and above the joint to make it quite firm then ladder stitch the opening at the top of each limb.

Attach the completed limbs to the body,

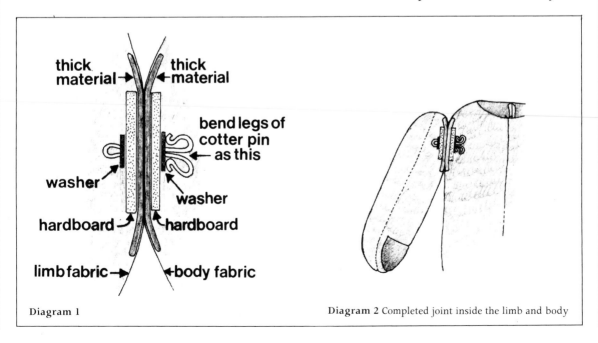

Diagram 1

Diagram 2 Completed joint inside the limb and body

before it is stuffed, as follows. Push the cotter pin protruding from the limb through the marked point on the body fabric then thread on a circle of material, a hardboard disc and, lastly, a washer. Now using the round-nosed pliers and taking each leg of the cotter pin in turn, pull upwards very hard and firmly bend it over into the shape shown in diagram 1 so that the leg is pressing hard against the washer. Diagram 2 shows a completed joint in position inside the limb and body. The joint should be as tight as possible.

After all the limbs are jointed on to the body, the body can be stuffed taking care to pack stuffing very carefully around each of the joints.

The teddy

For the arms: Join the pieces in pairs leaving a gap in the seam at upper edges as indicated. Turn right side out and stuff as far as the opening. Insert a joint on each arm taking care to make a pair. Finish off stuffing arms then ladder stitch the openings. Cut out two paw pads from felt or chamois leather following the dotted line on arm pattern. Stitch a paw pad in position on each arm as shown on arm pattern.

The legs: Join the pieces in pairs leaving the lower edges open and a gap in the seam at the upper edges as indicated on the pattern. Stitch a foot pad to the lower edges of each leg matching points A and B. Turn legs right side out, stuff, insert joints and finish off as for arms.

The body: Join the body pieces leaving the upper neck edges open and a gap in the seam at the back as indicated. Turn the body right side out, push cotter pins on limbs through the marked positions on the body and finish off the jointing on each limb. Stuff the body firmly then ladder stitch the back opening. Continue stuffing the body through the neck opening then run a gathering thread round raw edge of neck. Pull up gathers and fasten off, leaving about a 5 cm (2 in) opening in the neck. Continue stuffing through this opening to shape shoulders above the arms.

The head: Sew gusset to head pieces, matching points C, round top of head to D. Join the centre front seam of head pieces. Turn right side out and stuff very firmly. Run a gathering thread round neck edge, continue stuffing then fasten off thread leaving about a 5 cm (2 in) diameter opening.

Place the head on top of the body matching the centre front and back seams. Using very strong thread, ladder stitch the head to the body all round about 1 cm ($\frac{3}{8}$ in) from the raw edges, pull up thread tightly and make a back stitch every so often to hold the thread taut. Push more stuffing into neck between head and body if necessary to make quite firm before completing ladder stitching. Ladder stitch around the join twice more to make it quite secure.

The ears: Join ear pieces in pairs leaving the lower edges open. Turn right side out, turn in lower raw edges and oversew, pulling up stitches to gather slightly. Pin the ears on the head using the illustration, as a guide, then oversew them in place all round lower edges.

The nose and mouth: Clip the fur fabric short all round snout and mouth area. Using black yarn, work a straight stitch down from point of snout then a V on either side of this as illustrated. Cut a triangle of black felt 2 cm ($\frac{3}{4}$ in) across the base and 1·5 cm ($\frac{5}{8}$ in) at the apex. Sew this in place at end of snout as illustrated.

The eyes: Cut two 2 cm ($\frac{3}{4}$ in) diameter circles of brown felt. Place a button in the centre of each and using very strong thread sew buttons to head through felt circles at positions shown in illustration. The eyes should be set about 5·5 cm ($2\frac{1}{4}$ in) apart and level with the nose. The buttons can be replaced with circles of black felt sewing both circles in place on head.

To complete Teddy, tie a ribbon bow round his neck, trimming the ends of the ribbon into a V-shape for a smart finish.

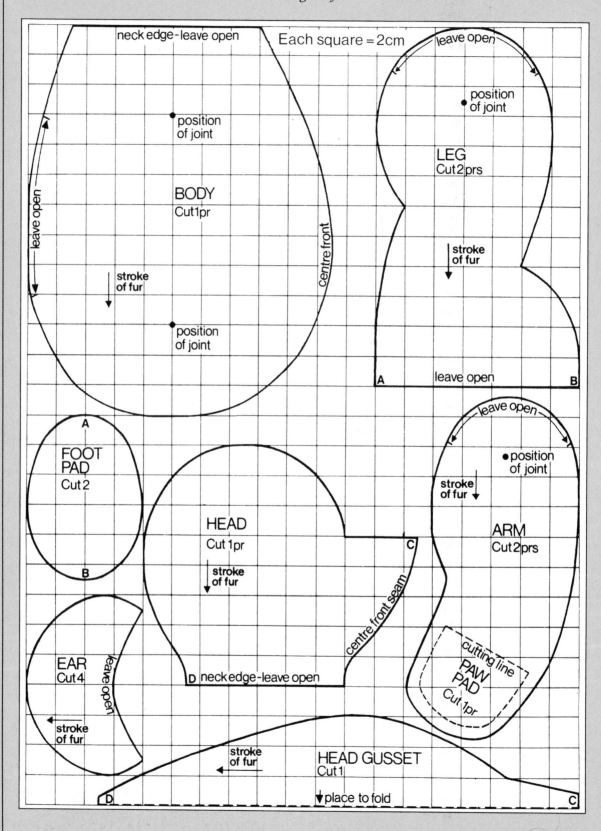

neck edge-leave open

Each square = 2cm

leave open

position
of joint

LEG
Cut 2 prs

leave open

BODY
Cut 1pr

stroke
of fur

position
of joint

Centre front

stroke
of fur

position
of joint

A   leave open   B

leave open

A

FOOT
PAD
Cut 2

stroke
of fur

position
of joint

B

HEAD
Cut 1pr

C

ARM
Cut 2 prs

stroke
of fur

centre front seam

cutting line

PAW
PAD
Cut 1pr

EAR
Cut 4

leave open

D neck edge-leave open

stroke
of fur

stroke
of fur

stroke
of fur

HEAD GUSSET
Cut 1

D

place to fold

C

Mr and Mrs Bunny

They're the best-dressed rabbits around – dandified Mr Bunny, in top hat, tail-frocked coat, waistcoat (with floppy cravat) and trousers; and his elegant partner, dressed up to the nines in Easter bonnet, prettily trimmed dress, petticoat and pantaloons. Each bunny measures about 46 cm (18 in) high

For each bunny you need: 25 cm ($\frac{3}{8}$ yd) of 138 cm (54 in) wide fur fabric; 250 g ($\frac{1}{2}$ lb) of stuffing; scraps of black, brown and white felt, and brown yarn for mouth; scraps of white fleece or felt for ear linings and tail; metric graph paper; adhesive.

Notes: Copy the patterns on to metric graph paper (each square on diagram equals 2 cm).

Cut out all bunny pieces as directed on patterns.

A seam allowance of 5 mm ($\frac{1}{4}$ in) is allowed on all pieces. Join all pieces with right sides facing.

Mark point A on each side head piece. Take a length of coloured thread through to right side of fur fabric to mark position of the dot on each side head piece.

The bunny

Join leg pieces in pairs, leaving the top edges open. Turn right side out and stuff almost to the top. Bring seams together and stitch across tops close to raw edges.

Take one body piece and sew tops of legs to lower edges, where shown on the body pattern, with right sides facing and raw edges level. Let the legs flop down below the body, then join both body pieces round edges, leaving lower edges open and a gap in seam at side, where shown on pattern. Turn body right side out, turn in and slip stitch remaining lower raw edge over seam at tops of legs. Stuff body very firmly through gap in seam, then ladder stitch gap.

Join side head pieces from point A to neck edge. Insert the gusset in top of head, matching points A and B. Turn the head right side out and stuff firmly. Run a strong gathering thread round, 1 cm ($\frac{3}{8}$ in) from neck edge. Pull up gathers as tightly as possible and fasten off. Position this gathered portion of head centrally on top of the body then ladder stitch head to body, working round a few times to secure.

Thread a needle with strong doubled thread and take it through front of face, from the position of one coloured thread to the other. Take thread back through again, about 5 mm ($\frac{1}{4}$ in) above the first stitch, then knot thread ends pulling very tightly. If the fur pile is fairly long, trim it slightly round face area before working facial features, as described below.

For each eye cut a 1·5 cm ($\frac{5}{8}$ in) diameter circle of brown felt. Stick eyes on to slightly larger ovals of white felt. Work a white highlight on each eye. Position eyes on face, at each side of coloured threads. Trim away fur pile under each eye then glue eyes securely in place and snip off coloured threads.

For mouth work a 2 cm ($\frac{3}{4}$ in) straight stitch down centre seam of face, 3 cm ($1\frac{1}{4}$ in) below point A. Work a curved line in straight stitches below this line. For the nose cut a tiny heart-shape from black felt and glue it in place above the first mouth stitch.

To make ears first trim off 5 mm ($\frac{1}{4}$ in) all round each contrasting lining piece. Join ear pieces to these, easing to fit and leaving lower edges open. Turn ears right side out, fold in half and oversew lower raw edges together. Ladder stitch ears at top of head, where shown by the dotted line on the side head pattern.

Join arm pieces in pairs, leaving a gap at top where shown. Turn and stuff to within 5 cm (2 in) of top. Turn in and slip stitch gap then sew arms to each side of body, about 2 cm ($\frac{3}{4}$ in) down from neck.

Cut tail from fleece or felt and slip stitch it to body where shown on pattern, enclosing a bit of stuffing.

Mrs Bunny's clothes

Notes: 1 cm ($\frac{3}{8}$ in) seams are allowed unless stated otherwise. Draw out the patterns on to metric graph paper as for bunny patterns.

Cut out all clothes as directed on patterns.

Petticoat and pantaloons

You will need: 50 cm ($\frac{5}{8}$ yd) of 91 cm (36 in) wide fabric; 1·60 m ($1\frac{3}{4}$ yd) of lace edging; 70 cm ($\frac{3}{4}$ yd) of narrow elastic; 50 m ($\frac{5}{8}$ yd) of narrow bias binding; two snap fasteners.

To make pantaloons: Hem lower leg edges, taking 1 cm ($\frac{3}{8}$ in) turnings twice, then sew on lace edging. Sew bias binding to the wrong side of each leg piece where shown by dotted lines on pattern. Thread lengths of elastic through each to fit round legs and securely sew elastic at each end.

Join pantaloon pieces at centre, clip seams at curves. Bring centre seams together and join inside leg edges. Hem waist edge, taking 1 cm ($\frac{3}{8}$ in) turnings twice, then thread through elastic to fit waist.

To make petticoat: Cut a fabric strip 20 by 60 cm (8 by $23\frac{1}{2}$ in). Join the short edges, leaving an 8 cm (3 in) gap at top of seam. Turn in and stitch raw edges of gap to neaten. Hem lower edge, taking 1 cm ($\frac{3}{8}$ in) turnings twice, then sew on lace trim.

Gather upper edge to measure 28 cm (11 in) then bind it with 6 by 32 cm ($2\frac{3}{8}$ by $12\frac{1}{2}$ in) straight strip of fabric, leaving 2 cm ($\frac{3}{4}$ in) at one end for an overlap.

Put petticoat on bunny, with top of waistband about 4 cm ($1\frac{1}{2}$ in) down from neck. Pin a strip of lace edging across front of band then up over each shoulder and across back of band to centre back, mitring the corners. Sew in position as pinned, then sew snap fasteners to back of band.

Dress

You will need: 30 cm ($\frac{3}{8}$ yd) of 91 cm (36 in) wide fabric; 1·50 m ($1\frac{5}{8}$ yd) of 4 cm ($1\frac{1}{2}$ in) wide broderie Anglaise or other lace trimming; 1·30 m ($1\frac{1}{2}$ yd) of narrow ribbon; two snap fasteners.

To make: For skirt cut a fabric strip 22 by 91 cm ($8\frac{3}{4}$ by 36 in). Make as for petticoat, trimming lower edge as illustrated. Gather top to measure 29 cm ($11\frac{1}{2}$ in); bind as for petticoat, with a fabric strip 6 by 33 cm ($2\frac{3}{8}$ by 13 in).

For each shoulder strap cut a fabric strip 6 by 15 cm ($2\frac{3}{8}$ by 6 in). Fold, bringing the long edges together, and join all round the raw edges, leaving a gap for turning. Trim seam, turn right side out and slip stitch gap.

Put skirt on bunny and place straps over shoulders, tucking and pinning ends 2 cm ($\frac{3}{4}$ in) inside waistband. Sew straps in place as pinned. Cut the 4 cm ($1\frac{1}{2}$ in) trimming to measure about 3 cm ($1\frac{1}{4}$ in) wide, turn in raw edge then sew trimming to straps and across waistband as illustrated, making tucks at each corner. Sew a ribbon bow to front and snap fasteners to back of band.

Hat

You will need: Small pieces of fabric, interlining and bias binding; 50 cm ($\frac{5}{8}$ yd) of trimming to match dress; oddments of ribbon, flowers, etc., for trimming.

To make: Cut two hat pieces from fabric and one from interlining. Place them together with right sides of fabric facing and the interlining pieces on top of them. Join round edges, taking 5 mm ($\frac{1}{4}$ in) seam and leaving a gap for turning. Turn right side out, slip stitch gap then top stitch round close to edge. Bind earholes to neaten.

Gather the 50 cm ($\frac{5}{8}$ yd) of trimming to fit round dotted line shown on pattern, and sew it in place. Put hat on bunny and take a strip of ribbon under chin, sewing it to positions shown on hat pattern. Trim hat with gathered rosettes of ribbon.

Parasol

Use a 30 cm ($\frac{3}{8}$ yd) strip of thick bootlace for the handle (the type used for sportswear). Push stuffing inside the strip from each end, using a knitting needle, until an 18 cm (7 in) section is stuffed. Trim off excess boot lace, then turn in raw edges and oversew to neaten.

Cut a 19 cm ($7\frac{1}{2}$ in) diameter circle of fabric and sew lace trimming all round raw edge.

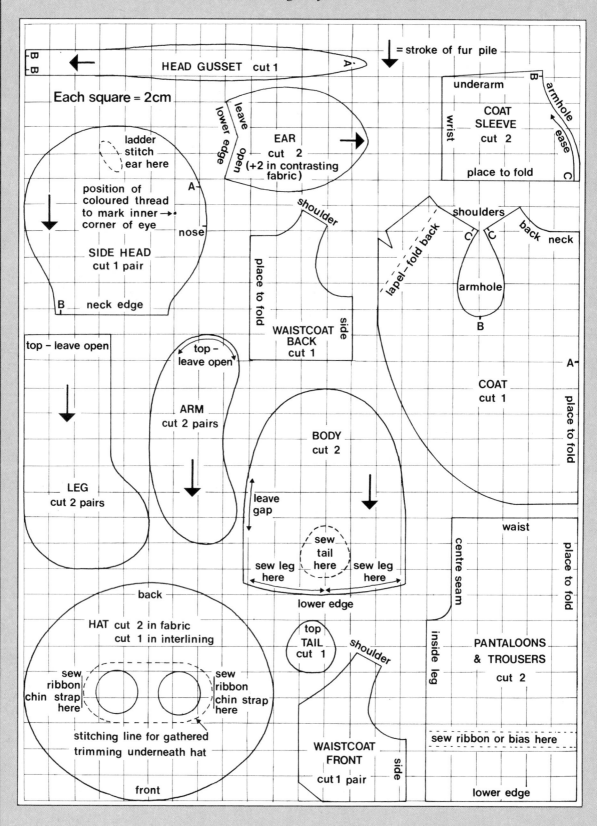

= stroke of fur pile

HEAD GUSSET cut 1

Each square = 2cm

ladder stitch ear here

position of coloured thread to mark inner → corner of eye

SIDE HEAD cut 1 pair

B neck edge

nose

A

leave lower edge open

EAR cut 2 (+2 in contrasting fabric)

shoulder

place to fold

WAISTCOAT BACK cut 1

side

underarm

COAT SLEEVE cut 2

wrist

armhole ease

B

C

place to fold

lapel−fold back

shoulders

back neck

C

C

armhole

B

A

COAT cut 1

place to fold

top – leave open

top – leave open

ARM cut 2 pairs

LEG cut 2 pairs

BODY cut 2

leave gap

sew tail here

sew leg here

sew leg here

lower edge

back

HAT cut 2 in fabric cut 1 in interlining

sew ribbon chin strap here

sew ribbon chin strap here

stitching line for gathered trimming underneath hat

front

top TAIL cut 1

shoulder

WAISTCOAT FRONT

cut 1 pair

side

waist

place to fold

centre seam

inside leg

PANTALOONS & TROUSERS cut 2

sew ribbon or bias here

lower edge

Mrs Bunny's parasol

Snip a small hole at centre of circle and push one end of handle through. Sew fabric to handle at this point and glue a bit of ribbon around. Gather round the circle below lace trim, pull up gathers and sew to handle. Sew a strip of ribbon round gathers.

The parasol can be fixed in place with a piece of Velcro touch-and-close fastener, sewing the other half to bunny's hand.

Mr Bunny's Clothes

Note: 5 mm ($\frac{1}{4}$ in) seams are allowed on all felt pieces. Copy patterns as before.

Trousers

Use striped fabric, and make as for pantaloons, omitting lace trim and leg elastic, etc.

Waistcoat

You will need: Small pieces of felt; buttons.

To make waistcoat: Join fronts to back at shoulders and sides. Top stitch close to edges. Sew buttons to right front edge and make buttonholes in left front.

Coat

You will need: A piece of felt 25 by 50 cm ($9\frac{3}{4}$ by $19\frac{1}{2}$ in).

To make coat: Cut centre back of coat open as far as point A. Top stitch all round coat, 5 mm ($\frac{1}{4}$ in) from edges except for armholes and shoulders. Fold back lapels at dotted line positions and press, then tack top edges to

shoulders. Join front shoulders to back shoulders.

Top stitch 5 mm ($\frac{1}{4}$ in) from wrist edges of sleeves. Join underarm edges of sleeves, turn right side out. Slip armhole edges of sleeves inside armhole edges of coat, matching points B and C. Sew sleeves into armholes, easing tops to fit as on pattern.

Top hat

You will need: A piece of felt 20 by 60 cm (8 by $23\frac{1}{2}$ in); the same amount of interlining; 30 cm ($\frac{3}{8}$ yd) of ribbon for hat band; adhesive.

To make: For a hat brim pattern, draw out a 14 cm ($5\frac{1}{2}$ in) diameter circle with a 9 cm ($3\frac{1}{2}$ in) diameter circle cut out of centre. Cut two brims from felt and one from interlining. Trim 5 mm ($\frac{1}{4}$ in) off outer and inner edges of interlining piece. Glue this centrally between felt brim pieces. Stitch round felt brim, close to outer and inner edges.

For crown of hat cut a felt strip 9 by 29 cm ($3\frac{1}{2}$ by $11\frac{1}{2}$ in), and an interlining strip 8 by 29 cm (3 by $11\frac{1}{2}$ in). Glue interlining centrally to felt. Join short edges.

For top of hat cut a 10 cm (4 in) diameter circle of felt and glue a 9 cm ($3\frac{1}{2}$ in) diameter circle of interlining to the centre. Place this on top of crown piece, with wrong sides outside, then back stitch all round through the 5 mm ($\frac{1}{4}$ in) felt edges. Turn right side out and place on top of hat brim, then oversew the 5 mm ($\frac{1}{4}$ in) felt edges together. Curl up the brim at each side of the hat and glue a ribbon strip round hat.

Cravat

Make a bow shape from a piece of wide ribbon, then use a strip of the same ribbon folded to make a narrower width for the neck band. Sew bow to front of band and a snap fastener to back edges.

Walking stick

Make as for parasol handle, stuffing it to make a 20 cm (8 in) length. Curve the top of the stick by running a thread along then pulling the thread tight and fastening off. Fix to hand as for parasol.

Puss in Boots

*This favourite character from nursery tale and pantomime comes to life as a cuddly toy.
He stands about 61 cm (24 in) high in his boots. These are stitched in place to form part
of the toy and in addition you can make a complete outfit of clothes; all of which can
be removed*

Puss in his boots

You will need: For Puss: 40 cm ($\frac{1}{2}$ yd) of fur fabric 138 cm (54 in) wide; 500 g (1 lb) of stuffing; scraps of pink black and blue felt; black 4-ply yarn and white thread.
For his boots: a 46 cm (18 in) square of felt; small pieces of strong card and black felt; two small buckles; 80 cm ($\frac{7}{8}$ yd) of braid for boot tops; 80 cm ($\frac{7}{8}$ yd) of broad bootlace; adhesive; a sheet of metric graph paper at least 46 by 60 cm (18 by 23 in).
Notes: The seam allowance is 1 cm ($\frac{3}{8}$ in)

On metric graph paper draw out all outlines and markings from diagram square by square (each square on diagram equals 2 cm). To get complete pattern for body, trace the full-size pattern off your graph paper on to folded tracing paper, placing the fold in tracing paper against fold line marked on pattern.

Cut out your patterns and pin them to the wrong side of fur fabric, then cut out pieces as shown in diagram 1, also cutting a strip 10 by 40 cm (4 by 15$\frac{3}{4}$ in) for tail. Transfer all markings onto the wrong side of the fur fabric.

Join seams with right sides of fabric facing unless otherwise stated.

Puss

Join body pieces round edges, leaving a gap in seam, and leaving lower leg edges open as shown on pattern. Machine along stitching lines between legs, then cut fabric open as on pattern. Clip seam at neck then turn right side out.

Stuff head and body firmly through side opening, then slip stitch this opening. Continue stuffing through lower leg edges. Tie strong thread very tightly round neck and sew thread ends into body.

Join ear pieces in pairs, leaving lower edges open as on pattern. Trim off points and turn right side out. Turn in lower edges 1 cm ($\frac{3}{8}$ in) and oversew them together, pulling stitches tight to gather slightly. Sew ears in place as shown on pattern.

Join long edges of tail strip, tapering slightly towards one end then rounding off seam across this end. Trim seam and turn tail right side out, using a thick knitting needle to do this easily. Stuff the tail very lightly,

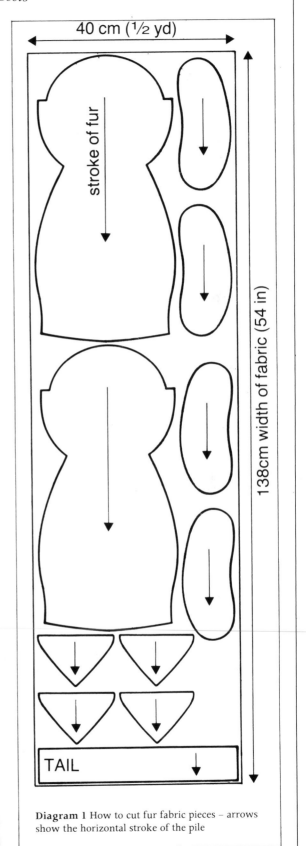

Diagram 1 How to cut fur fabric pieces – arrows show the horizontal stroke of the pile

pushing in small amounts of stuffing with knitting needle. Turn in remaining raw edge and slip stitch it to back of Puss as shown on the pattern.

Join arm pieces in pairs, leaving gaps in seams at top, as on pattern. Trim seams round paws and turn right side out. Stuff arms firmly to about halfway up, then stuff very lightly. Turn in and slip stitch raw edges, then sew tops of arms to Puss (see pattern).

Following pattern cut two oval eye shapes in blue felt, and two circles of black felt; glue them together in pairs. Using white thread work a highlight on each eye as shown in illustration. Cut nose from pink felt.

Carefully clip fur fabric a bit shorter at centre of face around mouth and nose area. Position eyes and nose on face with pins, using illustration as a guide.

With black yarn, work a stitch straight down from nose, then back-stitch remaining mouth lines, oversewing through each back stitch. Work whiskers with long straight stitches. Glue on eyes and nose, holding them in place with pins until glue dries.

Boots

Cut four uppers from felt. Join centre front and back seam. Trim seams and turn right side out. Cut two card soles and place one inside each boot at lower edge. Glue lower edges of boots 1 cm ($\frac{3}{8}$ in) onto soles all round, matching points A and B. Stuff boots very firmly. Cut two black felt soles and stick them over card soles. Glue strips of bootlace round lower edges of boots, as shown in illustration.

Cut two boot top pieces from folded felt, placing edge marked fold against fold in felt. Sew fancy braid to outer edge of each piece, then join short edges taking a tiny seam. Slip a boot top piece over each leg of Puss, with wrong sides out and braid edges uppermost. Pin the boots to the lower edges of legs, with the felt overlapping the fur fabric by 1 cm ($\frac{3}{8}$ in), and turning toes of boots outwards slightly. Slip stitch top edges of boots to legs as pinned, adding more stuffing as necessary to make legs and boots quite firm.

Bring inner edges of boot tops to top edges of boots and oversew them in place, matching centre back seams. Then turn top pieces

down over boots. Sew centre bar of each buckle to a boot front. Cut two buckle flaps from felt and thread one through each buckle, holding it in place with a few stitches.

Shirt

You will need: 40 cm ($\frac{1}{2}$ yd) of 91 cm (36 in) wide fabric; three small buttons; 140 cm ($1\frac{1}{2}$ yd) of lace edging, 6 cm ($2\frac{3}{8}$ in) wide.

To make: Cut two shirt pieces, placing edge marked fold to fold in fabric. Cut one piece open along fold line for centre front of shirt (the other piece will be the shirt back).

Trace sleeve pattern off shirt pattern, then cut two sleeves, placing edge marked fold to fold in fabric. Join one armhole edge of each sleeve to armhole edge of shirt back. Join remaining armhole edge of sleeve to armhole edge of each shirt front. Clip curves in seams and press seams towards sleeves.

Hem each lower sleeve edge then sew on a 40 cm ($15\frac{3}{4}$ in) strip of lace edging gathered to fit. Join entire side and underarm seams of shirt, including lace edging. Hem the lower edge of the shirt.

Turn in centre front edges 2 cm ($\frac{3}{4}$ in) and press. Turn in raw edges of these turnings and stitch them down.

Neaten the cut ends of remaining lace edging and sew it round neck edge of shirt, missing the turned-in edges at centre front. Gather neck edge all round to fit Puss's neck, leaving the turn-in edges at centre front ungathered. Bind neck edge with bias strip of fabric. Sew buttons to right front edge, and make buttonholes in left front.

Breeches

You will need: 30 cm ($\frac{3}{8}$ yd) of 91 cm (36 in) wide fabric; 80 cm ($\frac{7}{8}$ yd) narrow elastic.

To make: Cut two breeches pieces, placing fold line on pattern to fold in fabric. Join the pieces at centre edges, leaving a gap for tail in one seam as shown on pattern. Clip seams at curves and press open. Turn in and slip stitch raw edges at gap in seam, then join inside leg edges.

Turn in waist and lower edges 5 mm then 1 cm ($\frac{1}{4}$ in then $\frac{3}{8}$ in), and stitch to form casings

Belt

You need: A buckle; a strip of leather cloth or felt about 70 cm ($\frac{3}{4}$ yd) long, and wide enough to fit the centre bar of buckle.

To make: Attach one end of belt strip to centre bar of buckle, cutting a hole to fit over centre prong. Round off other end, then cut more small holes along centre of belt.

Cape

You will need: 30 cm by 60 cm (12 in by 24 in) of velvet and of lining fabric; 120 cm ($1\frac{3}{8}$ yd) of ric-rac or braid; 50 cm ($\frac{1}{2}$ yd) of narrow ribbon.

To make: For a pattern draw out a 58 cm (23 in) diameter semi-circle on paper then draw and cut out a 20 cm (8 in) diameter semi-circle at centre of straight edge for neck edge. Using the pattern cut cape from velvet and lining fabric.

Join both pieces round edges, leaving a gap in neck edge seam for turning. Trim the seam all round, turn right side out and press cape. Turn in and slip stitch gap.

Cut the ribbon in two and sew half to each end of neck seam, for ties. Sew ric-rac braid round close to the edges of the cape, as illustrated.

Hat

You will need: 50 cm ($\frac{1}{2}$ yd) of 91 cm (36 in) wide felt (or three 46 cm (18 in) squares); a 34 cm ($13\frac{1}{2}$ in) square of stiff interlining; 50 cm ($\frac{1}{2}$ yd) of braid for hatband; a few feathers; a large button; adhesive.

To make: For a hat brim pattern draw out a 34 cm ($13\frac{1}{2}$ in) diameter circle with a 12 cm ($4\frac{3}{4}$ in) diameter circle cut out of centre. Cut two of these shapes from felt.

From interlining cut a 33 cm (13 in) diameter circle with a 14 cm ($5\frac{1}{2}$ in) diameter circle cut out of centre. Spread glue round edges of interlining and stick it centrally over one felt piece. Stick the other felt piece on top

in the same way, sandwiching interlining between felt circles.

Stitch felt brim pieces together round outer edges, then stitch inner edges together 1 cm ($\frac{3}{8}$ in) from raw edges of felt. Clip inner edges all round, back to stitching.

For crown of hat cut a felt strip 44 cm by 16 cm ($17\frac{1}{2}$ in by $6\frac{1}{4}$ in). Join short edges, taking 5 mm ($\frac{1}{4}$ in) seam. Press seam open.

Slip one end of this tube, wrong side out, inside the centre hole of brim, with raw edges of felt level. Pin in place, then back stitch brim and crown together through stitching line all round, as shown in diagram 2. Trim seam then push the tube up through brim to turn it right side out. Note that the trimmed raw edges of back-stitched seam are now on the outside. Oversew these raw edges to crown, then cover them with braid.

Gather tightly all round top edge of crown and fasten off. Cover gathered edges with a felt-covered button. Sew feathers to hat.

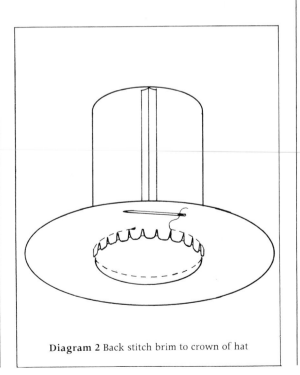

Diagram 2 Back stitch brim to crown of hat

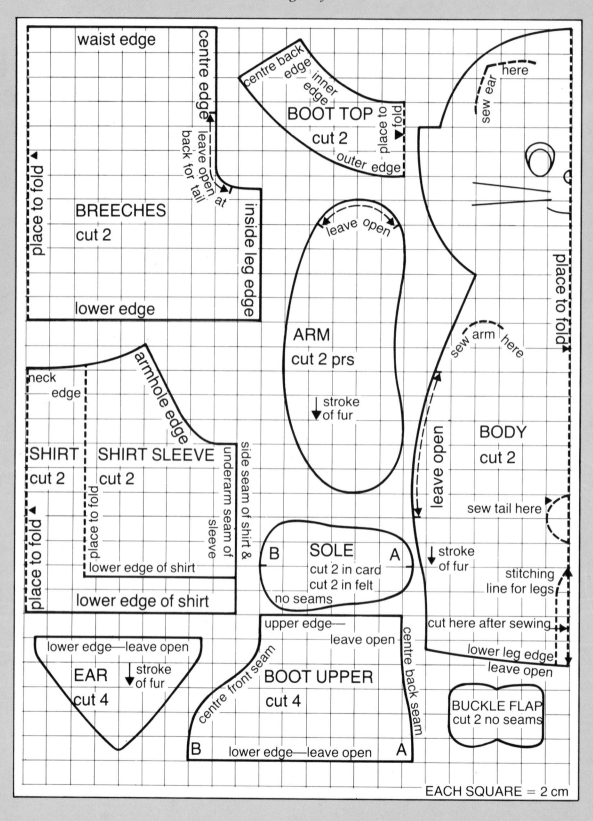

waist edge

centre edge

leave open at back for tail

inside leg edge

place to fold

BREECHES
cut 2

lower edge

centre back edge

inner edge

BOOT TOP
cut 2

place to fold

outer edge

sew ear here

sew arm here

place to fold

leave open

ARM
cut 2 prs

stroke of fur

BODY
cut 2

sew tail here

leave open

stroke of fur

stitching line for legs

cut here after sewing

lower leg edge
leave open

neck edge

armhole edge

place to fold

side seam of shirt & underarm seam of sleeve

SHIRT
cut 2

SHIRT SLEEVE
cut 2

place to fold

lower edge of shirt

lower edge of shirt

B **SOLE** A
cut 2 in card
cut 2 in felt
no seams

upper edge—
leave open

centre back seam

lower edge—leave open

EAR
cut 4

stroke of fur

centre front seam

BOOT UPPER
cut 4

B

A

lower edge—leave open

BUCKLE FLAP
cut 2 no seams

EACH SQUARE = 2 cm

Soulful Hound Dog

This lovable hound dog with his long droopy ears and doleful expression makes a cuddly bedtime toy for toddlers or an endearing mascot for the young at heart. He is 53 cm (21 in) long, from the tip of his nose to his tail

You will need: 50 cm ($\frac{5}{8}$ yd) of 138 cm (54 in) wide fur fabric; small pieces of light coloured fur fabric for ear linings; 500 g (1 lb) of stuffing; scraps of pink, black and blue felt for eyes; small piece of shiny fabric such as taffeta for nose; 1 m ($1\frac{1}{8}$ yd) of ribbon or braid.

Notes: Join all fur fabric pieces with right sides facing and taking 5 mm ($\frac{1}{4}$ in) seams.

Using the diagram draw out all the pattern pieces square by square onto metric graph paper (each square on diagram equals 5 cm). Transfer all markings on to each piece.

Cut out all the fur fabric pieces with the smooth stroke of the pile in the direction indicated by the arrows on the patterns. The body gusset should be cut out across the width of the fabric disregarding the direction of the pile.

The dog

Cut out one pair of body pieces, marking points A, B, C, D and E, then join them along their top edges from point A to point E. Cut gusset and mark all points as for body. Stitch gusset to body matching all marked points and leaving a gap in one seam between points C and D. Turn right side out, stuff firmly then ladder stitch the opening.

Cut out four foot pieces and join them in pairs leaving back edges open. Turn right side out and stuff. Turn in raw edges and slip stitch to close. Place feet side by side under dog so back edges of feet are about 36 cm (14 in) from point E. Ladder stitch feet to gusset and body where they touch.

Cut out one pair of tail pieces and join them leaving straight edge open. Turn right side out, stuff firmly, then turn in raw edges and ladder stitch to gusset about 15 cm (6 in) down from point E.

Cut out two ears and two ear linings. Join them in pairs, easing ears to fit linings and leaving top edges open. Turn right side out then turn in raw edges and slip stitch, pulling up stitches to gather slightly. Sew ears to top of head at positions shown on pattern.

Cut two eyes from blue felt, two eyelids from pink felt and two pupils from black felt. Sew pupils to eyes then sew on eyelids, with their lower edges overlapping top edges of eyes by 5 mm ($\frac{1}{4}$ in). Sew eyes in position on head about 1 cm ($\frac{3}{8}$ in) apart, 2 cm ($\frac{3}{4}$ in) below ears.

For the mouth, cut a 5 mm by 9 cm ($\frac{1}{4}$ in by $3\frac{1}{2}$ in) strip of black felt. Sew the strip to centre of gusset, starting about 8 cm ($3\frac{1}{8}$ in) below eyes and making a curved line as shown in illustration. You may need to trim the fur pile around the mouth strip. At the lower end of mouth, sew a 5 mm by 3 cm ($\frac{1}{4}$ in by $1\frac{1}{4}$ in) strip of black felt. For eyebrows cut two 5 mm by 2 cm ($\frac{1}{4}$ in by $\frac{3}{4}$ in) strips of black felt and sew one above each eye.

Cut six 5 mm by 4 cm ($\frac{1}{4}$ in by $1\frac{1}{2}$ in) strips of black felt and sew three to each foot to mark toes as shown in illustration.

From taffeta, cut one nose piece. Bring curved edges together and join along stitching lines as indicated by dotted lines on the pattern. Run a gathering thread round raw edge of nose and stuff very firmly, pulling up gathers until raw edges touch. Ladder stitch nose in position, slightly overlapping the top end of mouth strip. Tie ribbon round neck.

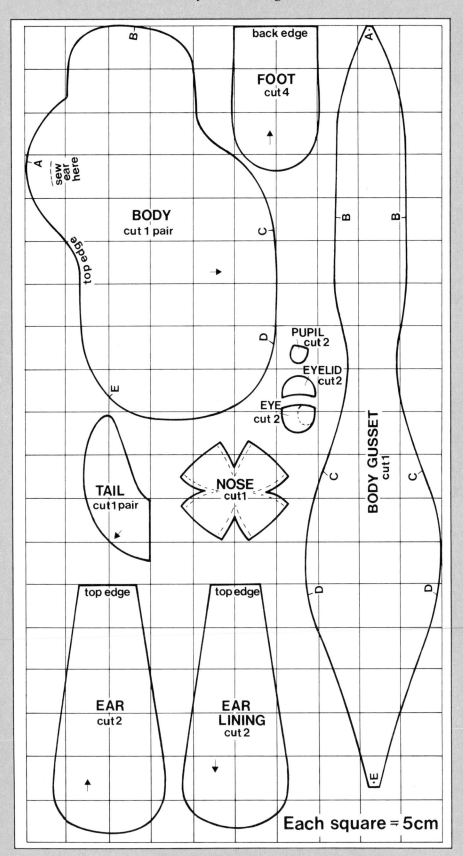

FOOT
cut 4

back edge

BODY
cut 1 pair

sew ear here

top edge

PUPIL
cut 2

EYELID
cut 2

EYE
cut 2

TAIL
cut 1 pair

NOSE
cut 1

BODY GUSSET
cut 1

top edge

top edge

EAR
cut 2

EAR
LINING
cut 2

Each square = 5cm

Mascot Teddy Bears

Twinkletoes Ted is a football mascot who can be kitted out in the strip of your favourite club team. The same basic pattern will also make up Superbear, a tubby teddy clad in leotard, mask and glittering cape. Both bears measure 48 cm (19 in) in height

For each bear you will need: 45 cm ($\frac{1}{2}$ yd) of 138 cm (54 in) wide fur fabric; 600 g ($1\frac{1}{4}$ lb) of stuffing; scraps of black, white, and brown felt and white thread; metric graph paper; adhesive.

Notes: On to 5 cm squared graph paper copy the pattern shapes, following the outlines on diagram square by square. For the head gusset and the mask patterns, trace the full-size patterns on to folded paper, placing the folded edge at the positions indicated on the patterns. Cut out, then open up the tracings to make whole pattern pieces.

The seam allowance is 5 mm ($\frac{1}{4}$ in) on all Teddy and garment pattern pieces unless otherwise stated.

When sewing seams on stretchy fabric, stretch the fabric slightly while stitching.

The Teddy Bear

Cut two pairs of arm pieces and join them in pairs leaving the top edges open. Turn right side out and stuff to within 3 cm ($1\frac{1}{4}$ in) of the top, then pin fur fabric here to hold stuffing in place. Tack top raw edges of each arm together.

Cut one pair of fronts and one pair of backs and join them in pairs at centre front and centre back edges from neck edge to points A. Now tack the top edges of the arms to the right side of body back pieces at positions shown on the pattern, with raw edges level and the arms pointing inwards.

Make sure also to have the curves of the arms pointing towards the neck edge.

Now tack the front body to the back at side edges and round the legs and feet to points A. Stitch the seams as tacked, then turn the body right side out. Remove the pins in the arms.

Stuff the legs and body, then run a strong gathering thread round neck edge, pull up the gathers to close completely then fasten off.

Cut one pair of head pieces and one head gusset. Sew the side dart in each head piece. Join the head pieces at the centre front, from point A to the neck edge. Insert the gusset, matching points A and B on the head and gusset pieces. Turn the head right side out, stuff, then gather the neck as for the body.

Place the head on top of the body, matching the gathered portions. Hold the head in place with three or four darning needles pushed into the head and body fabric. Ladder-stitch head and body together where they touch, using strong thread. Trim the fur fabric pile slightly shorter on the face below point A.

Cut the eye pieces from felt as follows – cut smallest ovals in black, medium ovals in brown and largest ovals in white. Glue eye pieces together as shown on the pattern then use white thread to work a highlight on each black oval as shown in illustration. Place the eyes in position (see illustration), about 4 cm ($1\frac{1}{2}$ in) apart. Trim away the fur pile underneath each eye then stick them in place and sew them securely round the edges.

Cut two nose pieces from black felt. Oversew them together all round the edges, but before completing the sewing push in a little stuffing. Sew the nose to the end of snout.

For the mouth cut a 5 mm by 8 cm ($\frac{1}{4}$ by 3 in) strip of black felt. Pin the strip in place, then sew it in position using back stitches. Trim off any fur pile which overlaps the mouth strip.

For eyebrows cut two 5 mm by 1·5 cm ($\frac{1}{4}$ by $\frac{5}{8}$ in) strips of black felt. Back stitch them in place above the eyes.

Cut four ear pieces and join them in pairs, leaving lower edges open. Turn them right side out and oversew the lower edges of each ear together, pulling the stitches to gather slightly. Sew ears to top of head, placing them about 8 cm (3 in) apart.

Clothes for Twinkletoes Ted

You will need: For the football shirt, pieces of stretchy fabric (from an old T-shirt, sweater or jersey dress); for the shorts, 20 cm ($\frac{1}{4}$ yd) of 91 cm (36 in) wide nylon or cotton fabric and a short length of elastic; for the socks, cuttings off a pair of old socks; for the boots, small pieces of black felt, 1·30 m ($1\frac{3}{8}$ yd) of 13 mm ($\frac{1}{2}$ in) wide white tape and a short length of sports laces.

Notes: The football strip should be suited to your chosen individual club. Any stripes to go on sleeves, body or shorts pieces should be stitched in place before sewing the pieces together.

To make the shorts: Cut two shorts pieces, placing the pattern to a fold in the fabric each time, as indicated. Hem the leg edges taking narrow turnings. Join the pieces to each other at the centre edges then clip the curves in seams. Bring centre seams together then join inside leg edges.

Take 1 cm ($\frac{3}{8}$ in) turnings twice on the waist edge, then thread elastic through to fit waist and join the ends.

To make the shirt: Cut front and back, placing pattern to a fold in the fabric each time as indicated and cutting neck edges as shown on pattern.

For neck bindings cut 3 cm ($1\frac{1}{4}$ in) wide strips of fabric. Mitre the strips for the front V-point, then sew to wrong side of neck edge, turn to the right side and press. Turn in the remaining raw edge of the binding and stitch down. Bind back neck edge in the same way, easing strip to fit curved neckline.

Join the front to the back at shoulder edges. Cut two sleeves and two cuff pieces, placing patterns to fold in fabric as shown on pattern. Join the edge of the cuff marked A-B to edge of sleeve marked A-B, with right sides facing and raw edges level.

Join armhole edges of sleeves to the armhole edges of shirt. Now join sides of shirt and underarm edges of sleeves and cuffs. Turn cuffs to inside and slip stitch the raw edge in place over the seam. Turn in lower raw edge of shirt and sew in place.

Cut two collar pieces, placing pattern to a fold in fabric as shown on pattern. Join the pieces round the edges, leaving a gap in the neck edge. Clip curves in neck edge then turn right side out, press, and slip stitch gap. Stitch all round outer edge of the collar. Slip stitch neck edge of collar to neck edge of shirt.

To make the socks: Use the leg portion of the socks only and also cut off any elasticated portion at the top. A 12 cm ($4\frac{3}{4}$ in) length is about right. Machine stitch round the cut edges of the sock, stretching the sock as it is stitched to prevent laddering. Slip a sock on each leg, with lower raw edge at approximate position of dotted line shown on body front and back patterns. Slip stitch lower edges in place, then roll down tops of socks as illustrated.

To make the boots: Cut four boot pieces from black felt. Fold tape in half along its length and press. Stitch three strips of tape to each boot piece (see pattern) taking care to make pairs.

Join the pieces in pairs at back edges for about 3 cm ($1\frac{1}{4}$ in), then bind the upper edges with tape. Join boot pieces round edges, leaving upper edges open. Turn right side out. Push a little stuffing in toes and heels, then put boots on feet and slip stitch the upper edges to socks. Make two bootlace bows and sew one to the front of each boot.

Clothes for Superbear

You will need: Pieces of stretchy fabric for the leotard (cuttings off an old T-shirt, sweater or jersey dress); small pieces of felt for the belt, buckle, mask, lightning motif and wristbands; 60 cm ($\frac{5}{8}$ yd) of 91 cm (36 in) wide shiny fabric for the cape; 1·50 m ($1\frac{5}{8}$ yd) of silver braid or trimming; four gold or silver buttons with shanks (or circles of felt if the mascot is for a young child); adhesive.

To make the leotard: Make the patterns from the front and back body patterns, trimming the lower edges along the dotted lines shown on the patterns. Cut one pair of fronts and one pair of backs. Join them in pairs at centre front and centre back edges, from neck to points A. Join the front and back pieces at the sides, from leg edge to points B. Turn in the remainder of the side edges and slip stitch in place. Bring the centre front and back seams together then join the inner leg edges from points A to C.

Turn right side out and put leotard on the bear. Turn in neck edge as necessary to fit close to the neck, then catch the neck and side edges together at each side above the arms. Catch the neck edge to the neck all round with large, loose stitches.

Turn in the leg edges as necessary to fit, then slip stitch them to the legs all round.

To make the belt: Cut a 4 cm ($1\frac{1}{2}$ in) wide strip of felt, long enough to go round the body (about 52 cm, or $20\frac{1}{2}$ in). Stitch the braid to the long edges of the belt. Place the belt on the bear and join the short ends at front, then sew the belt to the leotard.

Cut the buckle from two layers of felt glued together. Stitch all round the edge. Pierce four holes at positions shown on the pattern and push the button shanks through the holes. Sew the buttons to the felt at the back of the buckle, then catch each button to front of belt to hold it in place or sew on felt circles.

To make the lightning motif: Use the pattern to cut the shape from felt. Work lines of stitching on the felt as shown in illustration. Glue the motif in place on the leotard then slip stitch it in place all round the edges.

To make the mask: Cut the mask from two layers of felt glued together. Mark on the eye openings and cut them out using sharp scissors. Stitch all round the edge of the mask. Place it on the bear (see illustration), then glue the portion between and around the eyes in place. With a few stitches, catch the back of the mask to the head at the position of the crosses on pattern.

To make the cape: Make the cape pattern by drawing a 54 cm (21$\frac{1}{4}$ in) diameter semi-circle with a 10 cm (4 in) diameter semi-circle at centre of the straight edge.

Cut two cape pieces from this pattern and join them round the edges, leaving a gap in one straight edge. Turn right side out, press, then slip stitch the gap. Place cape round bear's neck and catch it to the shoulders at each side. Make the wristbands from strips of felt, sewing braid down centre of each strip.

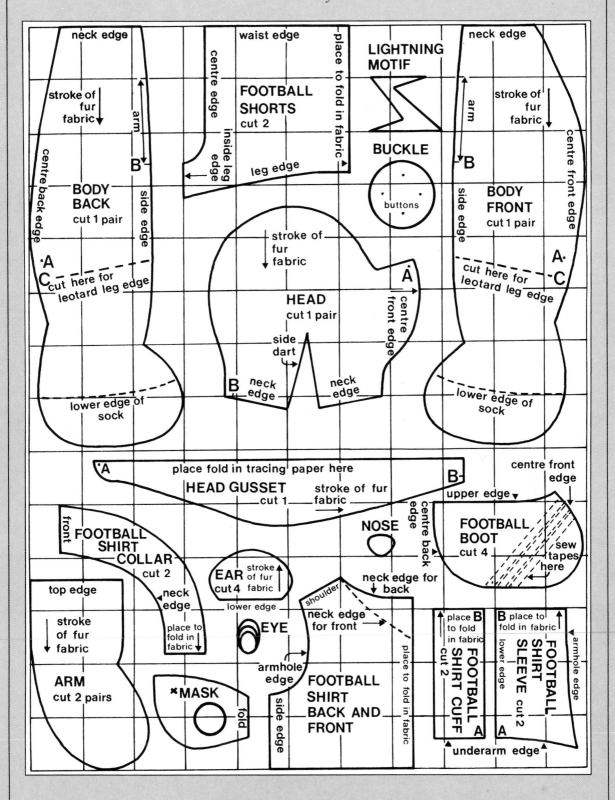

Hippos

A whole family of cuddly hippos made in fur fabric from very simple shapes. Mother and Father hippo each measure about 38 cm (15 in) long, and the babies about 20 cm (8 in).

You will need: For each large hippo – 50 cm ($\frac{5}{8}$ yd) of 138 cm (54 in) wide fur fabric (note: this will make two large hippos if you follow the cutting layout); 350 g (12 oz) of stuffing; scraps of felt, shoe lace and ribbon; metric graph paper; adhesive. For each baby hippo – small pieces of fur fabric and a small amount of stuffing; scraps of felt and ribbon; metric graph paper; adhesive.

Patterns for large hippo: Fold the graph paper in half down the length. Copy body, leg, ear and tail outlines from the scaled down **diagram on page 133 (each square on diagram = 2 cm)** square by square on to graph paper. When drawing the patterns be sure to position the edges marked 'FOLD' against the fold in graph paper. Leaving the paper folded, cut out the patterns then open them out to full size. Cut neck dart out of body pattern along dotted stitching lines shown on pattern. Trace the full-size eye and nostril patterns off the page.

Patterns for baby hippo: To make a smaller hippo, each square on the diagram = 1 cm. Copy pattern outlines and cut neck dart out of body pattern in same way as for the large hippo. Trace the full-size eye and nostril patterns off the page.

Note: Seam allowances are as stated in instructions.

Large hippo

For the upper body, pin body pattern to wrong side of fur fabric following the cutting-out layout. Cut out upper body level with outer edge of pattern. Now use a marker pen to draw neck dart on to fabric level with cut edges of pattern. Draw centre 'fold' line on fabric, from each pointed end of dart. Remove pattern. Fold dart along fold line then stitch dart through stitching lines. Trim dart 1 cm ($\frac{3}{8}$ in) away from stitching line.

For under body, pin pattern to fabric, cut out and mark neck dart as for upper body. Now, leaving pattern pinned to fabric, trim pattern along underbody dart stitching lines. Mark this dart on to fabric in same way as for neck dart. Remove pattern and stitch neck dart first then trim dart 1 cm ($\frac{3}{8}$ in) away from stitching line. Stitch and trim under body dart in same way.

Now join upper body to under body all round outer edges taking a 1 cm ($\frac{3}{8}$ in) seam. Clip seam at curves. To turn body right side out, unpick a little of the underbody dart seam. Turn, then stuff firmly and ladderstitch gap.

Cut eight leg pieces and join them in pairs taking a 1 cm (3 in) seam and leaving upper edges open. Clip seams at curves. Turn right side out and stuff legs then oversew top raw edges together. Sew tops of legs to body seam at positions illustrated. To keep legs in upright position, press them against body, then ladderstitch firmly to under body where they touch.

Cut out tail and oversew side edges together leaving top edges open. Turn right side out and oversew top raw edges together. Sew top of tail to centre back of body seam line.

Cut four ear pieces and trim fur pile a little shorter on each one. Oversew them together in pairs leaving lower edges open. Turn right side out then oversew lower edges together pulling stitches tightly to gather. Sew ears to head just in front of neck dart and 3 cm ($1\frac{1}{4}$ in) apart.

Cut blue or brown felt eyes and black pupils. Glue them together in pairs. Place eyes on head 2·5 cm (1 in) below ears and

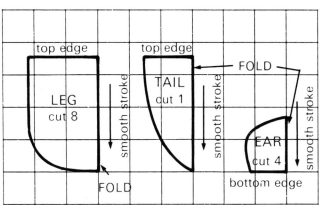

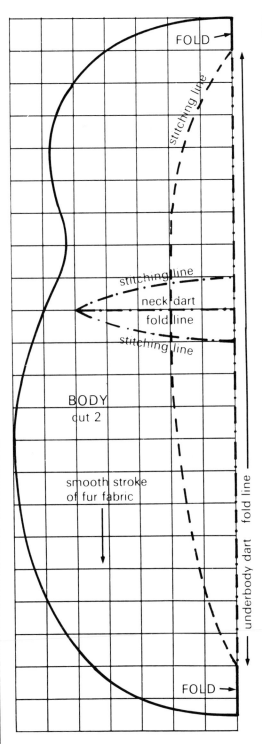

BODY
cut 2

smooth stroke
of fur fabric

For large hippo, each square = 2 cm
For small hippo, each square = 1 cm

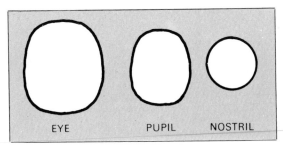

Diagram 1   Cutting-out layout for large hippos,
showing how to cut two toys from 138 cm wide fabric

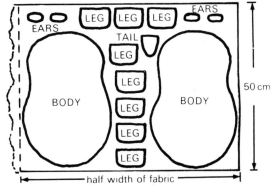

Diagram 2   Actual size patterns for large hippo's
facial features

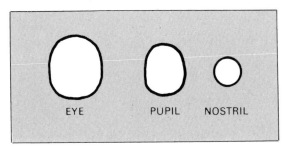

Diagram 3   Actual size patterns for small hippo's
facial features

2·5 cm (1 in) apart. Snip away fur pile beneath eyes, then stick eyes in place.

Cut nostrils from black felt and stick to head in same way as for eyes, placing them 2·5 cm (1 in) apart and 5·5 cm ($2\frac{1}{4}$ in) below eyes. Cut a 6 cm ($2\frac{3}{8}$ in) strip of shoe lace for mouth and sew in place as illustrated. Snip fur pile a little shorter around mouth. Sew ribbon bow to top of mother hippo's head.

Baby hippo

Make in the same way as for the large hippo but trim darts to 5 mm ($\frac{1}{4}$ in) from stitching lines and take 5 mm ($\frac{1}{4}$ in) seams when joining body and leg pieces.

Sew ears to head just in front of neck dart and 1·5 cm ($\frac{5}{8}$ in) apart. Cut eye pieces and glue in place as for large hippo, positioning them 1·5 cm ($\frac{5}{8}$ in) apart and 1 cm ($\frac{3}{8}$ in) below ears. Cut nostrils and stick in place, positioning them 1 cm ($\frac{3}{8}$ in) apart and 2·5 cm (1 in) below eyes.

Woman's Weekly Teddy

This 38 cm [15 in] teddy bear was specially designed to commemorate the 75th anniversary of Woman's Weekly. The clothes are removable – a sweater for a boy bear or pinafore dress for a girl bear, and both garments were knitted up in Women's Weekly pink and blue with the W W initials. You can of course knit them in colours of your choice, adding the appropriate initials to suit the chosen name of your own bear!

For the teddy you will need: Two 50 g
balls of pale yellow double knitting yarn;
length of black double knitting yarn for
embroidering mouth stitches; 340 g [12 oz] of
stuffing; a pair of 3 mm [No 11, USA 2]
knitting needles; scraps of black and light
brown felt for facial features; adhesive.

**To make both garments you will
need:** One 50 g ball of cerise and one 50 g
ball of blue double knitting yarn; oddments
of pale pink and royal blue double knitting
yarn; a pair of 3¾ mm [No 9, USA 4] and a
pair of 3¼ mm [No 10, USA 3] knitting
needles; seven small buttons; four small snap
fasteners.

Note: The above amounts of yarn required
for the clothes are for making matching
garments. If using different colours, you will
only need oddments of yarn.

Abbreviations: See page 17, as well as
below –

m 1   make one stitch by picking
up horizontal strand of
yarn lying between last
knitted stitch and next
stitch and knitting into
back of it.

yrn   yarn round needle, to make a
stitch.

K 2 tog tbl   knit two together through
back of loops.

To make the teddy

Right Leg

Begin at lower edge. Cast on 19 sts, mark last
st with coloured thread for centre front of
foot, cast on 11 sts – 30 sts.

1st row: Inc K wise into every st – 60 sts.
Beginning with a P row, st-st 13 rows.
Shape top of foot: *Next row:* K 8, (K 1, K
2 tog) 10 times, K 22 – 50 sts.
St-st 3 rows.
Next row: K 8, (K 2 tog) 10 times, K 22 –
40 sts.
St-st 23 rows then break off yarn and leave
sts on a spare needle.

Left leg

Begin at lower edge. Cast on 12 sts, mark last
st with coloured thread for centre front of
foot, cast on 18 sts – 30 sts.
1st row: Inc K wise into every st – 60 sts.
Beginning with a P row, st-st 13 rows.
Shape top of foot: *Next row:* K 22, (K 1,
K 2 tog) 10 times, K 8 – 50 sts.
St-st 3 rows.
Next row: K 22, (K 2 tog) 10 times, K 8 –
40 sts.
St-st 23 rows.

Body

Mark each end of next row with coloured
threads. With right side of work facing, K
across 39 sts of left leg, then K the last st of
left leg tog with first st of right leg from the
spare needle; K to end of remaining sts on
spare needle – 79 sts.
P 1 row.
Inc for body: *Next row:* K 5, (m 1, K 9) 3
times, (m 1, K 5) 3 times, (m 1, K 9) 3 times,
m 1, K 5 – 89 sts.
St-st 43 rows.
Shape shoulders: *Next row:* K 18, (K 2
tog, K 1) 3 times, K 2 tog, K 31, K 2 tog, (K 1,
K 2 tog) 3 times, K 18 – 81 sts.
St-st 5 rows.
Next row: K 19 (K 2 tog) 3 times, K 31, (K
2 tog) 3 times, K 19 – 75 sts.
P 1 row.
Dec for neck: *Next row:* (K 1, K 2 tog) to
end – 50 sts.
Cast off loosely marking centre of row with
coloured thread.

Head

Begin at lower edge and cast on 50 sts,
marking centre of row with coloured thread.
P 1 row.
Next row: (K 1, inc in next st) 3 times, inc
in next 13 sts, (K 1, inc in next st) 6 times,
inc in next 13 sts, (K 1, inc in next st) 3 times
– 88 sts.
Beginning with a P row, st-st 3 rows.
Inc for snout: *Next row:* K 37, inc in next
14 sts, K 37 – 102 sts.
St-st 15 rows.

Dec for top of snout: *Next row:* K 39, (K 2 tog) 3 times, K 12, (K 2 tog) 3 times, K 39 – 96 sts.

P 1 row.

Next row: K 40, (K 2 tog) 8 times, K 40 – 88 sts.

St-st 17 rows.

Shape top of head: *1st row:* K 16, (K 2 tog) twice, K 6, (K 2 tog tbl) twice, K 28, (K 2 tog) twice, K 6, (K 2 tog tbl) twice, K 16 – 80 sts.

2nd and every following alternate row: P.

3rd row: K 14, (K 2 tog) twice, K 6, (K 2 tog tbl) twice, K 24, (K 2 tog) twice, K 6, (K 2 tog tbl) twice, K 14 – 72 sts.

5th row: K 12, (K 2 tog) twice, K 6, (K 2 tog tbl) twice, K 20, (K 2 tog) twice, K 6, (K 2 tog tbl) twice, K 12 – 64 sts.

7th row: K 10, (K 2 tog) twice, K 6, (K 2 tog tbl) twice, K 16, (K 2 tog) twice, K 6, (K 2 tog tbl) twice, K 10 – 56 sts.

9th row: K 8, (K 2 tog) twice, K 6, (K 2 tog tbl) twice, K 12, (K 2 tog) twice, K 6, (K 2 tog tbl) twice, K 8 – 48 sts.

11th row: K 6, (K 2 tog) twice, K 6, (K 2 tog tbl) twice, K 8, (K 2 tog) twice, K 6, (K 2 tog tbl) twice, K 6 – 40 sts.

13th row: (K 2 tog) to end – 20 sts.

15th row: (K 2 tog) to end – 10 sts. Break off yarn leaving a long end, thread it through remaining sts, pull up tightly and fasten off.

Arms [make two alike]

Begin at hand and cast on 20 sts.

P 1 row.

Shape hand: *1st row:* (K 1, inc in next st, K 6, inc in next st) twice, K 2 – 24 sts.

2nd and every following alternate row: P.

3rd row: (K 1, inc in next st, K 8, inc in next st) twice, K 2 – 28 sts.

5th row: (K 1, inc in next st, K 10, inc in next st) twice, K 2 – 32 sts.

7th row: (K 1, inc in next st, K 12, inc in next st) twice, K 2 – 36 sts.

St-st 13 rows.

Shape arm: *Next row:* K 14, (K 2 tog) 4 times, K 14 – 32 sts.

P 1 row.

Next row: K 14, inc in next 4 sts, K 14 – 36 sts.

St-st 3 rows then inc 1 st at each end of

next row – 38 sts.

St-st 19 rows then cast off P wise.

Ears [make four pieces alike]

Begin at lower edge and cast on 17 sts.

1st row: K 6, inc in next st; inc into front, back, then front again of next 2 sts; inc in next st; K 7 – 23 sts.

Beginning with a P row, st-st 5 rows.

Dec 1 st at each end of next and the following 4th row – 19 sts.

P 1 row.

Dec 1 st at each end of the next 4 rows – 11 sts. Cast off.

Foot soles [make two alike]

Begin at back of foot and cast on 5 sts.

1st row: Inc K wise into every st – 10 sts. Beginning with a P row, st-st 21 rows.

Next row: (K 2 tog) to end – 5 sts. Cast off, marking centre of cast off row with coloured thread for centre front of sole.

To make up teddy

Join cast off row of body to cast on row of head, matching coloured threads at centres. Join row ends of head, then body as far as coloured threads at tops of legs, leaving a gap in body for turning and stuffing.

Join row ends of each leg. Oversew cast on edge of each leg to edges of foot soles, matching coloured threads on legs and soles. Turn teddy right side out. Stuff head, taking care to push in stuffing well at sides above neck seam. Stuff snout. Stuff feet, legs and finally body. Ladder stitch gap in seam.

For mouth work a 3 cm [1⅛ in] long stitch in black yarn, from centre of second snout dec row downwards. Work a shallow W at base of this stitch. Glue two layers of black felt

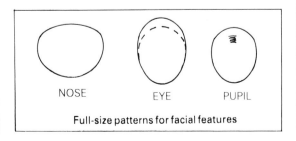

NOSE   EYE   PUPIL

Full-size patterns for facial features

together then cut out nose using the pattern on page 137. Oversew all round edges of felt, then sew nose in place at top of vertical mouth line.

Cut eyes from light brown felt and pupils from black felt using the patterns on page 137. Glue them together in pairs. Use white thread to work a highlight on each pupil as shown on the pattern. Sew eyes in place having lower edges level with first group of dec sts for snout.

Join ear pieces in pairs leaving cast on edges open. Turn right side out then oversew cast on edges of each ear together. Sew ears in place just behind dec sts at top of head nearest to face, placing them 8 cm [3 in] apart at top of head.

Join row ends of arms and across cast on sts. Turn right side out and stuff. Sew open ends of arms to sides of body having seams at underarms and placing tops of arms level with second shoulder dec row.

The clothes

The sweater

Front
Using cerise and $3\frac{1}{4}$ mm [No 10, USA 3] needles, cast on 52 sts and work 4 rows single rib.

Change to 3¾mm [No 9, USA 4] needles, join on blue and work in st-st beginning with a K row. Work 8 rows in two row stripes of blue and cerise alternately. Break off blue and cerise.

Join on pink and continue in this colour.

Shape armholes: Dec 1 st at each end of next 8 rows – 36 sts.

St-st 2 more rows then break off pink.

Join on cerise and st-st 2 rows. Join on blue and continuing in alternate two row stripes as before, st-st 8 more rows.

Keeping stripes correct, shape neck: *Next row:* K 9, turn, then work on this group of sts for left side of neck, leaving remaining 27 sts on a spare needle.

* Dec 1 st at neck edge on next 4 rows – 5 sts.

P 1 row, then cast off in blue P wise.

Slip 18 sts from spare needle onto a safety pin for neckband. With right side of work facing, rejoin blue to neck edge of remaining 9 sts and K to end. Now work as for left side of neck from * to end, joining on cerise at neck edge when required to keep sequence of stripes correct.

Right back

Using cerise and 3¼mm [No 10, USA 3] needles cast on 26 sts and work 4 rows single rib. Change to 3¾mm [No 9, USA 4] needles, join on blue and work in st-st beginning with a K row.

Work 8 rows in two row stripes of blue and cerise alternately. Break off blue and cerise, join on pink and continue in this colour. **

Shape armhole: St-st 8 rows, decreasing 1 st at beginning of every K row and end of every P row – 18 sts.

St-st 2 more rows then break off pink.

Join on cerise and st-st 2 rows. Join on blue and continuing in alternate two row stripes as before, st-st 8 more rows.

Next row: K 9, then slip remaining 9 sts onto a safety pin for neckband.

*** Keeping stripes correct, shape neck: Working on remaining 9 sts, dec 1 st at neck edge on next 4 rows – 5 sts.

P 1 row, then cast off in blue P wise.

Left back

Work as for right back as far as **.

Shape armhole: St-st 8 rows, decreasing 1 st at end of every K row and beginning of every P row – 18 sts.

St-st 2 more rows then break off pink.

Join on cerise and st-st 2 rows. Join on blue and continuing in alternate two row stripes as before, st-st 8 more rows then break off blue and cerise.

Next row: Slip first 9 sts onto a safety pin for neckband, rejoin blue to remaining 9 sts and K to end.

Now work as for right back from *** to end, rejoining cerise to neck edge when required.

Sleeves [make two alike]

Using cerise and 3¼mm [No 10, USA 3] needles cast on 46 sts and work 4 rows single rib.

Change to 3¾mm [No 9, USA 4] needles, join on blue and work in st-st beginning with a K row. Work 16 rows in two row stripes of blue and cerise alternately. Cast off P wise using cerise.

Neckband

Oversew cast off shoulder edges of front to backs. Work neckband in cerise on 3¼mm [No 10, USA 3] needles, as follows.

With right side of work facing, begin at left back and K 9 sts off safety pin, pick up and K 6 sts from left back neck edge and 6 sts from left side of front neck edge; K across 18 sts from safety pin; pick up and K 6 sts from right side of front neck edge and 6 sts from right back neck edge and finally K across 9 sts from safety pin – 60 sts.

Work 3 rows single rib then cast off in rib.

Left back band

With right side of work facing, using cerise and 3¼mm [No 10, USA 3] needles, pick up and K 30 sts along row ends of left back edge. Work 4 rows single rib then cast off in rib.

Right back band

Pick up and K 30 sts as for left back band

along right back edge and work 1 row single rib.

Buttonhole row: Rib 3, yrn, K 2 tog, (rib 4, yrn, K 2 tog) 4 times, rib 1.

Work 2 more rows single rib then cast off in rib.

To make up the sweater

Join cast off edges of sleeves to armholes of sweater. Join row ends of sleeves and side edges of sweater. Sew five buttons to left back band.

Bow tie

Using pink and $3\frac{1}{4}$ mm [No 10, USA 3] needles, cast on 54 sts then cast off. Tie in a bow then sew to neck edge of sweater at front.

Initials

Make initials of your choice if desired. Use $3\frac{1}{4}$ mm [No 10. USA 3] needles and royal blue or contrast yarn. The initials are knitted by simply casting on a number of sts, then casting off. You should experiment with different numbers of sts to suit the letters which you require. As an example, for the letter W on the sweater, cast on 26 sts, then cast off.

To sew on the letters, put sweater on teddy and fasten it at back. Slip a piece of paper between teddy and sweater at front. Now pin on your knitted initial, forming it to shape by pushing in pins at right angles to teddy. Sew in place round edges using matching sewing thread.

Pinafore dress

Note: Use $3\frac{3}{4}$ mm [No 9, USA 4] needles throughout.

Skirt

Using cerise begin at lower edge and cast on 150 sts.

G-st 4 rows.

Join on blue and beginning with a K row, work in st-st. Work 22 rows in two row stripes of blue and cerise alternately. Break

off blue and continue in cerise decreasing for waist as follows.

Next row: (K 2 tog, K 2 tog, K 1) to end – 90 sts.

G-st 4 rows for waistband then cast off.

Bib

Begin at top edge of bib and using pink cast on 22 sts and st-st 2 rows.

Shape bib: *Next row:* K 3, m 1, K to last 3 sts, m 1, K 3 – 24 sts.

Next row: P.

Repeat these 2 rows once more – 26 sts.

St-st 10 rows then cast off.

With right side of work facing and using blue begin at cast off edge and pick up and K 16 sts up right side of bib; pick up and K 21 sts along cast on edge; pick up and K 16 sts down left side of bib – 53 sts.

P 1 row then break off blue.

Join on cerise and g-st 4 rows. Cast off loosely P wise.

Straps [make two alike]

Using cerise cast on 44 sts and g-st 5 rows then cast off loosely.

Initials

Knit as for teddy's sweater, noting that for a letter W only 22 sts were required instead of 26, because of the smaller bib area.

To make up the pinafore dress

Slip cast off edge of bib inside centre front of skirt waistband and slip stitch it in place. Join row ends of skirt. Put skirt on teddy having waistband level with underarms.

Pin one end of each strap inside waistband on either side of back seam at an angle, so that they cross over each other and pass over shoulders. Sew these ends of straps in place. Sew halves of two snaps inside each top corner of bib, one at corner of pink and other at g-st band further up. Sew corresponding snap halves to strap ends. Sew buttons to outside of bib on top of snaps at pink corners. Sew on initials as for sweater.

5
SMALL
TOYS

Eight Sock Animals

Eight little animal characters – each one about 15 cm (6 in) tall (just the size to nestle into a child's hand), can all be made from stretchy towelling socks. You can make an owl, chick, penguin, mouse, teddy, pig, panda or a rabbit, using very simple pattern shapes.

You will need: Men's stretch towelling socks, size 6–11 shoe (one sock for each animal – note that panda and penguin will also need cuttings from another black or white sock); stuffing; oddments of felt, printed fabric and ribbon; adhesive.

To make each basic animal: (See also the additional instructions for some animals.) Use colours for animals as shown in illustration on pages 142–3. Turn the sock wrong side out.

Cut a 16 cm (6¼ in) length off leg of sock for body and head of animal as shown in diagram (*below left*). Lay foot portion of sock aside until required later on. Stitch round cut edge of leg to form a pointed oval shape as shown in diagram (if you like, cut a piece of paper to this shape, pin it to sock and stitch close to edge of paper). Trim off corners of seam and turn right side out.

Stuff the animal so that it measures about 25 cm (9¾ in) around. Run a gathering thread round remaining edge, pull up gathers tightly and fasten off securely. To form the neck, tie a strong thread tightly round body, 9 cm (3½ in) from top seamed edge. After knotting, sew thread ends into body.

Make all feet as follows: Cut foot pattern (the same for all the animals) from thin paper. Pin pattern to foot portion of sock, about 3 mm (⅛ in) from edge as shown in diagram. Stitch round close to edge of pattern, leaving straight edges indicated on pattern unstitched. Trim fabric level with straight edges of pattern, then remove the pattern and cut out foot close to stitching line.

Keeping the foot wrong side out, turn down raw edges 5 mm (¼ in) and tack loosely. Turn foot right side out and stuff. For all animals except the penguin, owl and chick, make four feet and pin open edges of feet to animal at each side of body as shown in **illustration on pages 142–3**, then sew securely in place. For penguin, owl and chick, make two feet and oversew open edges of feet together. Place them in position at front of animal as shown, and sew in place.

For ears and wings use patterns as given for individual animals, referring to illustration for requirements. Sew ears and wings as for feet, but use one layer of sock fabric and one layer of printed fabric,

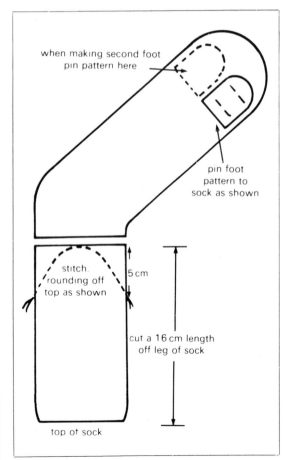

when making second foot pin pattern here

pin foot pattern to sock as shown

stitch, rounding off top as shown

5 cm

cut a 16 cm length off leg of sock

top of sock

How to cut out the sock

placing them right sides facing. Turn down and tack raw edges as for feet then turn right side out. Oversew edges together, pulling stitches to gather slightly. Sew ears and wings to animals as shown in illustration.

Cut individual facial features from felt, using patterns, then glue them to face. Sew ribbon bows to animals.

Additional instructions

Rabbit: For tail, gather and stuff a 6 cm ($2\frac{3}{8}$ in) diameter circle of sock fabric and sew it to back of rabbit.

Penguin: Before sewing on feet and wings, add chest piece as follows: Cut a piece of white sock fabric 7 by 9 cm ($2\frac{3}{4}$ by $3\frac{1}{2}$ in). Round off corners at one short edge. Turn in all raw edges 5 mm ($\frac{1}{4}$ in) and tack. Sew chest to front of penguin, with short straight edge level with neck.

Mouse: For tail cut a strip off length of sock, 3 by 10 cm ($1\frac{1}{4}$ by 4 in). Fold and join long edges with a 5 mm ($\frac{1}{4}$ in) seam at one end, tapering to other end and rounding off this end also. Trim seam, turn tail right side out with a knitting needle then sew tail to back of mouse.

Pig: For tail cut a strip off length of sock, 4 by 16 cm ($1\frac{1}{2}$ by $6\frac{1}{4}$ in). Join long edges taking a 5 mm ($\frac{1}{4}$ in) seam and stretching the fabric as seam is stitched so that the tail will curl up. Round off one short edge also. Turn tail right side out with a knitting needle and sew it to back of pig. After sewing on ears, bend them forward and catch them to head.

Owl: Trim a little off lower edge of ear pattern as indicated, for owl. Do not gather the base of ears.

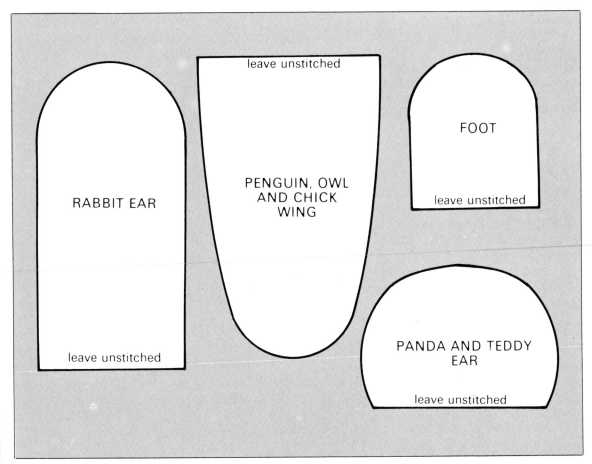

RABBIT EAR

leave unstitched

leave unstitched

PENGUIN, OWL AND CHICK WING

FOOT

leave unstitched

PANDA AND TEDDY EAR

leave unstitched

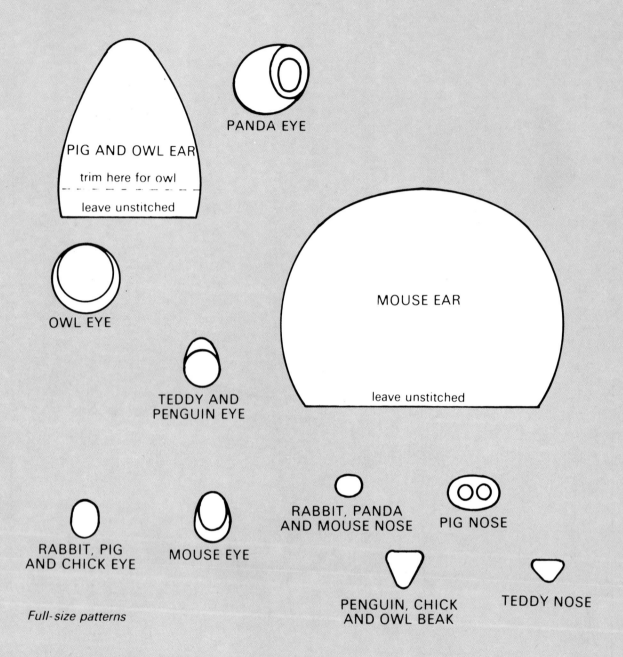

PANDA EYE

PIG AND OWL EAR

trim here for owl

leave unstitched

OWL EYE

MOUSE EAR

leave unstitched

TEDDY AND
PENGUIN EYE

RABBIT, PANDA
AND MOUSE NOSE

PIG NOSE

RABBIT, PIG
AND CHICK EYE

MOUSE EYE

PENGUIN, CHICK
AND OWL BEAK

TEDDY NOSE

Full-size patterns

Jungle Beanies

These miniature lion and tiger bean bags are just 9 cm (3½ in) in length. They are easy to make using the full-size patterns.

You will need: Small pieces of yellow and orange fleecy fabric; yellow fur fabric; felt; lentils for filling animal bodies (or they can be stuffed); stuffing for heads; permanent black marker pen; adhesive.

Lion

Trace tail, ear, eye and nose patterns off the page on page 148 on to writing paper and cut out. Trace off halved body pattern complete with all details on to folded writing paper, placing fold to dot-and-dash line on pattern and copying dart and gap stitching lines on to both halves; cut out folded pattern and open it out flat.

Pin body pattern on to two layers of yellow fleece, right sides facing. Stitch all round close to edge of pattern, leaving a gap in stitching at back of body as indicated. Before removing pattern, mark dart on one body piece. Remove pattern and cut out body

close to stitching line. Pull fabric layers apart and stitch dart as marked, then trim dart. Turn body right side out using the knob of a knitting needle to push through the narrow parts. Fill body with lentils using a paper funnel to help you. Ladderstitch gap in seam.

For head cut a 9 cm (3½ in) diameter circle of yellow fleece. Gather round edge then stuff. Pull up gathers tightly then fasten off.

For mane, cut a 9 cm (3½ in) diameter circle of yellow fur fabric. Turn in raw edge slightly and catch in place. Run a gathering thread round edge of mane then put head inside, gathered side down. Pull up gathers tightly round head and fasten off. Sew gathered edge to head.

Before working face, position head so that smooth stroke of fur fabric mane will be going away from forehead down back of head. For mouth work a vertical stitch in doubled black sewing thread, from centre of face downwards, then work a V-shape at base of stitch.

When glueing features in place, hold each on end of a pin to spread with glue, then position it on face. Cut nose from brown felt and stick in place. Cut black felt eyes (use a leather punch if available, to get perfect circles), and stick them in place.

Cut ears from felt to match body colour then sew lower edges to mane above face as shown in illustration on page 147.

Position head at front of body, turning it slightly to one side, and pin it in place. Ladderstitch head to body as pinned.

Cut tail from yellow fleece, using pattern. Bring long edges together, right side outside, and ladderstitch them together pulling stitches tightly to curve tail slightly. Push scrap of fur fabric inside narrow end of tail and sew it in place. Sew tail to back of lion.

Tiger

Make body as for lion, but using orange fleece. Use a black marker pen to mark stripes across body and legs as shown in illustration on page 147, blotting markings with a paper tissue as they are made, to press them into the surface of the fabric.

Trace off and cut out tiger head pattern (*below*) as for other pieces. Pin it to two layers of orange fleece, stitch, cut out and turn as for body. Work small stitches across base of each ear through both layers of fabric. Stuff head then ladderstitch gap. Make mouth, nose and eyes as for lion. Mark stripes on face as shown on face pattern. Sew head in place as for lion.

Make tail as for lion, marking on stripes before joining long edges; turn in end of tail and ladderstitch. Sew tail to back of tiger.

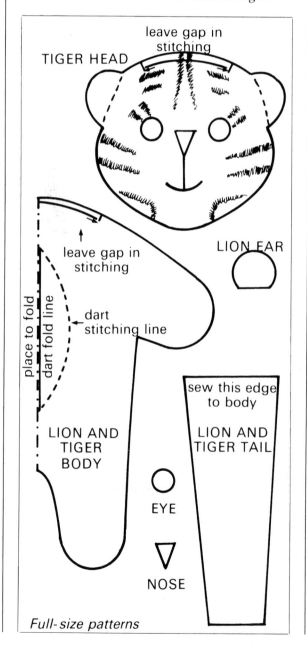

Full-size patterns

Four Small Animals

These four little animals, about 18 cm (7 in) high and 21·5 cm (8½ in) long from nose to tail, are all made from the same basic body pattern. Each one is given its individual characteristics by the addition of the appropriate eyes, nose, tail, etc.

You will need: Small pieces of fur fabric in colours illustrated on page 46; alternatively, 20 cm of 138 cm (8 in of 54 in) wide fur fabric will make two toys; small amount of stuffing; scraps of felt, ribbon, chunky knitting yarn; adhesive.

Notes: Trace all pattern shapes off pages 152–3 and mark on details. 5 mm (¼ in) seams are allowed on fur fabric pieces unless otherwise stated.

To make the basic body: Join body pieces together around head and back, from points A to B. Join underbody gusset pieces at upper edges from points A to B, leaving a gap in seam for turning. Now, matching points A and B, join one gusset to each body piece round legs. Turn body right side out and stuff firmly, then ladderstitch gap in gusset.

The lamb

Make basic body. For feet, cut eight foot pieces from felt. Join them in pairs, oversewing edges together and leaving upper edges open. Turn feet right side out and stretch felt slightly to make smooth, rounded shapes. Place a foot over each leg, pinning upper edges in place. Slipstitch upper edges to legs.

Join lamb's ear pieces, oversewing them together in pairs round edges and leaving lower edges open. Turn right side out. Fold ears in half at lower edges and oversew all raw edges together. Sew ears to lamb's head as shown in the illustration overleaf.

Fold tail, and oversew side edges together pulling stitches tightly to gather slightly. Then sew across end of tail. Turn tail right side out and sew to lamb as shown overleaf.

Trim fur pile a little shorter round end of lamb's face. Cut eyelids from pink felt, eyelashes and nose from black felt. Glue eyelids to eyelashes, overlapping lower edges of eyelids on to upper edges of lashes. Sew eyelids to lamb as shown in the illustration, leaving eyelashes free. Sew nose in place. Tie a length of ribbon in a bow around neck.

The bull

Make basic body. Make ears and feet and sew in place as for lamb. Cut eyes from blue felt, eyelids from pink and pupils from black felt. Glue them together as shown on eye pattern on page 151, then sew eyes to face. Trim fur pile a little shorter round end of face. Cut nose from pink felt and nostrils from black felt. Stick nostrils to nose, then sew nose in place. Cut tail from felt to match body colour and cut two tail end pieces from fur fabric. Oversew long edges of tail together. Oversew tail end pieces together, leaving upper edges open. Turn right side out. Slip lower edge of tail inside tail end piece and sew in place. Sew tail to bull.

Cut horns from white felt and oversew pieces together round edges leaving a gap in lower edge for turning. Turn right side out, stuff, then slipstitch gap. Sew centre of horns to head between ears. Cut horns' centre strip from fur fabric and place it over centre of horns. Sew front and back edges to bull's head and side edges to horns.

The donkey

Make basic body. Make feet and sew in place as for lamb. Make ears as for lamb using

donkey's ear pattern (*overleaf*), then sew them to head in upright position as shown in the illustration opposite. Trim fur pile a little shorter round end of face. Cut eyes from blue felt and pupils from black felt then stick pupils to eyes. Cut nostrils from pink felt, centre circles from black felt and stick them together. Sew eyes and nostrils in place.

For tail, wind yarn ten times around four fingers. Sew all these loops together at one end then sew to donkey. For the mane, make six more bunches of looped yarn in the same way as for tail. Sew two between ears to hang down towards face, then sew remaining four to head seam to hang down back on either side.

The dog

Make basic body. Oversew dog's tail pieces together, leaving lower edges open. Turn right side out, stuff, then sew tail in place.

Make ears as for lamb using dog's ear pattern (*overleaf*). Oversew upper raw edges of ears together then sew to dog as shown in the illustration opposite. Catch ears to head with a few small stitches about halfway down ears. Cut nose from black felt and run a gathering thread round edge. Stuff centre, pull up gathers tightly and fasten off. Cut eyes from blue felt and pupils from black felt and stick them together. Sew nose and eyes in place. Tie a length of ribbon in a bow around neck.

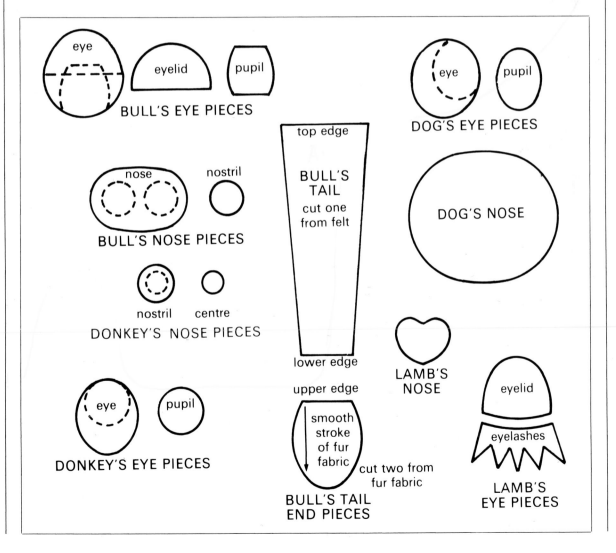

BULL'S EYE PIECES

DOG'S EYE PIECES

BULL'S NOSE PIECES

DONKEY'S NOSE PIECES

BULL'S TAIL cut one from felt

DOG'S NOSE

LAMB'S NOSE

DONKEY'S EYE PIECES

BULL'S TAIL END PIECES

LAMB'S EYE PIECES

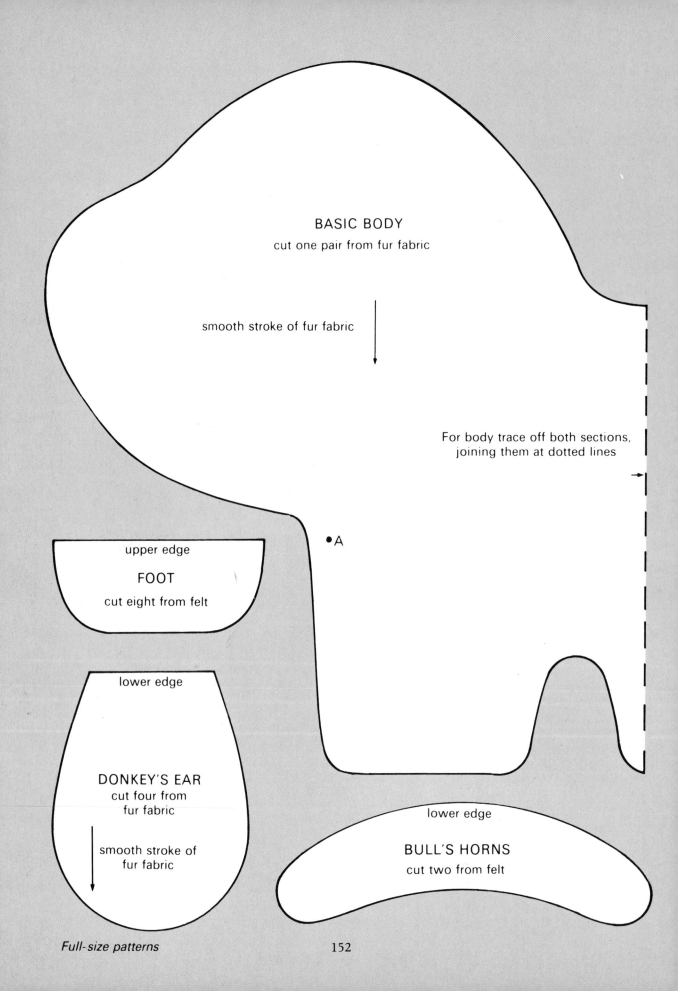

BASIC BODY

cut one pair from fur fabric

smooth stroke of fur fabric

For body trace off both sections,
joining them at dotted lines

●A

upper edge

FOOT

cut eight from felt

lower edge

DONKEY'S EAR
cut four from
fur fabric

smooth stroke of
fur fabric

lower edge

BULL'S HORNS

cut two from felt

Full-size patterns

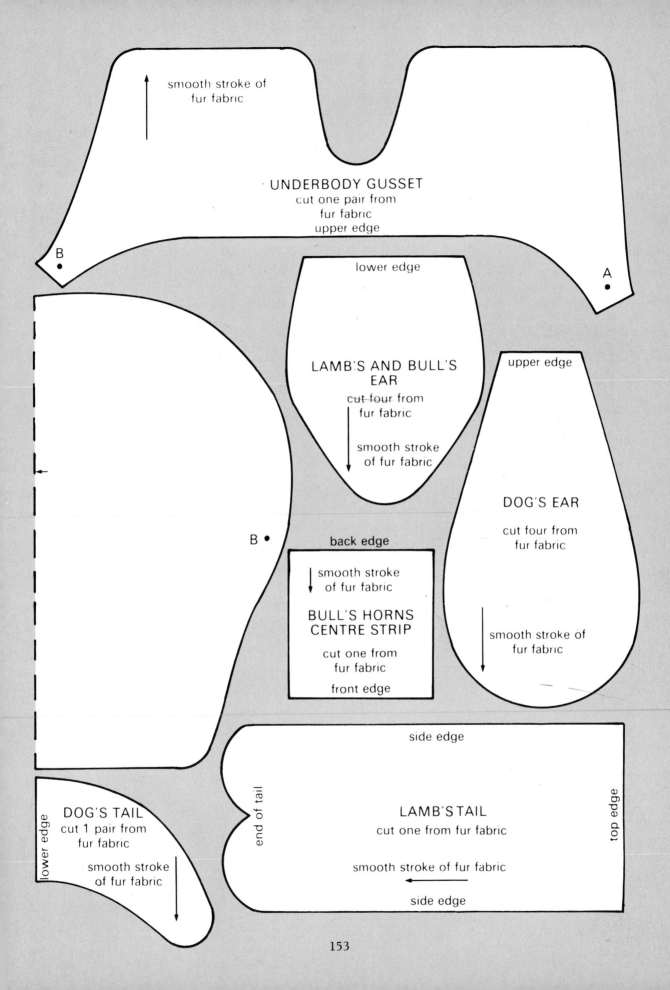

smooth stroke of fur fabric

UNDERBODY GUSSET
cut one pair from
fur fabric
upper edge

lower edge

B

A

LAMB'S AND BULL'S EAR

cut four from fur fabric

smooth stroke of fur fabric

upper edge

DOG'S EAR

cut four from fur fabric

smooth stroke of fur fabric

B

back edge

smooth stroke of fur fabric

BULL'S HORNS CENTRE STRIP

cut one from fur fabric

front edge

side edge

lower edge

DOG'S TAIL
cut 1 pair from fur fabric

smooth stroke of fur fabric

end of tail

LAMB'S TAIL

cut one from fur fabric

smooth stroke of fur fabric

side edge

top edge

Moo and Chew

These two irresistible miniature cows are about 9 cm (3½ in) long and are just the size to nestle in a toddler's hand, or fit into a pocket

You will need: Small pieces of white fleecy fabric; black and brown permanent marker pens; scraps of pink, black, brown and white felt; strands of brown and green embroidery thread and white yarn; stuffing; small bells and narrow ribbon; adhesive.

Note: The outline on the cow patterns is the stitching line.

The chewing cow

Trace the body and head patterns off the page on to folded pieces of paper, placing folds in paper to dotted lines shown on patterns. Cut out folded patterns and open up to give full-sized patterns.

Pin body pattern on to double layer of fleece, right sides together. Now machine stitch all round close to edge of pattern leaving a gap in seam at front end. Remove pattern and cut out body close to stitching line. Turn body right side out and stuff, then slip stitch gap. Run a gathering thread along centre of one body piece from back to front of body. Pull up thread slightly and fasten off. Fold body along this line bringing legs close together. Ladder stitch along fabric at fold to hold legs in this position.

Make head, turn and stuff as for body leaving gap in seam at top. Slip stitch gap. To make the patched markings on body and head, work irregular areas with brown marker pen as illustrated dabbing with a paper tissue to press colour into fabric. Work over again if necessary to penetrate fleece and deepen colour.

Cut ears from brown felt to match markings. Fold in half at lower edges, oversew these edges then sew to position on head as illustrated. Cut two horns pieces from white felt and oversew them together all round edges leaving a gap at lower edge. Horns may now be turned right sides out and then stuffed. Oversew gap. Cut a 1 by 2 cm ($\frac{3}{8}$ by $\frac{3}{4}$ in) strip of brown felt and wrap length of strip around centre of horns, oversewing short edges together at lower edge. Sew centre of horns in place behind ears.

Cut nose from pink felt and mark on dots for nostrils with black pen. Cut eyes from white felt and smaller ovals from black felt. Glue eye pieces together as shown on head pattern then stick eyes and nose to head.

Use a length of brown thread to work a 1 cm ($\frac{3}{8}$ in) stitch for mouth along seam line at front. For the 'grass' take green threads through from back of head to centre of mouth line and trim to irregular lengths. If available, sew a small guipure flower to one strand of

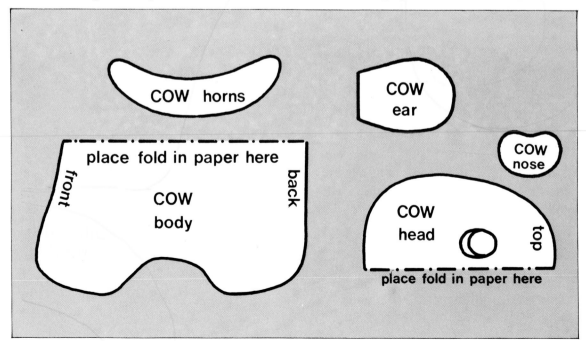

grass. Now position head on body as illustrated and sew them together.

For tail cut a 1 by 4 cm ($\frac{3}{8}$ by $1\frac{1}{2}$ in) strip of brown felt. Taper strip slightly towards one end. Oversew long edges together and across short tapered end enclosing a few strands of white yarn. Tease out yarn strands and trim to about 2 cm ($\frac{3}{4}$ in). Put a touch of glue on ends of strands and twist together to form the shape illustrated. Sew tail to back of cow. Thread bell on to ribbon and tie in a bow round cow's neck.

The mooing cow

Make as for chewing cow using black pen for for the markings with white felt for the ears and black for the tail. Sew head in position illustrated. Using white thread take a stitch through head seam at position of mouth, from one corner of mouth to the other. Pull thread tightly and fasten off. Cut a small black felt oval for mouth and stick in place as illustrated. Cut eye ovals from pink felt. Trim a little off across lower edges and stick small strips of black felt to these edges. Snip black felt into eyelashes.

Twelve Simple Toys

A toymaker's dozen of furry creatures, all designed without having to use a single pattern. The toys are made from simple shapes – squares, circles and oblongs – using fur fabric and felt. Finished sizes range from around 23 cm (9 in) high for the koala, owl and penguin, and 23 cm (9 in) long for the puppy and lion, down to 10 cm (4 in) nose to tail for the busy bee and the ladybird

For all the animals you will need: Oddments of fur fabric; stuffing; scraps of felt, fleecy fabric, trimmings and ribbon; adhesive; strong thread for gathering fur fabric.

Notes: All the animals are made from fur fabric with felt for features. 1 cm ($\frac{3}{8}$ in) seams are allowed unless otherwise stated.

Some animals are made from fur fabric circles. For this run a strong gathering thread round close to circle edges, pull up gathers slightly, insert stuffing then gather tightly and fasten off. Cover gap by sewing on a 5 cm (2 in) diameter felt circle.

Have the smooth stroke of fur fabric going from front to back or from top to bottom of the toys. Snip away fur pile under facial features before glueing in place.

On rectangular pieces with rounded-off corners, trim off excess fabric at these corners before turning right side out.

The bee

Gather and stuff an 18 cm (7 in) diameter circle of yellow fur fabric. For stripes cut three 2 cm ($\frac{3}{4}$ in) wide strips of black fur fabric; place strips round body, catch ends together beneath body, sew them in place.

For eyes glue 5 mm ($\frac{1}{4}$ in) diameter felt circles on larger ovals. Use a smaller fur fabric circle for nose. Make loops of black thread above eyes as illustrated.

For each wing cut a 12 cm ($4\frac{3}{4}$ in) diameter circle of net. Fold in half and gather folded edge, sew wings to bee.

The ladybird

Make as for bee, gathering a 16 cm ($6\frac{1}{4}$ in) diameter red fur fabric circle. Sew on black ric-rac trimming and ten 1 cm ($\frac{3}{8}$ in) diameter black felt circles for spots.

The tortoise

Gather and stuff a 30 cm (12 in) diameter circle of fur fabric. Sew on flower trimming for shell markings, as illustrated.

For head cut two 9 by 11 cm ($3\frac{1}{2}$ by $4\frac{1}{4}$ in) strips of contrasting fleece. Join round edges, rounding off corners at one short edge and leaving other short edges open. Turn, stuff, gather raw edges and sew to tortoise close to base. Catch head to body a little further up to hold it upright. Make eyes and nose as for bee.

For each foot cut two 6 cm ($2\frac{3}{8}$ in) squares of fleece. Join as for head, turn and stuff, then oversew raw edges to body as illustrated. Sew frilled trimming in place to complete.

The octopus

Gather and stuff a 30 cm (12 in) diameter circle of fur fabric. Cut eight fur fabric strips 8 by 24 cm (3 by $9\frac{1}{2}$ in), join long edges of each and across one short edge, rounding off corners. Turn right side out. Sew raw ends to octopus – round edge of felt circle. For eyes glue 2 cm ($\frac{3}{4}$ in) diameter felt circles on larger ovals, as illustrated.

The hedgehog

Cut two 22 cm (8¾ in) radius quarter-circles of fur fabric. Mark both at centre point of circle, noting that this is the back of the hedgehog, close to base. Round off one of the remaining corners using a big curve for humped back of hedgehog. Round off remaining corner slightly for snout. Join pieces leaving a gap in base. Turn and stuff, then slip stitch gap.

To turn up the snout run a strong gathering thread from snout 8 cm (3 in) up back seam, pull up gathers and fasten off.

For face piece cut a 14 cm (5½ in) diameter semi-circle of felt. Fold it into a quarter-circle and round off point. Oversew along straight edges and round point. Turn, put a little stuffing in point, slip this over snout and catch to head.

For each foot cut two 6 cm (2⅜ in) squares of felt. Make as for tortoise.

For nose gather and stuff a 3 cm (1¼ in) diameter felt circle and sew in place. For eyelids cut 1·5 cm (⅝ in) felt squares, rounding off top corners. For eyelashes cut 1 cm (⅜ in) wide felt strips and snip along one edge, glue to eyelids as illustrated.

The owl

Cut two fur fabric pieces 18 by 26 cm (7 by 10¼ in). Join them round edges taking large curves on corners at one short edge and smaller curves at other short edge, and leaving a gap for turning. Turn and stuff, then slip stitch gap. The large curves are the top of the head. Tie strong thread round 13 cm (5 in) down from upper edge.

For each ear cut two fur fabric triangles measuring 10 cm (4 in) across the base by 6 cm (2⅜ in) high. Join in pairs, leaving bases open. Turn, oversew bases to head as illustrated.

For each wing cut a triangle of fur fabric and one of felt measuring 12 cm (4¾ in) across the base by 12 cm (4¾ in) high. Join, rounding off top point and leaving bases open. Turn and oversew raw edges, pulling stitches to gather slightly. Sew to owl.

For each foot cut two 9 cm (3½ in) diameter semi-circles of felt. Join round curves, turn, push in a little stuffing and oversew remaining edges under owl at front, gathering slightly.

For eyes cut felt circles 2, 3 and 4 cm (¾, 1¼ and 1½ in) in diameter. For nose cut a felt triangle 2·5 cm (1 in) across base by 2 cm (¾ in) high; round off corners of triangle. Sew features in place.

The koala

Make body as for owl. Sew an 8 by 12 cm (3 by 4¾ in) piece of white fleece to the front, rounding off the corners. Make ears as for owl, using 7 by 10 cm (2¾ by 4 in) fur fabric rectangles and rounding off corners at one long edge.

For each arm cut two 7 by 8 cm (2¾ by 3 in) fur fabric pieces. Join, rounding off corners at one short edge, leaving opposite edge open. Turn and stuff, then sew to koala as illustrated. For nose cut a fur fabric triangle 4 cm (1½ in) across the base by 4 cm (1½ in) high. Round off corners then sew nose to face, pushing a little stuffing underneath. For eyes use felt circles 1·5 and 2 cm (⅝ and ¾ in) in diameter.

The mouse

Cut a 20 cm (8 in) radius quarter-circle of fur fabric. Fold it, bringing straight edges together, and round off centre point. Oversew round point and along straight edges, pulling up stitches until seam measures about 14 cm (5½ in). Turn, gather round remaining raw edge, stuff and fasten off.

For tail cut a triangle 2·5 cm (1 in) across the base by 15 cm (6 in) high. Round off top point and oversew long edges together then sew tail to back of mouse.

For ears cut two 2·5 by 4 cm (1 by 1½ in) felt pieces, rounding off corners at one long edge. Sew to head gathering ears at base. Make eyes and nose as for bee. Use white threads for whiskers, stiffening them with glue after sewing in place.

The rabbit

Make as for mouse, using a 28 cm (11 in) radius quarter-circle of fur fabric, snipping 7 cm (2¾ in) off centre point and pulling up oversewn seam to measure 18 cm (7 in). Tie strong thread round, 8 cm (3 in) from upper edge.

For each foot cut two 5 by 6 cm (2 by 2⅜ in) pieces of fur fabric. Make as for koala, rounding off corners at one long edge, then sew in place as illustrated. Gather and stuff a 5 cm (2 in) diameter fur fabric circle for tail.

For each ear cut an 8 by 10 cm (3 by 4 in) piece of fur fabric and of fleece. Join them, rounding off corners at one short edge and leaving opposite edges open. Turn and sew to head as illustrated, gathering raw edges. For eyes glue 1·5 cm (⅝ in) diameter felt circles to larger ovals. For nose use a 1·5 cm (⅝ in) diameter circle of felt.

The dog

For body cut two fur fabric pieces 15 by 18 cm (6 by 7 in). Join them, rounding off two corners at one short edge and leaving opposite edges open. Turn, stuff and oversew raw edges, pulling stitches tight to gather slightly.

For each foot cut two 8 cm (3 in) squares of fur fabric. Make as for body. Sew two to front of dog and two to seam at sides for back legs. Bring back legs to standing position and catch them to body to hold them in place.

For head cut two 12 by 14 cm (4¾ by 5½ in) pieces of fur fabric. Join, taking large curves on corners of one short edge, and smaller curves on opposite edge, leaving a gap for turning. Turn and stuff then slip stitch gap. Sew head on body as illustrated, with the small curves at top of head.

For each ear cut an 8 by 13 cm (3 by 5 in) piece of fur fabric and of felt. Make as for rabbit ears and sew to head as illustrated.

For tail cut a triangle measuring 10 cm (4 in) across the base by 8 cm (3 in) high. Join side edges, turn and stuff then sew in place. For eyes glue 1·5 cm (⅝ in) diameter circles of felt over slightly larger ovals; for nose use a 1·5 cm (⅝ in) diameter felt circle.

The penguin

Cut two pieces of black fur fabric 16 by 24 cm
($6\frac{1}{4}$ by $9\frac{1}{2}$ in). Round off two corners at one
short edge for top of head, taking large
curves, and round off one remaining corner
for front of penguin. Leave the remaining
corner square to form the penguin's tail. Join
pieces leaving a gap, turn and stuff. Slip stitch
gap. Tie thread round, 10 cm (4 in) down from
top. Cut a piece of white fleece 9 by 12 cm
($3\frac{1}{2}$ by $4\frac{3}{4}$ in). Round off corners and sew to
front as illustrated.

For each foot cut two 7 cm ($2\frac{3}{4}$ in) squares
of felt; make and sew them in place as for the
rabbit.

For beak cut a triangle measuring 8 cm
(3 in) across the base by 7 cm ($2\frac{3}{4}$ in) high.
Round off top point then join sides and round
point. Turn, stuff, then sew to face as
illustrated. Make eyes as for lion.

For each wing cut a fur fabric and a felt
triangle measuring 9 cm ($3\frac{1}{2}$ in) across the base
by 17 cm ($6\frac{3}{4}$ in) high. Snip 7 cm ($2\frac{3}{4}$ in) off top

points then round off. Join and sew in place
as for owl's wings.

The lion

Make as for dog, except for head. For this
join two 14 cm ($5\frac{1}{2}$ in) diameter circles of fur
fabric, leaving a gap. Turn, stuff and slip
stitch gap then sew to body as for dog.

For mane cut a 4 by 36 cm ($1\frac{1}{2}$ by 14 in)
strip of shaggy fur fabric and join short
edges. Place mane round face, with right sides
together and long raw edge about 2 cm ($\frac{3}{4}$ in)
away from seam on head. Sew long edge in
place then turn mane back over head.

For tail cut a 4 by 16 cm ($1\frac{1}{2}$ by $6\frac{1}{4}$ in) strip
of fur fabric. Join long edges and across one
short end then turn right side out. Sew a bit
of shaggy fur fabric to end of tail.

For eyes use 1·5 and 2 cm ($\frac{5}{8}$ and $\frac{3}{4}$ in)
diameter felt circles. For nose cut a felt
triangle 2 cm ($\frac{3}{4}$ in) across the base, 2 cm
($\frac{3}{4}$ in) high and round off the corners slightly.

Mamas and Babes

A cuddlesome bunch of tiny toys which are oh-so-quick to knit. The largest, Mrs Hedgehog is just 9 cm [3½ in] long, while the baby bee and ladybird measure less than 5 cm [2 in].

You will need: Oddments of double knitting yarn in assorted colours, appropriate to the various creatures as shown in the illustration; a pair of 3¼ mm [No 10] knitting needles; small amount of stuffing; oddments of felt, ribbon, lace edging, and guipure flowers; adhesive.
Abbreviations: See page 17.

Mother hedgehog

9 cm [3½ in] long
Begin at back of hedgehog and using brown cast on 15 sts.

Next row: Inc K wise into every st – 30 sts.
Work the looped pattern: *1st row:* K 6; * insert right hand needle K wise into next st, place first finger of left hand at back of st, wind yarn anti-clockwise round needle and finger twice, then round tip of right hand needle only, draw through the 3 loops; repeat from * until 6 sts remain; K 6.

2nd row: K 6; * K 3 tog, pulling loops down firmly as you go; repeat from * until 6 sts remain; K 6 – 30 sts.

Repeat these last two rows 8 more times.
Break off brown and join on fawn for head.
Now beginning with a P row, work in st-st, decreasing 1 st at each end of every row until 12 sts remain. Break off yarn leaving a long end then thread it through remaining sts, pull up tightly and fasten off.

To make up

Oversew row ends of work together leaving cast on edge open. Turn right side out and stuff. Gather round cast on edge, pull up gathers tightly and fasten off.

Work a few stitches for nose in brown. Cut out and stick on 5 mm [¼ in] diameter circles of black felt for the eyes.

For the hat cut a 4 cm [1½ in] diameter circle of felt then sew it to head through the centre of the circle. For the crown of the hat cut a 2 cm [¾ in] diameter circle from two layers of felt glued together. Stick this to the hat then decorate it with flower trimming and a ribbon bow as shown in the illustration.

Baby hedgehog

6.5 cm [2½ in] long
Begin at back of hedgehog using brown and cast on 10 sts.

Next row: Inc K wise into every st – 20 sts.
Work the looped pattern: *1st row:* K 4; * insert right-hand needle K wise into next st, place first finger of left hand at back of st, wind yarn anti-clockwise round needle and finger twice, then round tip of right-hand needle only, draw through the 3 loops; repeat from * until 4 sts remain; K 4.

2nd row: K 4; * K 3 tog, pulling loops down firmly as you go; repeat from * until 4 sts remain; K 4 – 20 sts.

Repeat these two rows 5 more times.
Break off brown and join on fawn for head.
Now beginning with a P row, work in st-st decreasing 1 st at each end of every row until 8 sts remain.

Finish off and make up as for mother hedgehog, omitting the hat and making the eyes slightly smaller.

Mother mouse

8.5 cm [3¼ in] long
Begin at back of mouse and using pink cast on 14 sts, leaving a long end of yarn for making tail later on.

Next row: Inc K wise into every st – 28 sts.
1st pattern row: K 4, P 20, K 4.
2nd pattern row: K.
Repeat these last two rows 7 more times.

Now beginning with a P row, work in st-st decreasing 1 st at each end of every row until 12 sts remain. Break off yarn leaving a long end, thread it through remaining sts then pull up tightly and fasten off.

Ears [make two alike]

Cast on 3 sts.

1st row: Inc K wise into every st – 6 sts.

Now beginning with a P row, st-st 5 rows.

Break off yarn leaving a long end and then thread it through sts, pull up tightly and fasten off.

To make up

Gather along cast on sts of body, pull up tightly and fasten off. Twist the long end of yarn for the tail tightly, then allow it to curl up, making tail about 10 cm [4 in] in length.

Fasten off end of yarn.

Oversew row ends of work together leaving a gap for turning. Turn right side out and stuff, then oversew gap. Sew gathered edges of ears to head. Work pink stitches for the nose then cut the eyes as for mother hedgehog and stick them in place.

Gather up a bit of lace trimming tightly for the hat, sew a ribbon bow to the centre then sew hat to head.

Baby mouse

6.5 cm [2½ in] long

Begin at back of mouse and using pink cast on 10 sts, leaving a long end of yarn for making the tail later on.

Next row: Inc K wise into every st – 20 sts.
1st pattern row: K 3, P 14, K 3.
2nd pattern row: K.

Repeat these last two rows 5 more times.

Now beginning with a P row, work in st-st decreasing 1 st at each end of every row until 8 sts remain.

Finish off as for mother mouse.

Ears [make two alike]

Make as for mother mouse but st-st 3 rows instead of 5.

To make up

Make up as for mother mouse omitting the hat and making the eyes slightly smaller.

Make the tail in same way as mother mouse but 8 cm [3 in] in length.

Mother ladybird

6 cm [2¼ in] long

Begin at back of ladybird and using red cast on 5 sts.

Next row: Inc K wise into every st – 10 sts.
Next row: Inc P wise into every st – 20 sts.
** *1st pattern row:* K.
2nd pattern row: K 3, P 14, K 3.
Repeat these last two rows 5 more times **.
Break off red and join on black, then repeat 1st and 2nd pattern rows 3 more times.
*** *Next row:* (K 2 tog) to end – 10 sts.
Next row: (P 2 tog) to end – 5 sts.
Break off yarn leaving a long end then thread it through remaining sts, pull up tightly and fasten off.

To make up

Gather along the cast on sts then pull up tightly and fasten off. Oversew row ends of work together leaving a gap for turning. Turn right side out and stuff, then oversew gap.

Cut 5 mm [¼ in] diameter circles of white felt for the eyes then using a black pen, mark a small semi-circle at one side of each eye. Stick the eyes in place.

Work a long black stitch down the centre of the body then work two black spots on each side.

Gather up a bit of lace trimming and sew it around the face as shown in the illustration.

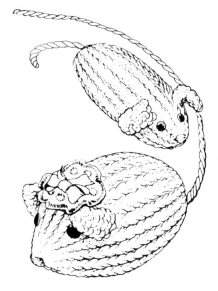

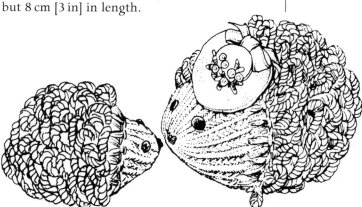

Baby ladybird

4 cm [1½ in] long

Begin at back of ladybird and using red cast on 4 sts.

Next row: Inc K wise into every st – 8 sts.
Next row: Inc P wise into every st – 16 sts.
** *1st pattern row:* K.
2nd pattern row: K 2, P 12, K 2.
Repeat these last two rows 3 more times **.
Break off red and join on black, then repeat 1st and 2nd pattern rows twice more.
*** *Next row:* (K 2 tog) to end – 8sts.
Next row: (P 2 tog) to end – 4 sts.
Finish off and make up as for mother ladybird, omitting the lace trim and making the eyes slightly smaller.

Mother bee

6 cm [2¼ in] long

Begin at back of bee and using brown cast on 5 sts.

Next row: Inc K wise into every st – 10 sts.
Next row: Inc P wise into every st – 20 sts.
Join on gold and work as for mother ladybird from ** to **, working in two row stripes of gold and brown. Break off brown and continue in gold only.
St-st 6 rows.
Now work as given for mother ladybird from *** to the end.

Wings [make two alike]

Using white cast on 4 sts.
1st row: Inc K wise into every st – 8 sts.
G-st 13 rows.
Break off yarn leaving a long end, thread it through remaining sts then pull up tightly and fasten off.

To make up

Make up the body as for the ladybird. Cut eyes and stick in place as for mother hedgehog. Work a loop of black yarn above each eye and a small pink stitch for mouth.
Sew the gathered up edges of wings to the first brown stripe behind the head.
Make the hat as for mother hedgehog but use a 2 cm [¾ in] and a 1 cm [⅜ in] diameter circle of felt.

Baby bee

4 cm [1½ in] long

Begin at back of bee and using brown cast on 4 sts.
Next row: Inc K wise into every st – 8 sts.
Next row: Inc P wise into every st – 16 sts.
Join on gold and work as for baby ladybird from ** to **, working in two row stripes of gold and brown. Break off brown and continue in gold only.
St-st 4 rows.
Now work as for baby ladybird from *** to end.

Wings [make two alike]

Using white cast on 3 sts.
1st row: Inc K wise into every st – 6 sts.
G-st 9 rows.
Break off yarn and finish off as for mother's wings.

To make up

Make up as for mother bee omitting the hat and making the eyes slightly smaller.

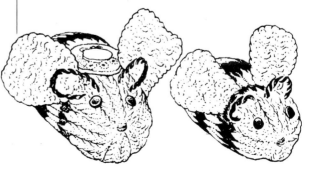

6
SIT-UPON
TOYS

Leo the Laughing Lion

Leo the friendly Lion is more than just a toy to sit on and hug; at 84 cm (33 in) long and 40 cm (16 in) high from paw to mane, he will guard your door so well that no draught will ever dare to enter!

You will need: 1·20 m (1⅛ yd) of 138 cm (54 in) wide short pile fur fabric; 40 cm (½ yd) of 138 cm (54 in) wide long hair fur fabric (see suppliers' list on page 139); 1·5 kilo (3 lb) of stuffing; scraps of black, blue and white felt; thick black football laces for mouth and pawlines; metric graph paper.

For the patterns: Copy the outlines from scaled-down diagram on to metric graph paper, noting that each square on diagram equals 5 cm.

Cut out all the patterns, then cut a second body pattern, making the outline exactly the same as the first. On one body pattern cut out the circular shape shown by the broken line on pattern (this is the *upper body* pattern). Mark points C and D on this piece also.

On the other body pattern mark the dart lines as shown on pattern – this is the *under-body* pattern. Mark all lettering on each pattern piece.

Notes: All pieces are cut from short-pile fur fabric except for the mane and tail end (cut these from long-hair fabric).

Pin patterns to wrong side of fabric as shown on the cutting-out layout.

Mark all points, A, B, C, etc., shown on the pattern pieces on the wrong side of fur fabric pieces.

The seam allowance is 1 cm (⅜ in) on all pieces unless otherwise stated. Join all pieces with right sides facing.

Leo the Lion

Start with the head. Join centre front edges of face pieces as far as points A. Sew sides of face gusset to top edges of face pieces, matching points A and B. Join centre front and centre back edges of back head pieces,

leaving a gap in centre back seam as shown on pattern. Now join back head and face pieces to each other at the side face edges, matching the centre front seams.

Sew the lower edges of head to the cut-out circular shape in the upper body, matching points C and D on both pieces. On the under-body piece stitch the dart as marked. Now join both body pieces all round edges, leaving the back leg edges open. Clip the seam at front between legs.

Join the inner and outer back leg pieces round the foot from points E to F, leaving the top edges open. Now join the back legs to the body as follows. First sew top edges of the outer leg pieces to the leg edges of the upper body, easing the leg edges to fit the body and matching points E and F. Now sew the top edges of the inner leg piece to the leg edges of the underbody.

Turn the lion right side out through the gap in head seam. Stuff the lion firmly, beginning with the front legs, then the back legs followed by the body and head. Ladder stitch the opening in the seam.

Join the side edges of the tail, leaving top edges open. Turn right side out and stuff lightly. Join the tail end pieces together, turn right side out and stuff as for tail pieces. Slip narrow end of tail inside top edges of tail end piece, then turn in raw edges and sew them to tail. Turn in and sew top of tail very securely to back of body below centre back seam.

Join centre front and centre back edges of mane pieces. With mane wrong side out, place face edge over lion's face, making sure the raw edge is level with lion's side face seam. Also place centre front of mane at centre front of lion's face under chin. Back stitch mane to head 3 cm (1¼ in) away from raw edge at top of head, tapering to 1 cm (⅜ in) away from raw edge beneath chin. Pull mane back over lion's head, turning it right side out. Slip stitch lower raw edge of mane to back and sides of lion's body where they touch.

Join ear pieces in pairs, leaving lower edges open. Turn right side out then turn in lower edges. Oversew lower edges together, pulling stitches tightly to gather slightly. Brush long pile on mane forward at top of head, then sew ears to face just in front of mane seam and each side of face gusset.

For mouth lines cut two 13 cm (5⅛ in) lengths of bootlace. Back stitch centre of strips to face as shown by broken line on face pattern. Clip fur pile slightly shorter above

mouth lines up to position of nose. Cut nose from black felt and sew it to face, with lower end just overlapping top of mouth lines.

Cut all eye pieces as directed on the pattern and sew them together. Work a highlight on each pupil in white thread. Sew eyes to face each side of face gusset, 5 cm (2 in) up from nose.

For lines on each paw, cut three 8 cm (3 in) long strips of bootlace. Back stitch them in place as shown in illustration.

Cutting-out layout for short pile fur fabric pieces

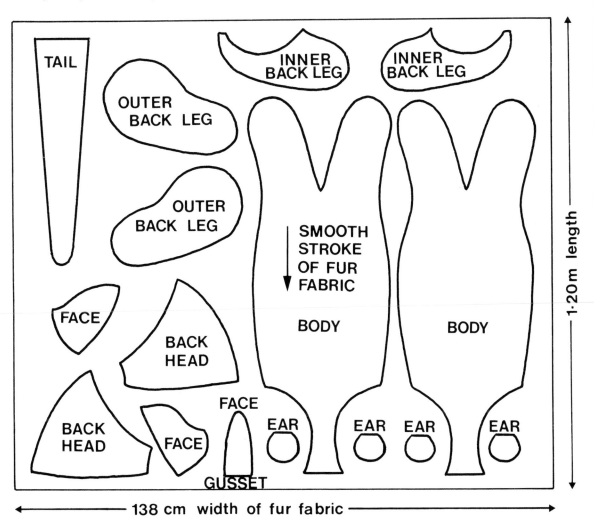

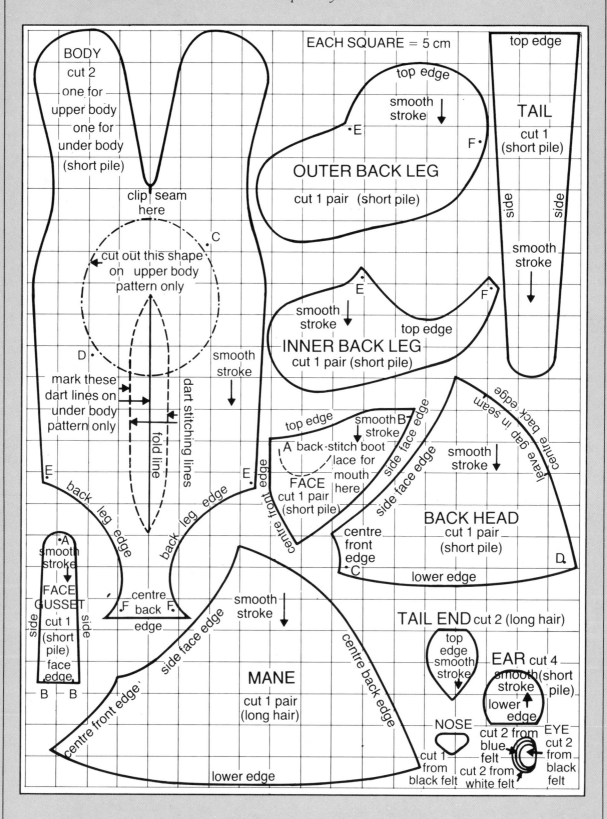

EACH SQUARE = 5 cm

BODY
cut 2
one for
upper body
one for
under body
(short pile)

clip seam
here

cut out this shape
on upper body
pattern only

C

D

mark these
dart lines on
under body
pattern only

dart stitching lines

fold line

smooth
stroke

E

back leg edge

back leg edge

E

centre front edge

top edge

smooth
stroke

E

OUTER BACK LEG
cut 1 pair (short pile)

F

TAIL
cut 1
(short pile)

top edge

side

side

smooth
stroke

E

smooth
stroke

INNER BACK LEG
cut 1 pair (short pile)

top edge

F

smooth B
stroke

A back-stitch boot
lace for
mouth
here

FACE
cut 1 pair
(short pile)

centre
front
edge

C

side face edge

side face edge

side face edge

smooth
stroke

leave gap in seam

centre back edge

BACK HEAD
cut 1 pair
(short pile)

D

lower edge

A
smooth
stroke

FACE
GUSSET
cut 1
(short
pile)
face
edge

side

side

B   B

centre
back
edge

F   F

centre front edge

side face edge

smooth
stroke

MANE
cut 1 pair
(long hair)

centre back edge

TAIL END cut 2 (long hair)

top
edge
smooth
stroke

lower
edge

EAR cut 4
smooth (short
stroke pile)

lower
edge

NOSE
cut 1
from
black felt

cut 2 from
blue felt
cut 2 from
white felt

EYE
cut 2
from
black
felt

lower edge

170

Ladybird, Ladybird

Mother ladybird – a giant-sized pouffe for the nursery – measures 46 cm (18 in) long, while her baby, only about 23 cm (9 in) from head to tail, makes an appealing small soft toy

For both ladybirds you will need: 40 by 138 cm (16 by 54 in) of red fur fabric; 50 by 138 cm (20 by 54 in) of black fabric; 1·5 kg (3 lb) stuffing; felt and thread for facial features; 1 m (1⅛ yd) of frilled lace edging and 1·50 m (1⅝ yd) of broad ribbon for large ladybird; small pieces of lace trimming and narrow ribbon for small ladybird; metric graph paper.

Notes: The seam allowance is 1 cm (⅜ in) on all pieces unless stated otherwise. Join the fabrics with right sides facing.

Copy all the pattern pieces square by square, on to graph paper (each square on diagram equals 2 cm). Mark all details on patterns.

Ladybird pouffe

Cut out a pair of large upper body pieces from red fur fabric; and a pair of large face pieces and one large underbody from black fabric (note that underbody pattern should be placed to a fold in fabric where directed on pattern). Mark points A, B, C and D, and positions of legs, on wrong side of fabric pieces.

Join each face piece to an upper body piece, matching points A-B. Now join the entire body and face pieces along top seam, from points C to C, leaving a gap in seam where shown on upper body pattern.

Cut six pairs of large leg pieces from black fabric. Join them in pairs leaving the straight edges open. Trim seams, turn right side out and stuff legs lightly, then sew straight edges of each leg together.

Place legs on underbody piece at positions shown on pattern, with legs pointing towards centre of underbody and raw edges of legs and underbody level.

Join the upper body to underbody, matching points C and D and easing upper body to fit underbody all round. Turn right side out and stuff very firmly, then ladder stitch the opening.

For the spots cut seven 9 cm (3½ in) diameter circles of black fabric. Turn in the raw edges 5 mm (¼ in) and tack. Pin one spot on top of the ladybird, and three on each side (as shown in illustration). Slip stitch the spots in place.

Cut eyes, pupils and nose from felts, using the patterns (see illustration as a guide to colours). Sew the pupils to the eyes and work a few white stitches on each pupil for a highlight. For cheeks cut two 7 cm (2¾ in) diameter circles of felt.

For mouth draw a U-shaped line on face, 7 cm (2¾ in) up from seam at the front. Work mouth in red thread, then position and sew on felt features, using illustration as a guide.

Sew two rows of lace frilling round the face, then sew ends of ribbon lengths to each side of frilling to tie in a bow below the mouth. Sew the bow in place. Make two ribbon rosettes and sew one to each side of the ribbon.

The baby ladybird

Make this in exactly the same way as for the large ladybird, using the small pattern pieces. For the spots cut 6 cm (2⅜ in) diameter circles of fabric, and 5 cm (2 in) diameter circles of felt for the cheeks. Work the mouth 3 cm (1¼ in) up from seam.

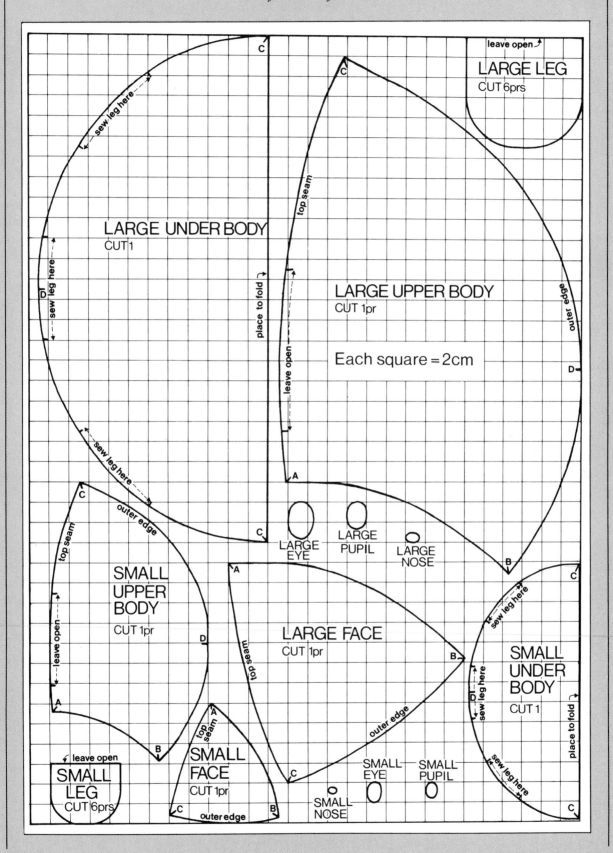

Sit-upon Elephant

Dumbelle is a giant-sized soft toy elephant (about 43 cm (17 in) high, 67 cm (26½ in) from trunk to back). You can make her from fur fabric and synthetic stuffing so she is washable – and satisfyingly squashy; and she is plenty large enough for toddlers to sit on.

You will need: 1·1 m (1¼ yd) of fur fabric, 138 cm (54 in) wide; 2·25 kg (5 lb) of stuffing; scraps of felt for eyes; oddment of knitting yarn for tail end; oddments of plain and patterned fabric; 1 ball of double knitting yarn for tassels; 1 m (1⅛ yd) of jumbo ric-rac braid; metric graph paper.

To make patterns: Copy the pattern outlines square by square from the diagram. Each square on diagram = 5 cm. After drawing the main body piece, draw the underbody piece separately as marked on the main body pattern. Mark the leg darts on the underbody piece only. Mark all other details on to each pattern piece.

Notes: Follow the cutting-out layout for the placing of patterns on the piece of fur fabric. Take care to reverse the pattern when necessary for cutting a *pair* of pieces. Mark darts and other details on wrong side of each piece. 1 cm (⅜ in) seams are allowed on all pieces unless otherwise stated.

The elephant

Make a small pleat at inner edge of each ear piece as follows. With the right side of ear towards you, fold top dotted line down to meet lower dotted line, making a 1 cm (⅜ in) pleat. Tack pleat in place.

Now join ear pieces in pairs, leaving inner edges open. Trim lower corners, turn right side out, then tack inner edges of each ear together.

On each body piece cut a slit for inserting ear as shown on the body pattern. Slip inner edges of ear between the slit, with raw edges level, then fold body at solid line beyond the slit at each end and tack ear in place. Tack,

then stitch, at position of dotted stitching lines shown on body pattern, thus enclosing ear in stitching.

Join long edges of tail, leaving upper and lower edges open. Turn right side out. Tack upper edges of tail together then sew them to one body piece at position shown on body pattern, with raw edges level.

Now join body pieces together from point A, round trunk and head to point B at back, leaving a gap in seam as shown on pattern. Pull the two layers of fabric apart at end of trunk and stitch dart across end of trunk as shown on pattern.

Stitch the leg darts on each underbody piece. Join underbody pieces to each other at upper edges between points A and B. Now join underbody to body pieces, matching points A and B and leaving lower leg edges open. Sew a foot piece to each lower leg edge, matching the centre front and back points of each foot to the leg seams.

Turn elephant right side out and stuff very firmly in this order: trunk, back legs, front legs and face, then body and head. Ladderstitch gap in seam securely. For tail

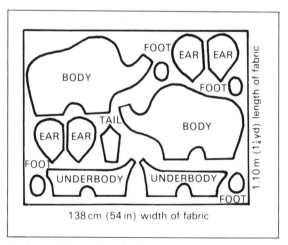

138 cm (54 in) width of fabric

Cutting-out layout for elephant

end, cut twelve 12 cm ($4\frac{3}{4}$ in) lengths of yarn, and tie a length of yarn round centre. Fold in half at tied position then push the folded ends into end of tail. Gather round end of tail, pull up gathers and oversew securely to hold yarn strands in place. Trim ends evenly.

Cut two eye pieces from white felt, using outline of eye pattern; cut two from blue felt to middle line, and two from black felt to smallest outline. Using white thread, work a highlight on each black pupil, then sew all the eye pieces together. Sew the eyes in place about 6 cm ($2\frac{3}{8}$ in) apart, with upper edges slightly lower than the height of the end of the trunk.

The saddlecloth

Cut two strips of patterned fabric 18 by 52 cm (7 by $20\frac{1}{2}$ in). For the plain borders, cut four strips of plain fabric 18 by 5 cm (7 by 2 in). Sew ric-rac braid down centre of two plain strips. Join a trimmed plain strip to each short edge of one patterned strip, right sides facing. Sew the remaining plain strips to each end of the other patterned strip, in the same way. Press seams open. Then join complete pieces together round edges, right sides facing leaving a gap in seam for turning. Trim off corners and turn right side out, then slipstitch gap.

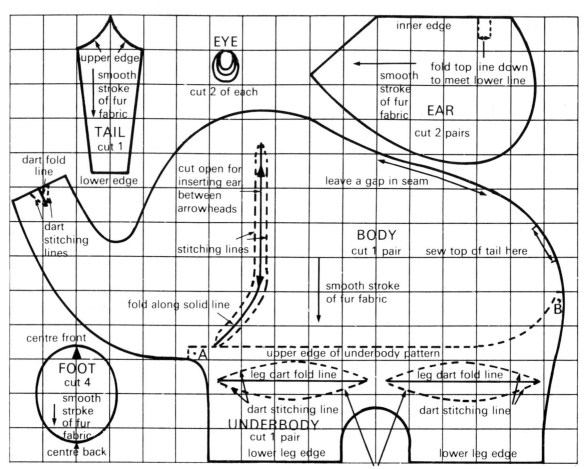

each square = 5 cm

mark darts on underbody pieces only

Make twelve tassels as follows. Wind yarn ten times round four fingers. Slip wound yarn off fingers and cut once through the strands. Knot a short length of yarn round centre of strands, then fold at centre and tie another strand of yarn round, about 1·5 cm ($\frac{5}{8}$ in) from top fold. Sew ends of first and second strands down into the tassel. After making all the tassels, slip them on to a thin knitting needle, pushing it through the tops, and steam them over a pan of boiling water to straighten the strands. Trim ends of all tassels to even lengths. Sew six tassels to each short end of saddlecloth, spacing them evenly. Put cloth over elephant's back with ric-rac trimmed borders uppermost, and sew each corner of the cloth to the elephant's body, to hold it securely in place.

The head-dress

Cut two 15 cm (6 in) squares of plain fabric and one 9 cm ($3\frac{1}{2}$ in) square of patterned fabric. Turn in and tack raw edges of patterned square then sew it to centre of one plain square. Join plain squares round edges, right sides facing, leaving a gap for turning. Trim corners then turn right side out and slipstitch gap. Stitch ric-rac round plain border.

Make sixteen tassels in same way as for saddlecloth. Sew one to each corner and three, evenly spaced, along each side. Place head-dress on elephant's head as shown in illustration (page 175) and sew corners to head.

7
PLAY HOUSES AND PUPPET BOOTH

Wendy House

Like every good Wendy house, this design has a smart front door, windows to look out of, and plenty of space inside (about 145 cm (57 in) long, 104 cm (41 in) wide, 135 cm (53 in) tall – to the pitch of the roof). Unlike most Wendy houses, though, this one is made from fabric – and it is constructed like a tent, with pitched roof, end poles and guy ropes.

You will need: For the walls – 4 m (4⅜ yd) of non-woven curtain fabric 172 cm (68 in) wide; for the roof – 1·6 m (1¾ yd) of similar fabric in a contrasting colour; for decorating walls, windows and doors – oddments of non-fray fabrics and felt; net fabric for window glass; fringed braid; narrow white tape; for tent poles – two 152 cm (5 ft) long broom handles, or similar lengths of 2·5 cm (1 in) diameter wooden dowelling; 1 m (1⅛ yd) of strong tape or bootlace for the guy rope loops and tent peg loops; 13 m (14¼ yd) of strong cord or string for guy ropes; twelve tent pegs; black and brown permanent marker pens; adhesive.

Notes: If possible, it is best to use non-fray fabrics (such as non-woven curtain fabric and felt) for all appliqué pieces on the walls. If you are using woven fabrics, allow 1 cm (⅜ in) extra on all raw edges for turnings.

Use dabs of adhesive to hold appliqué pieces in place before sewing them. (Small pieces such as the felt flowers need not be sewn in place if they are stuck down firmly.)

When making up the house take 3 cm (1¼ in) seams on all pieces. Other seams and turnings are stated in the instructions.

The roof

From roof fabric cut two pieces 78 by 150 cm (30¾ by 59 in). Mark a 3 cm (1¼ in) seam allowance along both short edges of each piece. Cut a piece of card to the size and shape shown in diagram 1 (*above right*). Place this card template on one piece of roof fabric, within the seam allowance as shown in diagram 1. Using black marker pen, draw dotted line round V-shape at lower end of

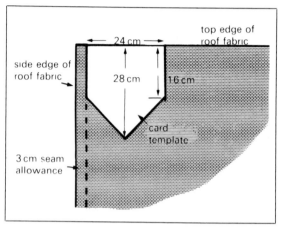

Diagram 1   Marking the pattern on the roof fabric

template. Continue like this, moving template along the roof and drawing round lower edge. Next draw a shallow curved shape (using the edge of a dinner plate) between V-shapes, as shown on the roof illustrated on pages 178–9. Repeat this pattern on the other roof piece. Draw shading below all lines, using a brown marker pen.

The walls

Using the cutting layout shown in diagram 2 (*opposite, top*), cut out the fabric walls to the sizes in diagrams 3 and 4 (*opposite, centre and below*).

To make the front wall (with door and window): Mark on, then cut out, door and window openings to size given in diagram 3. For window and door frames cut 10 cm (4 in) wide strips of fabric to fit sides and lower edges of window, and sides and top of door. Stitch them in place, with inner raw edges level. Turn in all inner raw edges of window

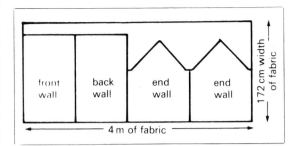

Diagram 2   Cutting layout for the walls

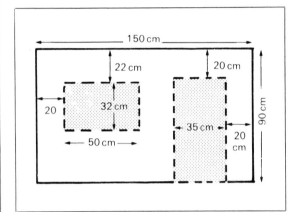

Diagram 3   Front wall, with door and window openings. Cut out back wall the same size, placing window as stated in instructions

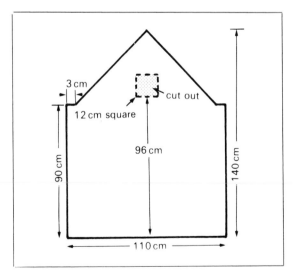

Diagram 4   How to cut out each end wall, with attic window

and door openings 2 cm ($\frac{3}{4}$ in) and press, clipping fabric at corners. Stitch down raw edges.

For mullion window, cut a piece of fabric 40 by 58 cm (15$\frac{3}{4}$ by 23 in). Draw a line all round, 2 cm ($\frac{3}{4}$ in) from raw edges. Mark this

rectangle into six equal 18 cm (7 in) squares. In each square draw round a saucer (about 14 cm (5$\frac{1}{2}$ in) in diameter), centrally placed. Cut out circles. Place window over a piece of net fabric 40 by 58 cm (15$\frac{3}{4}$ by 23 in), to represent glass. Sew pieces together around edges, and around edges of circles. To divide the window into panes, sew on strips of white tape between circles. Now sew window in place behind window opening.

For the striped awning above window, cut a strip of fabric 20 by 75 cm (8 by 29$\frac{1}{2}$ in). Sew this centrally above window; sew a strip of fringe to lower edge of awning.

Turn in lower edge of wall 3 cm (1$\frac{1}{4}$ in) and stitch it down. At lower edge of wall under window, sew an irregular strip of green fabric for grass. Cut groups of coloured felt flowers as shown in illustration on pages 178–9 and glue them in place. Sew centre of each flower to the wall.

For the door cut a piece of fabric 58 by 76 cm (23 by 30 in). Turn in all raw edges 2 cm ($\frac{3}{4}$ in) and stitch them down. For letterbox cut a 12 cm (4$\frac{3}{4}$ in) long slit across centre of door, about 28 cm (11 in) up from lower edge. Turn in raw edges of slit 1 cm ($\frac{3}{8}$ in) and stitch, clipping fabric at corners.

For letterbox flap, cut two pieces of fabric 8 by 20 cm (3 by 8 in). Join them round edges, taking a 1 cm ($\frac{3}{8}$ in) seam and leaving a gap for turning. Trim seam, turn right side out and slipstitch gap. Stitch round close to edges then mark on lines with black pen, 1 cm ($\frac{3}{8}$ in) from edges. Sew top of letterbox flap above slit in door. Use black pen to mark door panels on door, making the upper panel about 28 cm (11 in) square and lower panel 28 by 18 cm (11 by 7 in).

For doorknob, cut two 9 cm (3$\frac{1}{2}$ in) diameter fabric circles. Join them round edge, taking a 1 cm ($\frac{3}{8}$ in) seam. Trim seam. Cut a small slit in centre of one piece, turn circle right side out through slit then stuff. Oversew slit and sew knob beside letterbox. Sew top of door in place at back of door frame, with lower edge of door 2 cm ($\frac{3}{4}$ in) above lower edge of wall.

For curtains cut two pieces of fabric 45 by 50 cm (17$\frac{3}{4}$ by 19$\frac{1}{2}$ in). Narrowly hem all edges of each piece, except for one short edge. Take 1·5 cm ($\frac{5}{8}$ in) turning twice on this edge. Thread a 70 cm ($27\frac{1}{2}$ in) length of tape through these curtain edges and sew tape ends to inside wall above window, keeping it taut. Sew centre of tape to wall.

To make the back wall: Make a window, awning and curtains at centre of back wall, exactly as for window on front wall. Hem lower edge of wall and sew on grassy strip in same way. Sew a green fabric shrub shape to wall each side of window, as shown in illustration on pages 178–9, then glue on flowers as for front wall.

To make the end walls: Cut a small attic window in each wall (see diagram 4). Sew on 8 cm (3 in) wide strips of fabric for window frames and neaten inner edges as for other windows.

For window glass cut a 20 cm (8 in) square of net fabric. Sew white tape across centre to form four small panes. Sew net square to back of window frame. Turn in lower edges of side walls 3 cm ($1\frac{1}{4}$ in) and stitch down, then sew on grassy strips as before.

End wall with birdbox: For the upright post on birdbox cut a strip of fabric 6 by 40 cm ($2\frac{1}{2}$ by $15\frac{3}{4}$ in). For sloping support pieces, cut two strips 4 by 20 cm ($1\frac{1}{2}$ by 8 in). For flat table top cut a strip 5 by 32 cm (2 by $12\frac{1}{2}$ in), and slope the sides slightly.

Place them all in position on walls as shown in illustration on pages 178–9, with upright post about 30 cm ($11\frac{3}{4}$ in) away from right-hand edge of wall. Sew all pieces in place.

For birdbox cut a 25 cm ($9\frac{3}{4}$ in) square of fabric. Using illustration as a guide, shape one edge into a pitched roof, and below this taper sides in towards lower edge. Sew paler fabric to front of box and mark on lines, then add a small black felt circle for nesting hole. Sew birdbox on top of bird table.

For climbing nasturtiums, cut leaves of various sizes in different shades of green felt. Mark lines on each leaf with brown pen. Arrange leaves on wall, with the largest leaves at lower edge, and smaller leaves climbing up the wall. Glue leaves in place. Cut red and orange felt flowers and glue them in place.

Cut simple bird shapes in blue and brown felt. Mark on eyes, cut small triangles of black felt for beaks then sew birds to wall.

End wall with hanging sign: For the tub cut a piece of fabric 16 by 24 cm ($6\frac{1}{4}$ by $9\frac{1}{2}$ in). Curve the two short edges to make a tub shape. Stitch on three 3 cm ($1\frac{1}{4}$ in) wide felt strips for the iron bands. Cut a 3 cm ($1\frac{1}{4}$ in) wide strip for trunk of shrub, and green fabric for foliage, as for shrubs on back wall of house. Sew them all to wall, with right-hand edge of tub about 10 cm (4 in) from right-hand edge of wall. Add nasturtiums on grassy strip to left of tub, as for the other end wall.

For house sign, cut a piece of dark fabric 30 by 40 cm ($11\frac{3}{4}$ by $15\frac{3}{4}$ in). Cut edges to curved shapes. Mark on the lettering of your choice with chalk, then embroider it with yarn.

For the sign bracket cut braid strips – one 52 cm ($20\frac{1}{2}$ in) and two 8 cm (3 in) long. Place sign about 20 cm (8 in) from left-hand edge of wall and about 8 cm (3 in) down from edge of window frame. Sew sign in place then sew bracket pieces above the sign.

Joining the pieces

Join roof pieces along top edges, leaving a 4·5 cm ($1\frac{3}{4}$ in) gap at each side of seam, 3 cm ($1\frac{1}{4}$ in) in from each end. (These gaps are for top ends of poles to pass through.) To reinforce the gaps, press seam open then glue small patches of fabric over wrong side of gaps. Turn roof to right side and stitch all round a few times close to edges of gaps. Cut slits in fabric patches to match the gaps.

For guy rope loops cut four 10 cm (4 in) lengths of strong tape or bootlace. Fold each in half to form a loop. Join lower edges of roof pieces to tops of front and back walls, enclosing a guy rope loop in each seam, 3 cm ($1\frac{1}{4}$ in) in from each end. Cut six more 10 cm (4 in) lengths of tape and fold them into loops. Join side edges of end walls to front and back walls, enclosing a loop of tape at hem edge of each seam. Sew a tape loop to each lower corner of doorway.

Join apex portion of end walls to sides of roof pieces, snipping roof seam. Snip off top corners of apex on end walls.

Sharpen 2·5 cm (1 in) at one end of each pole, for driving into the ground. Mark a line round each pole, 10 cm (4 in) from these sharpened ends. Drill a 5 mm ($\frac{1}{4}$ in) diameter hole through each pole, 2·5 cm (1 in) from other end of pole. To support the roof, knot a length of strong cord round and through holes in poles, making the total cord length 144 cm (56$\frac{1}{2}$ in) including thickness of poles.

Now place poles inside house, pushing tops through gaps in roof seam. Using very strong thread, sew roof fabric to poles at these points, working oversewing stitches at each side of gap and taking thread through holes in poles.

For guy ropes at each corner of roof, knot one end of a 170 cm (67 in) cord length through each guy rope loop at roof corner, then knot a loop at other end of cord.

For the guy rope on each pole cut a 210 cm (82$\frac{1}{2}$ in) cord length. Knot one end to fit over the top of the pole; make a loop at other end.

Make a groundsheet from waterproof fabric, to fit the base of the playhouse exactly. Sew a loop of tape to each corner.

To erect the playhouse

The ground should be as level as possible to ensure that the playhouse goes up without creases. Spread the ground sheet out and insert a tent peg at each corner. Now at the centre of each short edge of the ground sheet cut out a 2·5 cm (1 in) radius semi-circle. Push the sharpened ends of the poles into the ground at the centre of these semi-circles and drive the poles in up to the marked lines. Peg out each corner loop of the house and the doorway loops. Peg out the guy ropes coming from the roof corners and then the guy ropes on the poles. Adjust the guy ropes as necessary to achieve a smooth finish.

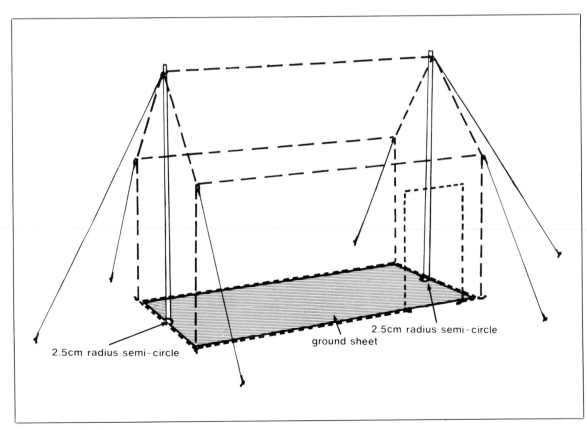

2.5cm radius semi-circle

ground sheet

2.5cm radius semi-circle

Erecting the playhouse

Punch and Judy Booth

A great favourite with children for generations past, Punch and Judy still pull the crowds at the seaside, at fairs and fetes throughout the year.
This Punch and Judy booth is designed for children to operate. It stands about 165 cm (5 ft 5 in) high, 84 cm (2 ft 9 in) wide, and 61 cm (2 ft) deep. It is fairly easy to make from fabric, and slotted into the corners are wooden poles, pared down at one end so they can be driven into the ground. The flag-decked guy ropes can be pegged out taut to keep the booth upright.
Six glove puppets complete the show.

The booth

You will need: Four 180 cm (6 ft) lengths of 2·5 cm (1 in) diameter wooden dowelling, for the corner posts; 3·4 m (3¾ yd) of 138 cm (54 in) wide striped ticking or other fabric, for the booth; 40 cm (½ yd) of 91 cm (36 in) wide fabric for decorating sides and top of stage; 70 cm (¾ yd) of 91 cm (36 in) wide fabric for the frill at lower edge of stage; 2·3 m (2½ yd) of 91 cm (36 in) wide plain fabric for top and back flap of booth; 1·6 m (1¾ yd) of fringe; 3 m (3¼ yd) of giant ric-rac braid; 9 m (9⅞ yd) of strong string or cord for the guy ropes; oddments of fabrics for the flags; four tent pegs; 20 cm (¼ yd) of Velcro touch and close fastener.

Making the booth

For the front cut a piece of fabric 170 cm long by 88 cm wide (67 by 34½ in). Cut the remaining 170 cm (67 in) length of fabric in half down its length for the side pieces of the booth. Hem top and bottom edges of all pieces, taking 2·5 cm (1 in) turnings twice.

Turn in 5·5 cm (2¼ in) on each long edge of front piece and press. *Note:* These creases mark the eventual seam lines when the booth pieces are assembled. All decorative pieces round the stage should be sewn on within these lines.

To make the stage opening on the booth front, pencil mark the outline (see solid line on diagram 1 (*right*)); draw another rectangle 5 cm (2 in) inside the first one then cut this

out. Snip to the corners of large rectangle then turn fabric to *right* side of booth and press along marked lines. Turn in raw edges 2·5 cm (1 in) and stitch down all round rectangle.

For the sides of stage cut two fabric strips 19 by 38 cm (7½ by 15 in). Turn in long edges 2 cm (¾ in) and tack. Sew these pieces in position (*see diagram 1, below*), keeping them within the crease lines and overlapping the stage opening about 5 mm (¼ in).

For the top of stage cut a fabric strip 18 by 79 cm (7 by 31 in). Trim one long edge to a curved shape (*see diagram 2, opposite top left*). Now cut another piece in the same way

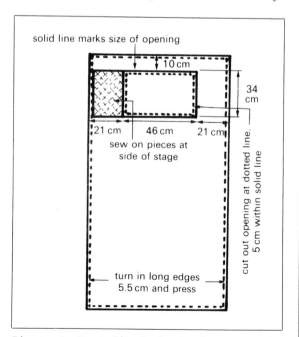

Diagram 1   Front of booth, showing the stage opening

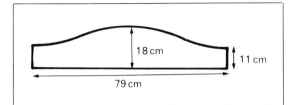

Diagram 2   Shaping for the pelmet at top of stage opening

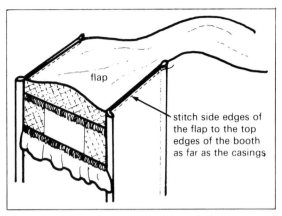

Diagram 3   Showing the fabric flap which covers top and back of booth

for lining (using ticking left over from the booth front). Join top pieces round edges, taking 1 cm ($\frac{3}{8}$ in) seam and leaving the long straight edges open. Trim seams, turn right side out and press. Sew on ric-rac trimming as shown in illustration on page 186.

Pin the top piece in place on booth front, with raw edges level with top edge of stage. Sew in place, taking stitching all round edges of top piece including the top curve. Slipstitch back of curved piece to top edge of booth front. Sew on fringe to cover lower raw edges.

For the frill cut fabric into two 35 by 91 cm (13$\frac{3}{4}$ by 36 in) strips. Join them at one short edge. Take narrow hems on side edges and a 2·5 cm (1 in) turning twice on one long edge. Sew ric-rac to this edge. Gather remaining raw edge to fit across the booth below the stage; sew in place. Sew on fringe to cover gathered raw edge.

Assembling the booth

With right sides facing, join each side of booth front to one long edge of each side piece, taking 1 cm ($\frac{3}{8}$ in) seam. Turn seams to bring wrong sides together and stitch again, 4·5 cm (1$\frac{3}{4}$ in) away from first seam line. This forms casings for the wooden poles at the two front corners (*diagram 3, above right*).

Turn in remaining long edges on the booth side pieces 1 cm, then 4·5 cm ($\frac{3}{8}$ then 1$\frac{3}{4}$ in). Stitch in place to form casings for the two remaining poles (see diagram 3).

For the flap which goes over the top and back of the booth, cut a 224 cm (88$\frac{1}{4}$ in) length of plain fabric, 84 cm (33 in) wide. Make 1 cm ($\frac{3}{8}$ in) turnings twice on all edges. Slipstitch one short edge to the top front edge of booth behind the stage pelmet. Machine the sides of strip to the top edges of

the booth sides as far as the casings for poles (see diagram 3). This forms the roof of the booth and the rest of the fabric hangs down the back as a loose flap.

Round off one end of each wooden pole for the top ends and pare the other ends to blunt points for driving into the ground. Bore a 5 mm ($\frac{1}{4}$ in) diameter hole through each pole, 5 cm (2 in) down from the top. Slip a pole into each casing, with the holes just showing above fabric. Using strong thread, sew fabric to poles through holes.

For each guy rope cut a 2 m (2$\frac{1}{4}$ yd) cord length. Tie one end through hole in pole, loop other end to take tent peg. For flags cut small fabric triangles. Narrowly hem edges then sew flags to cords.

Setting up the booth

Keep all corners square and the fabric taut when driving the poles into the ground. Drive in each pole a bit at a time until the fabric touches the ground, then peg out the guy ropes. Now tie another piece of cord across the back through the holes in tops of poles to provide a support for the back flap. To hold the flap in place, sew Velcro strips at intervals to the flap and booth.

The puppets

You will need: Pink felt for hands and heads of Punch, Judy and policeman,

crocodile's mouth and baby; white felt for
Joey's head and hands; green felt for
crocodile; pieces of felt or fabric for bodies;
scraps of felt, fur fabric, knitting yarn,
trimmings, ric-rac braid; iron-on Vilene,
ribbon and pieces of nylon stocking or

tights; 1 m (1⅛ yd) of fringe for Joey's hair;
four bobbles or beads for Punch; a 12 cm
(4¾ in) length of 1 cm (⅜ in) diameter
dowelling for Punch's stick; two beads for
crocodile eyes; four small and one larger
silvery button for policeman; thin card for

neck and hand tubes; black marker pen; red pencil for colouring faces; stuffing; adhesive; metric graph paper; tracing paper.

Notes: Using the diagram on page 190, draw out all pattern pieces square by square on to metric graph paper, following directions given on diagram. Join all pieces with right sides facing, taking 5 mm ($\frac{1}{4}$ in) seams unless otherwise stated. For an adult puppeteer, the body patterns may need to be enlarged.

Punch

For the head: Cut front and back head pieces from pink felt. Join front pieces at face edges and back pieces at centre back edges, trim seams. Join front and back round sides leaving neck edges open and a gap in the seam at the top of the head. Trim seams and turn head right side out. Cut a 7 by 20 cm ($2\frac{3}{4}$ by 8 in) strip of thin card for the neck tube, roll it up along the length to make a tube to fit the index finger (about 2 cm ($\frac{3}{4}$ in) in diameter for an older child, larger for an adult. Secure the end of the card with sticky tape then cover one end of the tube with sticky tape to seal it. Push the sealed end into the head so the neck edge of the head is level with the open end of the tube. Stick the neck edge of felt to the tube, easing felt to fit. Stuff the head firmly through hole in top of head, working evenly round the tube and pushing small pieces of stuffing very firmly into the nose and chin. Ladderstitch opening at top of head.

Colour nose, cheeks and chin with moistened red pencil then work colour into felt by gently rubbing with a wet piece of cloth. Cut out eye pieces and a narrow strip of red felt for mouth. Glue in place.

Cut one pair of hat pieces from red felt then join them leaving lower edges open. Trim seam, turn right side out and stuff the point. Sew hat to head as shown in illustration (*page 186*), pushing in more stuffing to make a firm shape. For hair, cut a 2 by 16 cm ($\frac{3}{4}$ by $6\frac{1}{4}$ in) strip of black fur fabric. Stick it round back of head, level with lower edge of hat. Stick trimming round

lower edge of the hat and then stitch a bobble or bead to point.

Cut ears from two layers of pink felt stuck together. Sew one to each side of the head just inside short edges of fur fabric.

For the body: Cut two body pieces from red felt and join them at side and shoulder edges. Clip into seam allowances at curves and turn right side out. Turn in neck edge 1 cm ($\frac{3}{8}$ in) and push neck edge of head inside it. Slipstitch neck edge of body to head. Cut one pair of hump pieces from red felt and join them leaving the straight edges open. Trim seam, turn, stuff, then sew to centre back of body about 3 cm ($1\frac{1}{4}$ in) down from neck edge.

For the hands: Cut two pairs of hand pieces and join them round the edges leaving wrist edges open. Trim seams and turn right side out. For hand tubes, cut two 3 by 12 cm ($1\frac{1}{4}$ by $4\frac{3}{4}$ in) strips of thin card. Roll up to fit inside hands then secure card and seal ends of tubes as for neck tube. Stuff ends of hands and thumbs then slip sealed ends of tubes inside hands, stick wrist edges to other ends of tubes.

Push hands 1 cm ($\frac{3}{8}$ in) inside wrist edges of body so thumbs are pointing upwards, sew in place. Stick trimming round wrists to match hat.

Cut a 36 cm ($14\frac{1}{4}$ in) length of 4 cm ($1\frac{1}{2}$ in) wide ribbon and gather along one edge. Join the short ends, pull up gathers then sew round neck for ruff. Sew bobbles or beads down front of body. Round off one end of dowel for Punch's stick.

Judy

Make head as for Punch except for hair and ears. For hair, sew the centre of a small hank of black yarn measuring 18 cm (7 in) across, to centre of forehead. Sew looped ends to head at each side.

For mob cap: Cut two 24 cm ($9\frac{1}{2}$ in) diameter circles of fabric. Join them round edges, leaving a gap for turning. Trim seam, turn right side out then slipstitch gap. Gather round cap 2·5 cm (1 in) from edge, pull up gathers to fit on head then fasten off. Stuff cap lightly then sew to head. Sew ribbon bow to top.

Make body and hands as for Punch but if using woven fabric, add 5 mm ($\frac{1}{4}$ in) to wrist edges and 1 cm ($\frac{3}{8}$ in) to lower edges for hems. Make hems before sewing to hands. Stick trimmings round wrists. For shawl, cut a 17 cm ($6\frac{3}{4}$ in) square of fabric and fray out the edges, fold diagonally and place round neck. Stitch to secure at centre front and back of body.

Policeman

Make head in the same way as for Punch but using the policeman's front head pattern. For nose, cut out a 2·5 cm (1 in) circle of pink felt, gather round the edge then stuff the circle firmly as you draw up the gathers. Sew nose in place about 6 cm ($2\frac{3}{8}$ in) up from neck. Cut moustache from brown felt and stick under nose. Cut a 3 by 16 cm ($1\frac{1}{4}$ by $6\frac{1}{4}$ in) strip of felt for hair and stick in place. Make ears as for Punch and sew in place. Cut eye pieces from felt and glue in place.

For chin strap on helmet, stick a strip of narrow ribbon under chin, up sides of face to top of hair as illustrated on page 6. Cut two helmet pieces from blue felt then join them leaving lower edges open. Trim seam, turn right side out then stuff top and place on head. Sew to head at top of hair line at position indicated by dotted line on the pattern, adding more stuffing if necessary. Stick narrow ribbon round sewing line. Sew large button to front of helmet.

Make body and hands as for Punch using blue felt for body. Stick a 1 cm ($\frac{3}{8}$ in) wide strip of blue felt around neck, then sew on buttons down front of body.

Joey the clown

Make head in the same way as for the policeman using white felt. Make the hands from white felt. Make nose as for the policeman but use a 3 cm ($1\frac{1}{4}$ in) diameter circle of red felt. Sew in place. Cut out eye and mouth pieces from felt and glue in place. For hair, sew strips of fringe to head from side to side placing the first strip level with nose. Sew fringe to top of head working outwards in a spiral.

Make body as for Punch if using felt or as for Judy if using fabric. Sew ribbon bow to neck at front.

For sausages: Cut a 4 by 22 cm ($1\frac{5}{8}$ by $8\frac{5}{8}$ in) strip of double thickness nylon stocking or tights fabric. Fold the strip down its length and join long edges. Gather up one end tightly then turn right side out. Stuff about 5 cm (2 in) of the casing for each sausage, tying thread round before stuffing the next one.

The baby

Cut two baby pieces from pink felt. Join them leaving a gap at the lower edge. Trim seam and turn right side out. Stuff, then ladderstitch the gap. Tie a strand of thread round neck then colour cheeks with moistened red pencil and work facial features with small stitches. Stick a bit of trimming to chest below neck. Cut a 20 cm (8 in) square of fabric for shawl and fray out the edges. Fold diagonally and wrap round baby. Make small stitches here and there to hold shawl in place.

Crocodile

Cut two crocodile body pieces from green felt. Trim a little off one piece at mouth end as shown by curved broken line on pattern, for lower jaw. Join pieces along sides from points A to B. Cut one gusset piece from pink felt using head portion of body pattern and placing the fold in the felt to the dotted line shown on the pattern. Trim off one end of gusset at broken line to correspond with lower jaw. Stick white ric-rac braid round edge of gusset so one wavy edge is level with the edge of the felt. Now stick or iron on a piece of Vilene interfacing to other side of gusset piece for reinforcing. Sew gusset in place at open end of body so ric-rac trimmed side of gusset is against the body pieces. Trim seam and turn crocodile right side out. Cut a piece of thin card in the same way as the gusset piece then trim 1 cm ($\frac{3}{8}$ in) off the outer edge all round. Place folded cardboard

piece inside mouth then open up mouth and sew the card to felt at the fold with a few stitches. Sew on beads for eyes and glue on tiny ovals of felt for nostrils as shown on the illustration on page 6.

Cut two pairs of leg pieces from green felt. Join them in pairs leaving a gap at the top edge. Trim seams, turn and stuff, then ladderstitch gaps. Sew a leg to each side of the body where indicated on pattern (*below*).

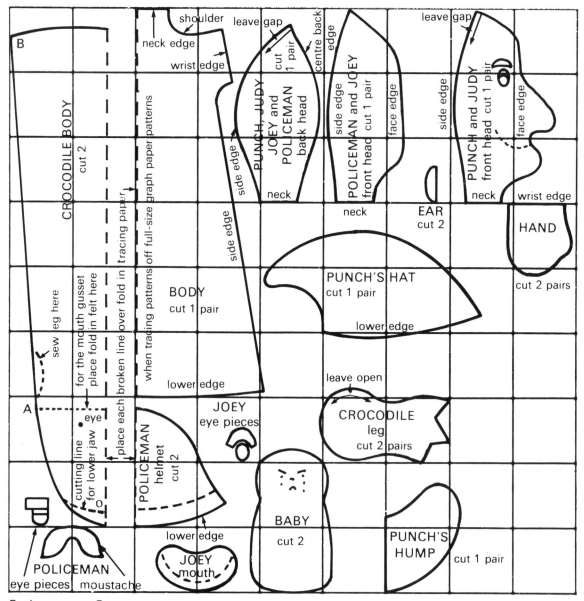

Each square = 5 cm

Wigwam

The wigwam measures roughly 1·68 m (5 ft 6 in) high at the peak – and there is plenty of room inside for two or more small braves. It stands on six bamboo canes, and there are fabric loops sewn at the base of the canes to take tent pegs or skewers.

You will need: 3·1 m ($3\frac{3}{8}$ yd) of calico sheeting 182 cm (72 in) wide (or old sheets); six 182 cm (6 ft) long bamboo garden canes; pieces of fabric (or fabric paints) for decorating the wigwam; 3·2 m ($3\frac{1}{2}$ yd) of tape about 1·5 cm ($\frac{5}{8}$ in) wide (or strips of fabric with raw edges turned in).

Notes: If fabric shapes are to be sewn on, use a little glue spread round the edges to stick them in place before sewing.

Add 1 cm ($\frac{3}{8}$ in) on all raw edges of fabric shapes for turnings, except for the edges which will be taken into the main wigwam seams.

The wigwam

To make: On large sheets of brown paper, or newspaper sheets joined together, draw out the pattern outline to the measurements given in diagram 1 (*opposite*). Then cut out the calico pieces (*see diagram 2, right*), cutting five complete triangles and two half triangles and adding 3 cm ($1\frac{1}{4}$ in) to the straight edges of these as shown (these are for the doorway section of the wigwam). Join the half triangular pieces, taking a 3 cm ($1\frac{1}{4}$ in) seam and leaving 69 cm (27 in) open at the lower edge of the seam for the doorway.

Decorate each section either with fabric pieces or paints, as shown in diagram 1. Turn in and stitch the raw edges of the doorway to neaten.

Sew three 30 cm ($11\frac{3}{4}$ in) lengths of tape or fabric to each of the doorway edges at even intervals, for the ties. Turn in the upper edge of each triangular section 1 cm ($\frac{3}{8}$ in) and stitch. Hem the lower edge of each section, taking 1 cm ($\frac{3}{8}$ in) turnings twice.

To assemble: Join two of the triangles at one side, with the right side of the fabric outside and taking a 5 mm ($\frac{1}{4}$ in) seam. Turn wrong side out and stitch again, taking a 2·5 cm (1 in) seam (this forms a casing for the bamboo cane). Stitch securely across the top edge of the seam to close it. Join all the side edges of the triangles in this way to form the complete wigwam.

The finishing touches: For tying the doorflaps back, sew a 30 cm ($11\frac{3}{4}$ in) length of tape or fabric to the edge of each seam inside, on either side of the doorway section, about 52 cm ($20\frac{1}{2}$ in) up from the lower edge.

For the loops at the lower edge (to take tent pegs) cut six 12 cm ($4\frac{3}{4}$ in) lengths of tape or fabric. Sew these to the lower edge of the wigwam, placing one beside each seam (*see diagram 3, bottom*). Now slip a bamboo cane inside each seam and oversew across the lower edges of all seams to hold the canes in place.

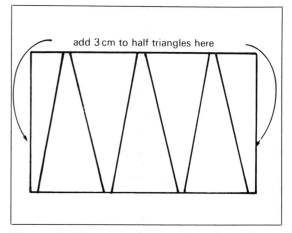

Diagram 2 Cutting out the main pieces from calico

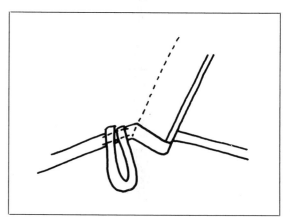

Diagram 3 Sewing the loops to the lower edge

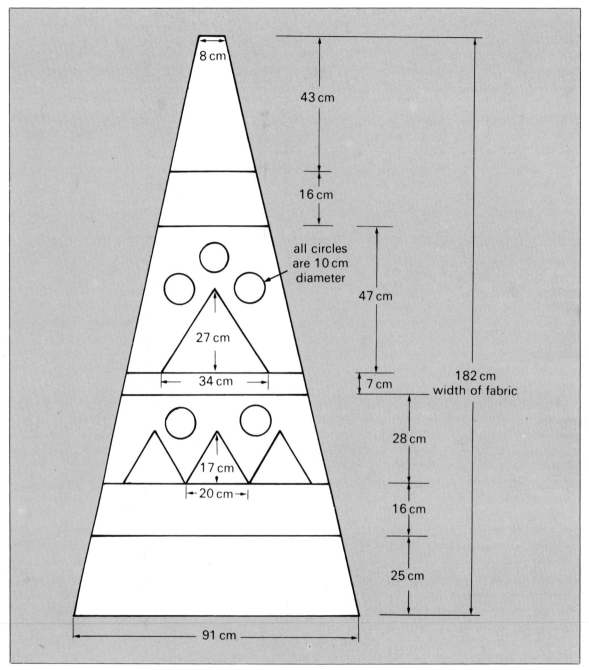

Diagram 1 Pattern pieces for the wigwam

8
TOY
HOUSES

Dormouse House

The dormouse (from the French word dormir – to sleep) *can sleep happily through the winter – either underground or in its own snug nest built into a hollow tree, and this family of toy dormice are like their real-life cousins. They are small and furry about 7·5 cm (3 in) high, with bushy tails slightly shorter than their bodies, and they sit up on their hind legs, using their forepaws to hold their food. Their tree house is a touch more fanciful than the usual variety – with two rooms luxuriously furnished down to the last detail. It measures about 33 cm (13 in) across, 18 cm (7 in) high, and it is made in two separate halves hinged together along one wall, with a zip fastener across the roof and down the opposite wall. You can make the complete toy as a soft, squashy dolls' 'house-for-animals' or copy some of the ideas for furnishing an existing dolls' house.*

For the house and furnishings you will need: 1·20 m (1⅜ yd) of heavy sew-in Vilene interfacing, 83 cm (32½ in) wide; 80 cm ⅞ yd) of polyester wadding, 91 cm (36 in) wide; for doorbell – a bell (the kind used for birdcage toys, available from pet shops); oddments of fabrics, felt, green fur fabric, double knitting yarn, stuffing, trimmings, braids, lace edging, bias binding, shoe lace and boot lace; a 50 cm zip fastener; dark and light brown permanent marker pens; a pair of tweezers for turning and stuffing very small pieces.

For the dormice you will need: Oddments of fawn fleecy fabric, matching felt, fabrics, trimmings, stuffing; for eyes – six circles of black felt if the toys are for a very young child (or six 3 mm ($\frac{1}{8}$ in) diameter black beads for toys for an older child); brown marker pen; transparent nylon sewing thread for whiskers.

General notes

Suitable fabrics and sewing methods: For the outer house walls (tree bark) use brown tweedy furnishing fabric or coatweight fabric. For the house roof (the cut section of the tree) use smooth fawn fabric. Seams, hems and turnings are 5 mm ($\frac{1}{4}$ in) except where stated otherwise.

Patterns for dormice, easy chair and hearth are given full size on page 202. Trace these off the page on to thin paper. Baby dormouse

patterns are given in broken lines, within the dormouse outlines.

Join fabric pieces with right sides facing unless stated otherwise. When sewing items to inside walls of the house, turn the rooms inside out to do this easily.

The stitch-around method: When this is mentioned in instructions, make the item as follows: pin the paper pattern on to layers of fabric stipulated, then stitch around close to the edge of the pattern, leaving a gap for turning. Remove pattern and cut out the item 3 mm ($\frac{1}{8}$ in) from stitching line. Turn right side out and slipstitch gap or proceed as given in the instructions.

The living room

Floor: Make a paper pattern as follows: draw a 36 cm (14$\frac{1}{4}$ in) diameter semi-circle then add 3 cm (1$\frac{1}{4}$ in) to straight edge. Use the pattern to cut two from interfacing, one from wadding and one from fabric suitable for the interior floor of the room.

Place interfacing pieces together, wadding on top and floor fabric right side up on top of wadding. Tack, then sew pieces together round edges. Work stitching lines round the floor to quilt it, parallel to the curved edge, about 2 cm ($\frac{3}{4}$ in) apart. After quilting, the straight edge will have curved inwards slightly. Trim this edge to straighten it. Bind the straight edge with a 4 cm (1½ in) wide straight strip of fabric to match the floor. Press floor.

Walls: Cut a paper pattern measuring 18 by 64 cm (7 by 25¼ in). Cut one pattern shape from bark fabric, one from interfacing and one from wadding. Tack them together round edges, sandwiching wadding between the other two pieces. Turn in bark fabric 2 cm (¾ in) at short edges and stitch this to interfacing. Use pattern to cut a fabric strip for interior walls. Place this on top of interfacing, turn in short edges of fabric strip 3 cm (1¼ in) so that they lie 1 cm (⅜ in) inside the turned-in edges of bark fabric, then sew in place. Tack remaining long edges of strip to interfacing. Now stitch through all thicknesses at long edges, then work vertical lines of stitching up the wall, about 3 cm (1¼ in) apart.

Using the diagram as a guide, cut out door and window openings to sizes given. Bind these edges to neaten them and form door and window frames. Cut two 8 cm (3¼ in) lengths of bias binding for window struts. Fold each in half along length and stitch, then sew turned-in ends of strips to inside of window frame to form four panes.

Sew braid round the outside of the window and the door frames on the outside of the house.

Roof: Cut pieces and stitch as for floor, making the upper piece of fabric the appropriate colour for a cut-section of tree. After trimming straight edge to straighten it, turn it in 1 cm (⅜ in) and slipstitch it in place.

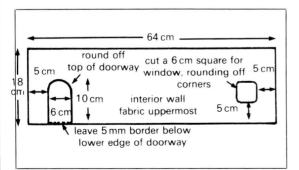

Diagram 1 Showing how to cut window and door openings in the wall

Press roof. Mark a few dark brown lines radiating from centre of roof, then use lighter brown to shade the stitching lines as shown in the illustration on pages 194–5.

Make a skylight window in roof, in same way as for wall window.

To assemble the pieces: Pin, then stitch one long edge of wall around the curved edge of the floor, with interior wall fabric against the floor fabric and raw edges level.

Cut a 6 by 64 cm (2½ by 25¼ in) strip of green fur fabric for grass. Oversew one long edge of the strip to seamline under floor on outside of house, with right side of fur fabric outside.

Cut the remaining long raw edge of fur fabric irregularly, then turn it up loosely on to the wall so that a little fur fabric lies along the ground. Sew the irregular edge to the wall.

Turn room inside out and pin upper edge of wall to curved edge of roof, with outer roof fabric against the tree bark fabric. Sew in place, taking a 1 cm (⅜ in) seam. Turn seam down and oversew raw edges to the inside wall of room. To cover these raw edges, sew the straight edge of lace trim or braid to seamline, then sew fancy edge of the trimming to the wall.

The bedroom: Make exactly as for living room, omitting the door.

To assemble the rooms

Place the rooms side by side, the bedroom on the left, living room on the right, with adjacent walls touching. Oversew these wall edges together securely where they touch, to form a hinge. Open the zip fastener and sew ends of tapes to hinge at top of walls. Pin the zip tapes just inside edges of each room along roof and down the remaining wall edges. Slipstitch edges of roof and walls alongside zip teeth, then oversew remaining outer edges of tapes in place.

Decorating the outside

Doorbell: The bellpull also acts as a tag for holding on to when closing the zip fastener. For a bellpull, cut a 30 cm (12 in) length of shoe lace. Thread this on bell and join lace ends. Make a loop at this end and sew it to top of wall outside the hinge between the rooms.

Window awning: Cut an 11 cm (4¼ in) length of pleated or frilled trimming, neaten ends then sew it above window.

Window box: Cut an 18 cm (7 in) length of 1·5 cm (⅝ in) wide braid. Join ends then sew lower edges together. Sew bits of green fur fabric inside box, then sew guipure flowers to fur fabric. Sew sides of box to wall below window.

Mushrooms: Use white stretchy stockinette, such as cuttings off a T-shirt. For a stalk roll up a 3 by 24 cm (1¼ by 9½ in) strip of fabric tightly and sew the end in place.

For mushroom top, gather a 7 cm (2¾ in) diameter circle of fabric, stuff; then push

stalk inside, turning in the gathered raw edges, pull up gathers and sew them to the stalk.

Make various sizes, using smaller strips and circles. Sew stalks to grass and tops to wall where they touch.

Toadstools: Make stalk as for mushrooms. For top, cut a 6 cm (2¼ in) diameter circle of red spotted fabric, and one of stockinette. On stockinette mark 'gills' with a brown pen, radiating from centre. Join the circles round edges, then cut a small hole in centre of stockinette and turn right side out. Stuff, then push in stalk and sew in place. Sew to house as for mushrooms.

Make smaller toadstools as for mushrooms, using a red spotted circle only for each top.

Leaves: Use pinking shears to cut oval leaf shapes from green and brown felt, about 3 by 5 cm (1¼ by 2 in), varying the sizes slightly. Mark on veins, then fold leaves in half and press. Sew brown leaves to grass, green leaves in groups to the bark.

Ladybird: Gather and stuff a 2·5 cm (1 in) diameter circle of red fabric. Hold the ladybird on a needle while marking the centre stripe, spots and face in black pen.

Snail in shell: Cut an 11 cm (4¼ in) length of white boot lace (the broad kind, used for sports shoes). Turn in and gather one end tightly. Stuff, then turn in remaining edge and sew, but do not gather. Rub the boot lace with brown pen then mark a few thin lines along length with darker pen. Grip gathered end with tweezers and roll snail up tightly, pinning then sewing it in place.

Doormat: Sew a piece of towelling outside the door, turning in raw edges.

Chimney: Cut a 7 by 50 cm (2¼ by 20 in) strip of bark fabric. Hem one long edge. Roll strip up tightly and sew in place. Now use sharp scissors to cut rolled-up raw edge at an angle, to fit against the outside wall of house. Sew a bit of wadding in centre top for smoke. Do not sew chimney in place at this stage.

Living room furnishings

Curtain rail and curtains: For the rail, knot ends of a 16 cm ($6\frac{1}{4}$ in) length of brown cord.

For each curtain, hem edges of a 6 by 11 cm ($2\frac{3}{8}$ by $4\frac{1}{4}$ in) piece of fabric, leaving one raw short edge. Turn in this edge a little, then fold it down 1·5 cm ($\frac{5}{8}$ in) and sew it in place. Stitch again 3 mm ($\frac{1}{8}$ in) from fold, then thread curtain rail through. Sew ends and centre of rail to wall above the window.

Door: Cut two 8·5 by 11·5 cm ($3\frac{3}{8}$ by $4\frac{1}{2}$ in) pieces of felt and two of interfacing. Round off one short edge of each piece, for top of door. Work vertical lines of stitching on pairs of felt and interfacing pieces, about 1 cm ($\frac{3}{8}$ in) apart. Join pieces, taking 3 mm ($\frac{1}{8}$ in) seam, leaving a gap for turning. Turn and slipstitch gap, then press.

Mark a 1·5 cm ($\frac{5}{8}$ in) line for letterbox halfway down door, then stitch round line a little away from it. Cut letterbox open, and trim close to stitching.

For flap, cut two oblong pieces of felt to cover letterbox and sew them together round edges, then sew flap above letterbox.

Now sew side of door to inside of doorway, level with inner edge of bias binding. For doorknobs, gather and stuff two 2·5 cm (1 in) diameter circles of felt and sew them to door.

Easy chairs: Pin chair and seat patterns to two layers of fabric. (Note that the seat pattern is the broken line printed within chair outline.) Make chairs using stitch-around method. Stuff lightly, then slipstitch gaps. Oversew lower edge of chair round sides and back of seat.

Make four legs as for doorknobs, and sew them to corners of seat. Sew a bit of lace trimming over back of chair.

Chimney breast, hearth and fire: Pin hearth pattern to two layers of felt and make hearth using stitch-around method. Turn and slipstitch gap. Press, then sew braid round outer edge for fender.

For log fire, roll up short strips of bark fabric and sew ends in place. Sew logs to hearth, with flames of red and yellow fabric, and wadding for smoke.

For chimney breast, cut two 14 by 17 cm ($5\frac{1}{2}$ by $6\frac{3}{4}$ in) strips of red fabric and one of wadding. Mark bricks on one red fabric piece with black pen.

For fireplace opening cut a 5 cm (2 in) wide by 6 cm ($2\frac{3}{8}$ in) high piece out of centre of one short edge of each piece, rounding off top corners. Join pieces round edges, with wadding under fabrics, tapering long edges slightly towards top and leaving top edges open. Trim side seams, and turn right side out. Sew narrow braid round the fireplace opening.

Now sew lower edges of chimney breast to hearth where shown on hearth pattern. Pin the entire assembly against the living room wall, off-centre (*see page 199*).
Sew side edges in place as pinned, then turn in top edges and sew them to top of wall.

Sew chimney to outside of house, to correspond with position of chimney breast.

Log basket: Join ends of a 12 by 3 cm ($4\frac{3}{4}$ by $1\frac{1}{4}$ in) strip of coarse cotton lace trimming. Sew a 3·5 cm ($1\frac{3}{8}$ in) diameter circle of felt to base. Make logs as for fire.

'Home Sweet Home' sampler: Mark words on a 2·5 by 3 cm (1 by $1\frac{1}{4}$ in) piece of fabric, then sew fancy braid round edge. Sew this to a larger rectangle of felt. Sew sampler to the chimney breast.

Rug: Plait six 2 m ($2\frac{1}{4}$ yd) lengths of knitting yarn to make a 1 m ($1\frac{1}{8}$ yd) length. Coil the plait round edge to edge, sewing it in place as you go. Press.

Toasting fork: Cut a 5 cm (2 in) length of narrow gold gift wrapping braid and knot one end. Sew a 2 cm ($\frac{3}{4}$ in) braid length to the other end, bending it into a curve. Sew fork to chimney breast.

Table: Pin a 7 cm ($2\frac{3}{4}$ in) diameter circle of paper to two layers of fabric (the same as you used for the roof). Stitch all round edge then cut out. Snip a small hole at centre of one piece and turn right side out. Stitch rings round table and colour it as for roof.

For table pedestal, cut a 3 by 40 cm ($1\frac{1}{4}$ by 16 in) strip of bark fabric. Turn in and hem long edges, then roll up the strip tightly and sew end in place. Sew pedestal under table.

Mugs of cocoa, and toast: For each mug roll up a 1 by 7 cm ($\frac{3}{8}$ by $2\frac{3}{4}$ in) strip of felt tightly and sew end in place. Make a thread loop for handle, and buttonhole stitch round the loop. Colour centre of mug brown to look like cocoa.

For plate, cut a 3 cm ($1\frac{1}{4}$ in) diameter circle of felt and sew on a guipure flower for a doyley. For each slice of toast, cut a 1·5 cm ($\frac{5}{8}$ in) square of felt. Colour the edges dark brown, and the surfaces light brown. For melted butter effect, spread the toast with adhesive and leave to dry. Cut toast in triangles.

Shelf and plant: Make the shelf as for table top, using a 6 cm ($2\frac{3}{8}$ in) diameter semi-circle of paper for pattern and leaving a gap in straight edge for turning. Turn right side out. Sew shelf to wall beside fireplace. Use a guipure flower for a lace mat.

For plant pot, cut a 1·5 by 10 cm ($\frac{5}{8}$ by 4 in) strip of felt. Cut a few spiky leaf shapes from green felt and place them at one end of strip. Roll up strip, sew end in place, and also green leaves.

Broom: Fray out one end of an 8 cm (3 in) square of bark fabric. Roll it up tightly and wind sewing thread tightly round and round handle. Bind round top of bristles with contrasting thread.

Bedroom furnishings

Curtains: Make as for living room curtains.

Bed: For base pattern, cut a 12 cm ($4\frac{3}{4}$ in) square of paper rounding off the corners. Pin this to two layers of fabric with one layer of interfacing on top, one layer of wadding underneath. Make bed by stitch-around method. Turn fabric sides out.

Make legs as for doorknobs, using 3 cm ($1\frac{1}{4}$ in) diameter circles of black felt.

For pillow pattern, cut a 4 by 12 cm ($1\frac{1}{2}$ by $4\frac{3}{4}$ in) piece of paper, rounding off corners. Pin this to two layers of fabric, make pillow by stitch-around method and stuff.

Patchwork quilt: Cut twelve 2 cm ($\frac{3}{4}$ in) wide strips of various printed fabrics, 20 cm (8 in) long. Join them at long edges, pressing seams open. Cut this piece across width into eight 2 cm ($\frac{3}{4}$ in) wide strips and join them, reversing alternate strips so that patches are not matched. Cut lining the same size as quilt, join them round edges, leaving gap. Turn and slipstitch gap.

For valance, cut a 3·5 cm ($1\frac{3}{8}$ in) wide strip to go round two short and one long edge of quilt plus 1 cm ($\frac{3}{8}$ in). Hem all except one long edge. Turn in this edge and sew it in place round quilt.

Bed drapes on wall: Hem edges of an 8 by 30 cm (3 by 12 in) strip of fabric. Gather the strip at centre and 5 cm (2 in) from each end. Tie ribbon bows round end gathers. Pin to centre back of wall above bed, then cut a piece of fabric to cover wall within these drapes. Hem edges of this piece and sew it to wall, then sew drapes to wall at gathers.

Bedside shelves: Make these as for the living room shelf.

Candlestick: Roll up and sew a small strip of white felt for candle; sew wick with black thread. Wind and sew a small strip of coloured felt round base of candle.

For candlestick base, stitch round a 2 cm ($\frac{3}{4}$ in) diameter circle of paper pinned to two layers of felt. Cut out and sew base to base of candle.

Family portraits: Use a fine black pen or pencil to trace portraits off page on to thin white fabric. Cut out oval shapes, then sew braid round edges. Sew portraits to wall.

Armchair: Make as for living room chairs. Add patchwork cushion, sewing this as for the bed quilt.

Baby's cot: Make the base as for big bed, using a 5 by 7 cm (2 by $2\frac{3}{4}$ in) paper pattern.

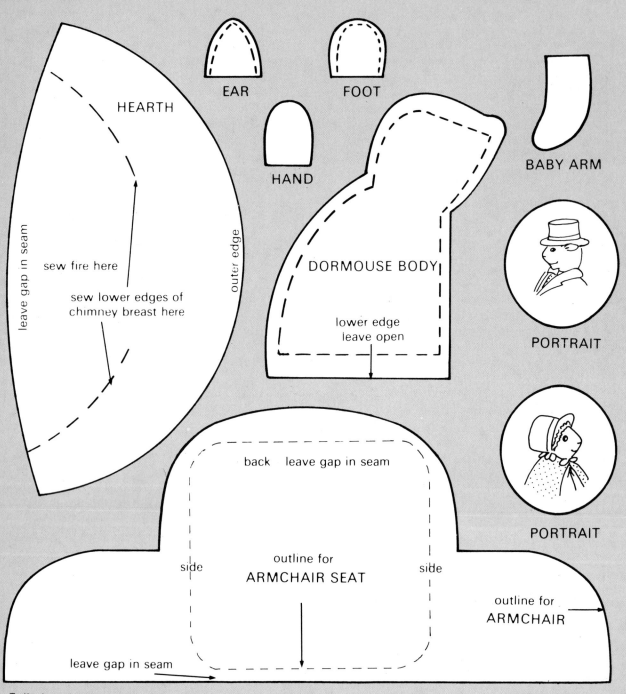

HEARTH

EAR

FOOT

HAND

BABY ARM

leave gap in seam

sew fire here

sew lower edges of
chimney breast here

outer edge

DORMOUSE BODY

lower edge
leave open

PORTRAIT

PORTRAIT

back   leave gap in seam

side

outline for
ARMCHAIR SEAT

side

outline for
ARMCHAIR

leave gap in seam

Full-size patterns

Use a 3 by 5 cm ($1\frac{1}{4}$ by 2 in) pattern for pillow.

For cot sides, use a strip of 4·5 cm ($1\frac{3}{4}$ in) wide coarse cotton lace edging, long enough to go round base plus extra for a seam. Join ends. Sew a 2·5 cm (1 in) wide strip of interfacing round inside of cot to stiffen it, with one long edge, level with base. Cut a slightly wider fabric strip, neaten edges and sew in place to cover the interfacing. Now sew lower edge of cot sides round edge of base. Sew a ribbon bow to one end of the cot.

For valance frill, cut a 4 by 40 cm ($1\frac{1}{2}$ by 16 in) strip of fabric. Join ends and hem long edges, then gather and sew round outside of cot as shown in illustration **on page 199**

For quilt, join two 5 by 6 cm (2 by $2\frac{3}{8}$ in) pieces of fabric. Turn and stuff, then sew a guipure flower to centre.

The dormice

To make mother: Pin body pattern to two layers of fleecy fabric. Trim fabric level with lower edge of pattern. Make mother using stitch-around method. Stuff, then gather lower edge, pulling up tightly and fastening off. Tie thread tightly round neck.

Sew felt circles (or beads) in place for eyes, taking the needle through from one side of head to other, pulling thread tightly to depress eyes into head. Mark nose with pen and work a small stitch for mouth, below nose. For whiskers, use four strands of nylon thread, passing needle through snout. Knot threads each side of snout and trim ends.

Use pattern to cut four ear pieces. Oversew them round edges, leaving straight edges open. Turn, then gather straight edges and sew to head (*see illustration on pages 194–5*).

Cut four foot pieces from fleece and make as for ears. Do not stuff. Sew straight edges under body at front.

For tail, cut a 2·5 by 6 cm (1 by $2\frac{3}{8}$ in) strip of fleece. Oversew long edges together and continue across one short edge, rounding off corner. Turn, then sew open end of tail to back of body.

For dress, join ends of a 5 by 14 cm (2 by $5\frac{1}{2}$ in) strip of fabric. Hem one long edge and sew on trimming. Turn in remaining raw edge and gather tightly round neck, then fasten off. Add ribbon bow to front.

Cut and make hands as for feet, using hand pattern. For each sleeve cut a 4 by 4·5 cm ($1\frac{1}{2}$ by $1\frac{5}{8}$ in) strip of fabric. Turn in long edges and press. Join remaining raw edges with a gathering thread, pull up slightly and fasten off. Turn sleeves right side out, slip hands in ends and sew in place. Stuff sleeves lightly, then gather top edges and sew sleeves to sides of dormouse, level with neck. Catch sleeves to body at elbows.

To make father: Make dormouse body, ears and facial features as for mother. Make feet and tail, but do not sew them in place.

Make shirt as for mother's dress, using a 4 by 12 cm ($1\frac{1}{2}$ by $4\frac{3}{4}$ in) fabric strip. Make sleeves and hands as before and sew in place.

For trousers, cut two 5 by 7 cm (2 by $2\frac{3}{4}$ in) fabric strips. Join short edges then turn in one remaining raw edge and press. Gather other raw edge tightly and fasten off. Put trousers on mouse and sew top edge to shirt. Now sew feet and tail in place.

Sew narrow ribbon round top edge of trousers for belt, then work a buckle in straight stitches, using sewing thread.

To make baby: Make as for mother except for dress, hands and tail, using the smaller patterns. Make tail as for mother, using a 2 by 5 cm ($\frac{3}{4}$ by 2 in) strip of fleece.

For dress, join ends of a 12 cm ($4\frac{3}{4}$ in) length of lace edging, about 3·5 cm ($1\frac{3}{8}$ in) wide. Gather this round neck as for mother. Make arms as for mother's hands, using baby arm pattern. Sew tops of arms to sides of dress, just below neck.

Dolls' House

No woodworking skill whatever is needed to make this smart bungalow for dolls. It is designed from grocery cartons, with some furniture made of matchboxes (mixed in with bought dolls' house furniture, for added ease).

Smart, modern four-roomed bungalow with garden. Large recep., sunny kitchen/dining room (fully equipped with latest kitchen units), sumptuous bedroom with built-in bed and fitted wardrobes, and luxury bathroom en suite, equipped with vanity unit and shower. Bungalow measures about 70 cm ($27\frac{1}{2}$ in) in diameter, 19 cm ($7\frac{1}{2}$ in) high. Would suit family of dolls roughly 10 cm (4 in) tall.

Notes: All the materials used throughout the house are too numerous to mention in detail here. However, the complete requirements can be ascertained by reading through the instructions for each room.

The four quarters (rooms) of the house are made and joined to each other room by room, as the work progresses.

The house is designed to suit the scale of bought dolls' house furniture and accessories, available from toy shops. The items used here are from the Lunby and 'Caroline's Home' range and, where necessary, bought items are mentioned in the instructions.

You will need: Cardboard grocery box or boxes measuring at least 34 by 34 cm by 18 cm high ($13\frac{1}{2}$ by $13\frac{1}{2}$ in, 7 in high). (Note that a smaller house can be made by drawing out a smaller radius quarter-circle when making the basic rooms.) Small pieces of fabrics and paper for floor- and wall-coverings, and curtains. Small cardboard boxes and cartons such as matchboxes, toothpaste tube and glue tube boxes. Card, paper and Cellophane. Three transparent tops off St Ivel Gold Spread (or transparent acetate film or Fablon). Small mirror tiles and

handbag mirrors. Brass paper fasteners. Cotton reels. Plastic lids of all kinds. Thin wooden dowelling. Discarded plastic sink mat or drainer for garden trellis. For garden plants, small plastic plants as used for aquariums, guipure flowers, green foam sponge. Printed pictures cut from magazines (for pictures, clock faces, etc.). For the kitchen equipment, record player, etc., printed pictures cut from magazines and leaflets from electrical suppliers. Sticky-backed plastic sheeting (such as Fablon) in white and colours and wood effect, for covering furniture. Adhesive. Plasticine. 4·5 m ($4\frac{7}{8}$ yd) of furnishing braid about 1 cm ($\frac{3}{8}$ in) wide.

To make the basic room: Draw out a 34 cm ($13\frac{1}{2}$ in) radius quarter-circle on the glued-down base of the box (*see diagram 1, below*). Now draw lines 18 cm (7 in) up the sides of the box and cut out this shape (see dotted lines on diagram 1). If the box is large enough, another room can be cut from the

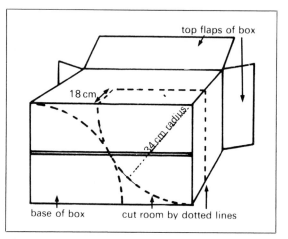

top flaps of box

18 cm

34 cm radius

base of box   cut room by dotted lines

Diagram 1 Cutting a room from a cardboard box. The box shown measures 34 by 58 by 46 cm ($13\frac{1}{2}$ by 23 by 18 in) – large enough to make all four rooms

box base as shown in the diagram. If the top flaps of the box are then glued down, two further rooms can be cut from the top end of box if it is more than 36 cm (14 in) high.

Diagram 2 (*below*) shows the room after cutting out. To make a level floor, fill in any missing pieces of card, as shown in diagram. Cover the walls and floor by glueing on fabric or paper, turning and glueing cut edges to wrong side of card. For skirting boards use strips of card 2 cm ($\frac{3}{4}$ in) wide. Note that all items are assembled by glueing unless otherwise stated.

The garden

Cut out basic room. From the centre of the right-hand wall cut out an opening for French windows 12·5 cm wide by 18 cm high (5 by 7 in). Cover right-hand wall. Place transparent lids at back of wall, with tops of lids facing towards garden. Attach sides of lids to back of wall with strips of sticky tape.

Trellis: Cover floor with green fabric or felt. For the trellis which frames the window, cut three strips of sink drainer or mat to fit across top and up sides. Tie strips together with strong thread where they meet. Thread

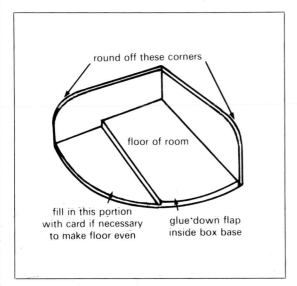

round off these corners

floor of room

fill in this portion with card if necessary to make floor even

glue down flap inside box base

Diagram 2 The shape of each room, after cutting out. Level up floor and trim wall corners as shown

a plastic plant through trellis then place trellis in position. Fix it to the wall with strong thread, taking thread through wall with a needle and knotting it at the back.

Crazy paving: Draw out a semi-circle the width of the window by 12 cm ($4\frac{3}{4}$ in) deep; add to this a 6 cm ($2\frac{3}{8}$ in) square for path and finally a 10 cm (4 in) diameter circle at end of path for fountain. Cut this shape from dark paper. Cut irregular pieces of lighter coloured paper and glue them on for paving. Glue all paved pieces in place and stick bits of foam here and there between the paving stones.

Balustrades: Cut card strips to fit round the curved edge of paving as far as the path – making the strips wide enough to cover ends of Drima thread reels. Mark the card strips to resemble stone then glue the reels between two matching strips as shown in the illustration. Glue the balustrade in place. Cut narrow strips of brown felt for soil on flowerbeds outside the balustrades; glue on foam and guipure flowers.

Urns: For the urns on balustrades use suitable buttons, tying them together through centre holes with thread. Tie in plastic plants too.

Fountain: For lower portion of fountain use a 7 cm ($2\frac{3}{4}$ in) diameter plastic lid off a cheese spread box and on to this glue the push-in centre of sticking plaster dispenser. Glue braid round edge of lid, and blue Cellophane inside lid for water.

For upper part of fountain use the base from a plastic aquarium plant turned upside down. (Alternatively half a table tennis ball could be used.) For the spray of water cut a strip of blue Cellophane 6 by 14 cm ($2\frac{3}{8}$ by $5\frac{1}{2}$ in) and snip this into strips along one long edge, leaving about 6 cm ($2\frac{3}{8}$ in) un-snipped at other long edge. Roll up strip tightly. Make a hole through upper and lower portions of fountain and join them together by glueing the spray of water through holes.

Kitchen window: On left-hand wall of garden cut opening for kitchen window, making it the size of transparent lid used.

Place the window 6 cm (2$\frac{3}{8}$ in) away from corner of garden and 2·5 cm (1 in) down from top of wall. Cover left-hand wall of garden.

Flowerbed: For wall of flowerbed under the kitchen window cut a 2·5 cm (1 in) wide strip of card the length of the wall. Cut a strip 3 cm (1$\frac{1}{4}$ in) long for end of wall. Mark strips to resemble stones and glue them to garden 3 cm (1$\frac{1}{4}$ in) from kitchen wall.

Fill flowerbed with pieces of chunky cork for soil, glueing them in place. Push plastic plants into cork as shown on page 210.

Garden table and stools: For table use a large cotton reel with a cheese spread lid glued to top. For stools use small lids and golf tees with points cut off (otherwise use Drima thread reels cut in half). Stick centre motifs cut off paper doyleys to tops of table and stools.

Umbrella: Use an umbrella cocktail stick, glueing braid round edge. Otherwise use three paper baking cases flattened out and stuck together, with cocktail stick handle.

The living room

Cut out basic room and place it behind the right-hand garden wall. Mark and cut out rectangle for French window to match the window on garden wall, making the opening slightly larger. Check that the windows will open freely on to the living room.

Cover walls and floor, then glue living room wall to garden wall, holding them together until glue dries with spring clothes pegs or bulldog clips. To fill in the 'threshold' gap between rooms at window, cut a card strip and glue in place. If the windows rub against the floor after carpet is in place, trim lower edges of windows.

Block prints: Cut pictures from magazines and glue them to larger pieces of black card.

Spotlamps: For lighting track, cut strip off edge of a rectangular margarine box. For spotlamps use lids off hair conditioner bottles

or anorak toggles, sewing them to the track. Glue beads inside for bulbs.

Sideboard: Use toothpaste tube box, covering it with wood-effect plastic. For doors cover small pieces of card to match. For handles use halves of self-adhesive spot labels.

Music centre: For record deck use a matchbox tray cut to 1 cm ($\frac{3}{8}$ in) deep. For lid use the transparent lid off a small ring or jewel box. Hinge lid to base with sticky tape. Cover base with wood-effect plastic, then glue on appropriate cuttings for the turntable, etc.

For each stereo speaker cut a matchbox tray in half and slip one half, turned over, inside the other half. Cover to match deck and glue black paper to fronts.

Records and holder: Cut these from magazine advertisement and glue to pieces of card. For record holder use the wire spiral off a small spiral-bound note pad.

Seating units: Each is made up from two matchboxes (or three for the settee unit). Cover each box separately, glueing a 10 cm (4 in) wide fabric strip round it. Snip fabric to corners of box and trim all edges to 5 mm ($\frac{1}{4}$ in) except for one wide edge at each side. Turn in the 5 mm ($\frac{1}{4}$ in) edges and glue down, then glue down remaining portions. Glue covered boxes together as shown in the illustration on page 210, then stick braid round lower edge of each unit.

Coffee table: Use a transparent cheese spread box with braid glued round the sides.

Telephone table: Use lid off hair spray can.

Large plant: Fill a fancy perfume bottle lid with Plasticine and push in dried flowers.

Bookcase: For base use two matchboxes, and two matchbox trays for upper portion. Cover to match sideboard then make and glue on drawer fronts as for sideboard.

Typewriter: Use novelty pencil sharpener.

Row of books: Use magazine cutting glued to a piece of matchbox.

Plant: Fill toothpaste cap with Plasticine and push in a dried plant.

Dog ornament: Use a lucky charm.

Curtains: Use thin wooden dowel for curtain rail with beads glued to ends. Push small screw-in eyes (as used for hanging pictures) into wall to carry the rail. Make curtains to fit, just clear of the floor.

The kitchen

Cut out basic room and place right-hand wall against left-hand wall of garden. Mark on window opening and cut out to match opening in garden wall. Glue walls together as for living room and garden, this time sandwiching the transparent lid between them for window.

Cover walls and floor then glue strip of card in place for window sill. Place bought kitchen sink unit under window.

Floor units and machines: For each cupboard and machine use two matchboxes glued together, standing them on end. Alternatively use one toothpaste or glue box to form several units linked together. Cover cupboards with wood-effect plastic sheet. Cut machine fronts from leaflets or magazine and glue in place. For handles on cupboards cut small oblongs of card and glue to top edge.

Work surfaces: Cut card strips to fit on tops of cupboards and machines, making them slightly wider. Cover with coloured plastic and glue them in place.

Hob unit: Cut hob from a leaflet and glue it to work surface above cupboards.

Double oven: Glue two matchboxes as for base units on to two others. Cover with white plastic and stick on leaflet cutting.

Tall cupboard: Use a suitable small cardboard box. Open it up so it lies flat then cover outside with wood-effect plastic, turning edges to other side of cardboard. Reassemble box, and glue in a card shelf.

Wall units: Cover two matchbox trays to match floor cupboards. Glue a card strip inside each one for a shelf. Link these together with a long shelf over the top then stick a shelf between them.

Extractor hood: Cut matchbox tray 5 mm ($\frac{1}{4}$ in) deep. Cover and glue leaflet cutting to front. Glue hood in place under shelf above hob unit.

Paper towel dispenser: Glue a strip of paper tissue round a thin dowel 2·5 cm (1 in) long. Cut strip of card to fit round dowel. Cover it, then glue all on to wall.

Accessories: For wall clock and posters use magazine cuttings. For chopping board cover card with plastic sheeting.

Dining table and chairs: Cover plastic lid with plastic sheeting then glue it to smaller lid. The chairs were bought.

Curtains: Gather strips of net fabric and glue them to each side of window, tying them back. Glue frill across top of window.

The bathroom

Cut out basic room and cover right-hand wall. For bathroom partition cut a piece of card 14 by 26 cm ($5\frac{1}{2}$ by $10\frac{1}{4}$ in). Round off one top corner, then cut an arched doorway 4 cm ($1\frac{1}{2}$ in) from outer edge, measuring 5 by 12 cm (2 by $4\frac{3}{4}$ in). Glue partition in place, as illustrated. To hold the wall securely glue strips of thin paper at right angles to wall and floor at lower edge. Cover remaining bathroom wall and floor. The shower unit, lavatory and accessories were bought.

Towel ring: Use a plastic ring (from a cracker) or curtain ring, fixing it through the wall with a paper fastener.

Vanity unit: Cover two matchboxes and a matchbox tray with coloured plastic sheeting then stick on contrast pieces for fronts. Make handles as for sideboard. Stand matchboxes on end and glue tray between them at top for drawer. For top surface of unit cut a piece of card 4 by 9·5 cm ($1\frac{1}{2}$ by $3\frac{3}{4}$ in). For basin use a small plastic lid, cutting a hole in unit top just large enough to take the lid, so it fits tightly. Cover the unit top and push lid in place. Stick unit top to unit.

For taps use the clip fittings off clip-on earrings. Bend them to shape then make small slits in top and push fittings in. For mirror back on unit cut a piece of card 8 by 9 cm ($3\frac{1}{8}$ by $3\frac{1}{2}$ in). Cover it to match unit then glue on mirror tiles and posters cut from a magazine. Glue unit and back to bathroom wall. Place small lids and caps on the unit.

Bathroom cabinet: Cover a matchbox tray to match unit, glue on mirror tiles.

Plant: Make as for living room plant.

The bedroom

Cover remaining walls and floor then glue braid round arched edge of doorway.

Door curtain: Fray out a piece of fabric to form a long fringe. Glue it over doorway and stick braid along top edge.

Wardrobes: Use three toothpaste or glue boxes the same size, with a Swan Vestas matchbox for dressing table top. Cover each box with coloured plastic sheeting then for front panels cut pieces of thin card 5 mm ($\frac{1}{4}$ in) smaller all round. Cover card with open-weave fabric to resemble rattan, turning raw edges to wrong sides of card. Fix paper fasteners through card for knobs then glue panels to boxes.

Stick wardrobes in place in bedroom. Place matchbox between wardrobes, if necessary cutting it to fit. Cover it as for wardrobes.

Glue a handbag mirror to wall between the wardrobes then stick dressing table top in

place about 4 cm ($1\frac{1}{2}$ in) up from floor.

Cut a piece of card to go right across tops of wardrobes; cover it to match and glue in place. Place small lids, glass or pearl buttons on dressing table.

Portable TV: Use a plastic novelty toy or a magazine cutting glued to a matchbox.

Stool: Cover a small lid with open-weave fabric and on top of it glue a card circle covered with contrast fabric.

Laundry basket: Cover a lid with fabric as for stool. Make lid of basket from a card circle covered with fabric, with a paper fastener pushed through for knob.

Bed: For raised platform cut a few pieces of card 13 by 16 cm ($5\frac{1}{8}$ by $6\frac{1}{4}$ in). Round off corners at one long edge. Glue card pieces together then cover them with fabric, turning raw edges to other side of card.

For mattress use six matchbox trays glued together (or a complete cardboard box about 11 cm ($4\frac{1}{4}$ in) square by 2 cm ($\frac{3}{4}$ in) deep. Cover mattress with fabric as for base.

For the sheet cut a piece of card 5 mm ($\frac{1}{4}$ in) smaller all round than mattress, cover it with fabric and glue to mattress.

Bedhead: Glue three slide-on matchbox covers together end to end, and cover with fabric to match bed. For headboard cut an arched piece of card the width of bedhead by 12 cm ($4\frac{3}{4}$ in) high. Cover it with open-weave fabric. Cut two 2·5 cm (1 in) wide card strips to fit round curved edge of headboard. Cover one strip with fabric to match headboard and the other to match bed. Glue strips in place. Stick bed to bedhead.

Make lighting track in bedhead as for living room, using small Christmas tree baubles for the spotlamps.

Pillow and quilt: Cut two 4 by 12 cm ($1\frac{1}{2}$ by $4\frac{3}{4}$ in) pieces of fabric for pillow and two 12 cm ($4\frac{3}{4}$ in) squares for quilt. Take narrow seams round edges, turn and stuff lightly then slipstitch gaps.

Books: Cut from magazines and glue to card.

Wall mirror: Use fancy handbag mirror or a small mirror badge.

Baby's bassinet: Stick tops of two matchbox trays together. Cover inside one tray with open-weave fabric then glue trimming round sides of bassinet.

For hood cut a piece of card 1 by 10 cm ($\frac{3}{8}$ by 4 in). Bend it in half and glue ends to sides of bassinet at one end. Glue trimming over this and at end, then make a small pillow and bedcover from trimming.

To complete the dolls' house

Glue final room in place. Cut four quarter-circles of card to fit underneath the rooms. Turn house upside down and glue these card pieces in place, taking care that the quarter-circles join in a different position from the rooms, to strengthen the base.

Glue braid along the top edge of bathroom partition, then across top edges of the rooms and finally right round the outside edges of the floors.

Dolls' house dolls

Parents about 10 cm (4 in) tall; baby about 4·5 cm ($1\frac{3}{4}$ in).

You will need: A pipe cleaner and 1 cm ($\frac{3}{8}$ in) diameter wooden bead for the baby; two 1·5 cm ($\frac{5}{8}$ in) diameter wooden beads and six pipe cleaners for parents; scraps of fabrics, cotton wool, nylon stockings or tights; knitting yarn for hair; marker pens or pencils for facial features; modelling clay or Plasticine for shoes; adhesive. *Note:* Take

3 mm ($\frac{1}{8}$ in) seams on clothes unless otherwise stated.

Baby

Cut a 10 cm (4 in) length of pipe cleaner for body and legs, fold it in half and glue fold into bead. For arms use remaining 6 cm ($2\frac{3}{8}$ in) length of cleaner, tying centre to body pipe cleaner below head with thread. Wrap a tiny bit of cotton wool round body, arms and legs, tying it in place with thread. Bend round 3 mm ($\frac{1}{8}$ in) at ends of pipe cleaners for hands and feet.

Mark on face and hair with pen or pencils then glue a bit of yarn to top of head to cover hole in bead. To cover hands pull scraps of nylon stocking fabric up around hands and tie it round wrists with thread. Trim off excess fabric.

Trace tights pattern on to thin paper and cut out; pin pattern to two layers of stretchy fabric (e.g. cuttings off a sock). Sew round pattern close to edge, leaving top edges open. Remove the pattern and cut out tights. Turn right side out and put tights on baby, glueing waist edge in place. Glue a bit of matching fabric round each arm for sleeves. To cover rest of body cut a strip of ribbon; cut arm slits then glue in place.

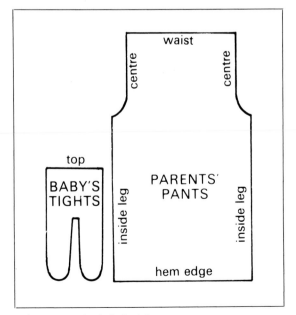

Left Pattern for baby's tights
Right Pattern for parents' pants

Father

Cut two 12 cm ($4\frac{3}{4}$ in) lengths of pipe cleaner for body and legs. Cut a 15 cm (6 in) length of pipe cleaner and fold it in half for arms. Glue the fold and other pipe cleaners into bead.

Wrap cotton wool round body, arms and legs tying it in place with thread. Bend round 1 cm ($\frac{3}{8}$ in) at end of each cleaner for hands and feet. Cover hands as for baby. Model shoes round pipe cleaner feet with clay or Plasticine. Colour clay when dry. Mark on face and hair and glue bits of yarn to head.

Use the pattern to cut two pants pieces from fabric. Turn in hem edges and glue. Join pieces at centre edges, bring these seams together and join inside leg edges. Turn pants right side out. Put them on doll and glue waist edge to waist.

For sweater front and back cut two 3 cm ($1\frac{1}{4}$ in) squares of stretchy fabric. Glue them in place, overlapping and sticking sides under arms and top corners on shoulders. Glue a strip of fabric round each arm for sleeves. Cut narrow strips of fabric, turn in long raw edges and glue down to neaten, then stick these strips round lower edge, wrists and neck edge of sweater.

Mother

Make doll as for father, cutting leg pipe cleaners slightly shorter. Cover head with yarn strands as illustrated. Make pants as for father.

For blouse sleeves cut two 4 cm ($1\frac{1}{2}$ in) squares of fabric. Overlap and glue two opposite edges on each piece. Slip sleeves on arms and sew top edges to body. Gather wrist edges round wrists and glue on trimming.

For body of blouse cut a fabric strip 4 by 10 cm ($1\frac{1}{2}$ by 4 in). Turn in one long edge and glue down then stick on trimming. Place on doll and make small slits at each side so arms can come through. Turn in and glue raw edges of slits. Place blouse on doll again and gather top edges tightly round neck. Glue trimming round neck and tie a narrow ribbon round waist for a belt.

Hickory Dickory Dock (mouse house and clock)

This toy will help the children to learn to tell the time without tears. The clock face is removable, and behind the face is a little mouse house, complete with a family of tiny white mice!

For the clock you will need: A man-size paper handkerchief box measuring about 31 cm long by 16 cm wide by 5 cm deep (12$\frac{1}{4}$ by 6$\frac{1}{4}$ by 2 in); pieces of thin card from cereal packets; scraps of fabric, felt, guipure flowers, ribbon, stuffing, trimmings, braids, thin twigs, medium fuse wire, Plasticine, dried flowers, paper; 2 cm ($\frac{3}{4}$ in) of Velcro Touch and Close Fastener; two metric size Drima reels for weights on clock; two imperial size Drima reels for small tables in house; a Swan Vestas matchbox for the fireplace; small cap off a washing-up liquid bottle and cap off a perfume bottle for plant pots; two small buttons with two holes; 1·2 m (1$\frac{3}{8}$ yd) of thin cord for pendulum and weights; adhesive; paints or permanent marker pens.

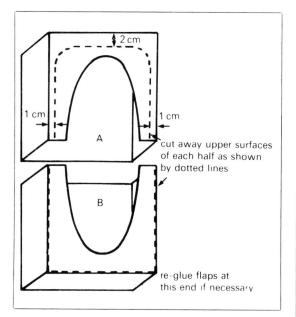

Diagram 1 Cut handkerchief box in half and cut away the upper surfaces

For the mice you will need: Scraps of white fleecy fabric and pink felt; tiny red beads for eyes; scraps of black felt, trimmings, stuffing and white thread; white Velcro Touch and Close Fastener; adhesive.

The clock

For the box at the back of the clock: Cut the paper handkerchief box in half and cut away the upper surface of each half as shown by the dotted lines in diagram 1 (*below left*). Re-glue the end flaps of the half marked B if they are loose. Now slide the half marked A inside the half marked B having first spread the surfaces which will be against each other with glue, to form the box shape shown in diagram 2.

Now glue two small loops of narrow ribbon to the top of the box at the back for hanging the clock on the wall (see diagram 2). Reinforce the box on all sides by glueing on pieces of card cut to fit. When glue is dry, pull the ribbon loops to check that they are securely stuck in place. Cover sides and back of box with fabric or felt.

Pierce three small holes in the base of the box as shown in diagram 2 with the pendulum hole 1 cm ($\frac{3}{8}$ in) from the back and the weights holes 8 cm (3 in) apart. Thread a 40 cm (15$\frac{3}{4}$ in) length of cord through the pendulum hole and knot on the inside of the box then knot the other end. Cut an 80 cm (31$\frac{1}{2}$ in) length of cord for the weights, thread one end up through one hole in the box, then across and down through the other hole.

Paint the metric size Drima reels and

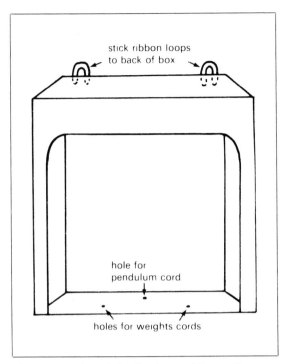

stick ribbon loops
to back of box

hole for
pendulum cord

holes for weights cords

Diagram 2 Pierce holes for the pendulum and weights cords in base of box and attach ribbon hanging loops to the top back

thread one on each end of the weights cord and knot the ends. Sew a 1 cm ($\frac{3}{8}$ in) strip of hooked Velcro around each cord just above the weights.

For the pendulum: Cut two circles of felt 8 cm (3 in) in diameter. Oversew the edges together all round, pushing a little stuffing between them as you go and enclosing the knotted end of the pendulum cord before completing stitching.

To complete: Cover the inside of the box with paper or fabric for the house walls. Make the floor of the house from thin card to fit inside the base of the box and to form a 'bridge' over the cords. Bend the floor to shape as shown in diagram 3 (*below*) making

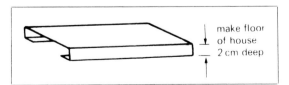

make floor
of house
2 cm deep

Diagram 3 Make a card floor to fit inside the box base

it 2 cm ($\frac{3}{4}$ in) deep. Cover the floor with paper or fabric and stick it in position in the house. Stick a narrow strip of card round the walls at floor level for the skirting board.

For the fireplace: Use the slide-on cover of the matchbox. Cut off one end so the remainder measures 5 cm (2 in) high. Cut out an arched shape for the fireplace opening measuring 2·5 cm (1 in) wide by 3·5 cm (1$\frac{3}{8}$ in) high. Colour the fireplace black and glue trimming round the arched shape and gold trimming across the lower edge for the front of the grate. Cut a 2 by 5·5 cm ($\frac{3}{4}$ by 2$\frac{1}{4}$ in) strip of card for the mantlepiece, stick it in place then stick trimming round sides and front as illustrated on page 215. Cut a 3 cm (1$\frac{1}{4}$ in) wide strip of card to fit across the fireplace for the hearth, make a tile design on it and stick in place under the fireplace with back edges level. Glue twigs, red paper and cotton wool for smoke inside the grate, then stick fireplace in position. Glue a tiny fabric strip in front of the hearth for a rug.

For the basket of logs: Cut a 2 cm ($\frac{3}{4}$ in) diameter circle of card and glue a strip of narrow braid round it then stick short twigs inside. For the plant pedestal table cut a 2 cm ($\frac{3}{4}$ in) section off one end of an imperial size Drima reel then glue a 2·5 cm (1 in) diameter circle of card to the cut end. Paint the table and stick on lace trimming for a mat. Push a little Plasticine inside the perfume bottle lid then cut small spear-shaped pieces of green paper and push them into Plasticine for leaves. Make the smaller table in a similar way. For the flowering plant, glue dried flowers inside the washing-up liquid cap.

For the gold candlestick: Begin with a 2 cm ($\frac{3}{4}$ in) piece cut off a matchstick. Glue narrow gold braid or cord round and round to cover the match leaving about 5 mm ($\frac{1}{4}$ in) exposed at one end for the candle. Glue a little extra braid round at the base so the candlestick will stand upright. Pare down the candle to make thinner.

For the 'Home Sweet Home' sampler: Cut a 2 by 2·5 cm ($\frac{3}{4}$ by 1 in) piece of card. Glue braid round the edge then mark on words.

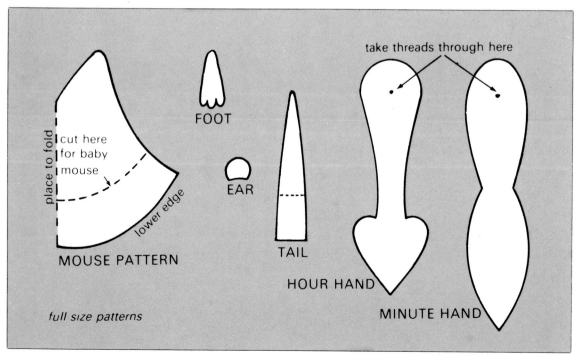

take threads through here

FOOT

place to fold

cut here
for baby
mouse

lower edge

MOUSE PATTERN

EAR

TAIL

HOUR HAND

MINUTE HAND

full size patterns

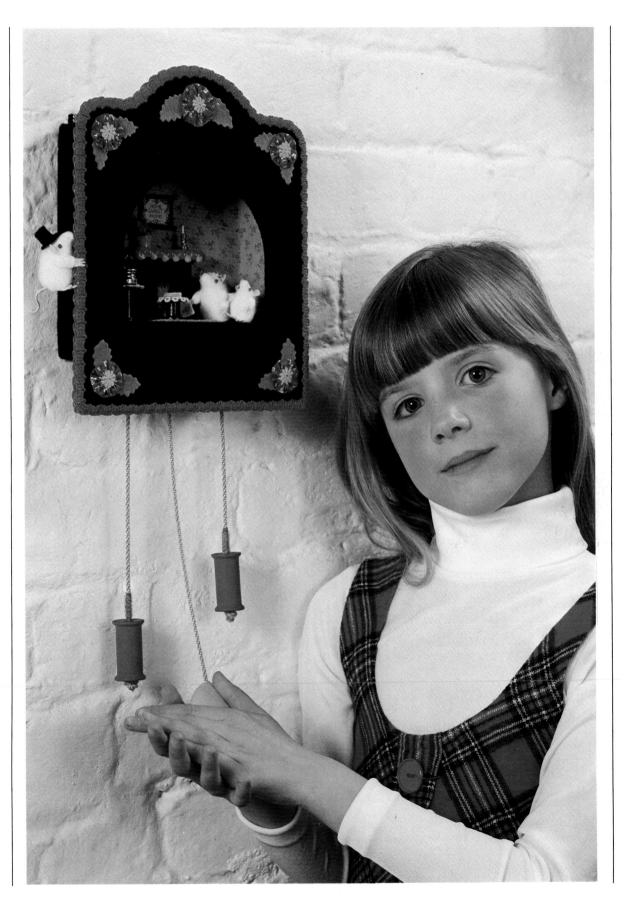

Stick narrow strips of card round the edges for the frame.

For the toast on a plate: Cut a 1·5 cm ($\frac{5}{8}$ in) diameter circle of card for the plate and stick on 1 cm ($\frac{3}{8}$ in) squares of light brown felt cut in half. Mark the top slice with darker brown pencil and spread with glue for a 'buttered' effect. For the toasting fork, cut an 8 cm (3 in) length of fuse wire and bend in half. Join in a 4 cm ($1\frac{1}{2}$ in) length of wire and twist all three together for 1 cm ($\frac{3}{8}$ in) then divide wires and bend to make a forked shape. Trim off excess wire and glue on a slice of toast made from felt.

For the clock front: Cut the clock front from card using the pattern shape shown in diagram 4 (*below*), then cut out the arched shape from the centre and discard it. Reinforce the clock front by glueing on one or two more layers of card cut to the same shape. Cover the clock front by sticking on a piece of fabric, cutting it level with the outer edges. Cut away the fabric covering the arched centre opening, leaving enough fabric

for turning and sticking to the other side of the card.

Stick braid round the outer edges of the clock front then stick the clock front in position on the 'mouse house' box so the floor of the house is level with the edge indicated on the clock front pattern.

Stick two 1 cm ($\frac{3}{8}$ in) strips of hooked Velcro to the clock front at the position indicated on the pattern. For the decorative flowers on the clock front cut four 4 cm ($1\frac{1}{2}$ in) diameter circles of fabric for the corners and one 6 cm ($2\frac{3}{8}$ in) diameter circle for the top. Gather round the edge of each circle and pull up the stitches until the raw edges meet then fasten off. Using pinking shears, cut out ten green felt leaf shapes about 3 cm ($1\frac{1}{4}$ in) long. Stick leaves and gathered flowers in place as shown in illustration on page 215, then stick a guipure flower to the centre of each fabric flower.

For the clock face: Cut two 17 cm ($6\frac{3}{4}$ in) diameter circles of yellow felt. Cut an 8 cm (3 in) diameter circle of contrasting felt and sew it to the centre of one large felt circle. Cut a 14 cm ($5\frac{1}{2}$ in) diameter circle of card and stick it centrally between the two larger circles with right sides of the felt outside.

Using black thread, machine the felt circles together, stitching close to the edge, then stitch round again close to the edge of the card. Glue twelve guipure flowers at even five minute intervals round the clock face between the lines of stitching. Cut numbers from black felt or alternatively mark them on the clock face with black marker pen. To make the felt figures, first spread the back of the felt with glue and allow to dry before cutting. Make the number one 5 mm by 2 cm ($\frac{1}{4}$ by $\frac{3}{4}$ in). To keep the other figures in proportion, cut each one from a 1·5 by 2 cm ($\frac{5}{8}$ by $\frac{3}{4}$ in) rectangle of felt. Stick the numbers in place.

Using the pattern shapes given on page 114, cut hour and minute hands from card and stick each of them on to a piece of felt. Cut the felt 3 mm ($\frac{1}{8}$ in) larger all round than the card then stick felt to the other side of the card in the same way. Oversew the edges of felt together all round. To fix the hands to the clock face, pass a double thickness of

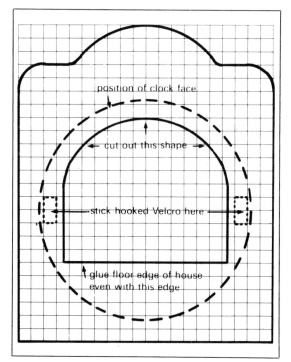

Diagram 4 Pattern for clock front
Each square = 1 cm

button thread through both holes of the button then thread all four ends of thread through a needle and take them through the minute hand then the hour hand and then the centre of the clock face to the back. Divide the threads into pairs again and pass through the holes in the second button. Knot thread securely. Sew two 1 cm ($\frac{3}{8}$ in) strips of furry Velcro to back of the clock face at the positions indicated on the clock front pattern.

The mice

Trace off patterns for mouse body, foot, ear and tail pieces given on page 214.

Father mouse: Cut the mouse from fleecy fabric placing the broken line on the pattern to the fold in the fabric. Oversew the raw edges together leaving the lower edge open. Turn right side out and stuff firmly then gather the lower edge up tightly and fasten off. Stick two layers of pink felt together and allow to dry before cutting out the feet. Stick feet in place under the body. Spread both sides of a piece of felt with glue and allow to dry before cutting out hands. For hands, use the foot pattern trimmed down a little. For arms, cut 1 cm ($\frac{3}{8}$ in) squares of fleecy fabric and glue these around the ends of the hands. Glue arms to body at each side. Cut a tail from felt, spread it with glue and roll up across the width then bend to shape and sew in place. Sew small red beads in place for eyes about 1 cm ($\frac{3}{8}$ in) back from the nose and taking the stitches through the head from side to side. For whiskers, sew strands of white thread through the face and fasten off then trim to length. Cut ears from glued felt and stick to head behind eyes.

For the top hat brim, cut a 1·5 cm ($\frac{5}{8}$ in) diameter circle of felt. For the crown, cut a 1 by 5 cm ($\frac{3}{8}$ by 2 in) strip of felt, spread it with glue and roll up along the length. Glue in position on the mouse's head. Sew a small strip of white furry Velcro to the front of the Father mouse for fixing him on to either of the weights cords.

Mother and Baby: Make in same way. For Mother glue lace to head and toasting fork to one hand. For Baby trim patterns along dotted lines, and reduce feet, hands, arms and ears slightly.

9
NOVELTY TOYS

Puppets for a Pantomime

Aladdin is one of the most popular traditional pantomines and here instructions are given for making the main characters – Aladdin, Widow Twankey, the Princess, wicked Abanazer and two genies of the lamp. The puppets are about 48 cm (19 in) tall and are held by rods hidden under clothing. Each main character has an additional rod attached to one hand which allows it to gesticulate and appear more life-like. Even the smallest child can hold and play with these puppets easily

For each puppet you will need: Small pieces of pink or white cotton stockinette fabric (such as a vest or T-shirt fabric); cotton wool, stuffing, a wire coathanger; one 45 cm (18 in) bamboo garden cane for each puppet except genies; oddments of fabrics; felt; thin fabric for genies; sequins; braid; trimmings; card; yarn for hair; coloured pencils; felt and threads for facial features; scrap of Velcro fastener for positioning Aladdin's un-wired hand; bits of junk jewellery; two curtain rings; one stud-type pierced earring for the magic ring; short lengths of cotton tape about 1·5 cm ($\frac{5}{8}$ in) wide; adhesive.

Notes: The seam allowance is 5 mm ($\frac{1}{4}$ in) on all basic puppet pieces and 1 cm ($\frac{3}{8}$ in) on garment pieces unless otherwise stated.

Cut out stockinette pieces with most stretch in fabric going across the measurement stated in instructions.

Copy pattern outlines square by square on to 5 cm squared graph paper.

Aladdin

Take the bamboo cane for centre rod of puppet and wrap cotton wool round the narrow end, securing with tape.

For head cut a piece of stockinette 13 by 16 cm (5 by 6$\frac{1}{4}$ in) with most stretch across the shorter measurement. Join the long edges. Gather round one remaining raw edge, pull up tightly and fasten off. Turn right side out and stuff top. Push padded end of rod inside head and stuff, working round the rod until head measures about 24 cm (9$\frac{1}{2}$ in) round. Run a gathering thread round, 2 cm ($\frac{3}{4}$ in) from remaining raw edge, pull up tightly and fasten off. Stick the raw edges to rod, then

glue tape around them, sticking the tape to rod also.

For body cut a piece of stockinette 12 by 18 cm (4$\frac{3}{4}$ by 7 in) with most stretch across the short measurement. Join long edges and turn right side out. Turn in one remaining raw edge and run a gathering thread round. Slip body onto rod and pull up gathers below head. Fasten off, then sew gathers to head. Stuff body to measure about 18 cm (7 in) round, keeping rod at centre. Gather and secure lower edge of body to rod as for head.

Cut two pairs of hand pieces from stockinette. Join one pair leaving wrist edges open. Join other pair as far as point A and leaving wrist edges open (the wire rod will be inserted in this hand). Trim seams and turn hands right side out.

Cut coathanger as shown in diagram 1, bend round one end to fit inside hand and straighten other end as shown in diagram. For the handle, bend round 8 cm (3 in) at straight end of wire as shown in diagram 2, then bind this end with tape, glueing it in place. At hand end of wire, pad round wire with cotton wool, sewing it in place, then slip wire inside hand and stuff hand to shape. Gather round wrist edge and fasten off, then slip stitch gap from wrist to point A. Stuff remaining hand to size of other hand and gather wrist.

For each sleeve cut a piece of fabric suitable for the puppet's undersleeves 10 by 16 cm (4 by 6$\frac{1}{4}$ in). Join long edges and turn right side out. Turn in one raw edge and slip it over gathered end of each hand. Slip stitch in place and stick on trimming. Stuff lower portion of sleeves then run a gathering thread across sleeves 6 cm (2$\frac{3}{8}$ in) from wrist edges. Pull up gathers and fasten off. Put a little stuffing in tops of sleeves, gather up raw edges tightly and sew one to each side of body

1 cm ($\frac{3}{8}$ in) down from neck, taking care to have thumbs pointing inwards to body.

Tunic: Cut two tunic pieces placing edge indicated on pattern to fold in fabric each time. Join pieces at shoulders from wrist edges to points A. Hem wrist edges taking 1 cm ($\frac{3}{8}$ in) turnings twice then sew on trimming. Join side and underarm edges and clip seams as shown. Turn right side out and hem lower edge. Slip tunic on puppet pulling wired hand through one sleeve, and the rod through neck opening. Bring shoulder edges together turning in raw edges, then slip stitch as far as neck keeping neck at centre. Sew to neck. Pin braid round neck then take to right-hand side seam of tunic as shown in illustration. Sew braid in place as pinned.

Face and hair: Cut eyes from black felt and stick in place halfway down face and 2·5 cm (1 in) apart. Cut a 2 cm ($\frac{3}{4}$ in) diameter circle of stockinette, gather round edge and stuff, for nose. Sew to face then work mouth and eye lines in thread. Colour cheeks and nose with red pencil.

Cut about thirty 70 cm ($27\frac{1}{2}$ in) lengths of black yarn. Back stitch centres to position of centre parting. Take strands to each side of head and sew there as for centre parting. Plait strands at back of head.

Hat: Cut hat from thin card. Stick fabric to one side of card then form into a cone-shape by overlapping and glueing straight edges as shown on pattern, with fabric on inside of

cone. Cut another piece of fabric slightly larger all round than hat pattern. Place right side out over outside of hat and pin straight edges together to fit. Seam as pinned, turn right side out and place over hat. Stick edges to hat all round, trimming off any excess fabric. Glue braid round edge of hat then stick hat to head.

Magic ring: Fix pierced earring through unwired hand when required. Sew small piece of hooked Velcro to this hand and furry piece of Velcro to tunic at front so that hand may be fixed in place and ring may be rubbed with other hand.

Magic lamp: Cut two from felt and oversew them together leaving lower edges open. Turn and stuff then oversew lower edges. Glue and sew braid round lamp as illustrated, leaving a loop of braid for handle large enough to fit round puppet's unwired hand. Add other ornamentation as available.

The princess

Make basic puppet and tunic as for Aladdin and trim tunic as illustrated. Make basic hair as for Aladdin sewing it to sides of head. Twist strands of yarn and take each to centre top of head then sew there. Take remainder of strands down back of head and tuck ends under then sew in place above neck. If necessary cover remainder of back of head with yarn strands in the same way. Cut eyes from black felt, eyelids from pink felt, then glue them in place and work eye, mouth and nose stitches as illustrated. Sew on beads for earrings, or use other scraps of jewellery.

Head-dress: Cut two from thin card. Cover each with fabric, turning raw edges of fabric to other side of card and glueing down. Stick wrong sides of card pieces together. Glue trimming round edge and jewel to front. For veil, cut a 30 cm (12 in) square of thin fabric and join two opposite edges. Place this seam at centre then join remaining raw edges leaving a gap in one seam. Turn right side out and slip stitch gap. Gather one short edge of veil to 4 cm ($1\frac{1}{2}$ in) and sew it to inner edge of

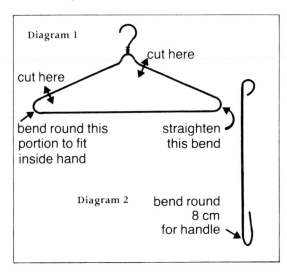

Diagram 1
cut here
cut here
bend round this portion to fit inside hand
straighten this bend

Diagram 2
bend round 8 cm for handle

head-dress. Sew trimming to other edge of veil. Place head-dress on head behind twists of hair then sew it to each side of head.

Widow Twankey

Make basic puppet as for Aladdin using stockinette pieces 15 by 16 cm (6 by 6¼ in) for head and 14 by 18 cm (5½ by 7 in) for body. Make arms but do not sew them to body at this stage. Make hair as for Aladdin, sewing to sides of head, then curl up the strands to form a sausage curl at each side. Sew curls to head. Sew on beads or other junk jewellery for earrings. Make nose as for Aladdin. Cut eyes from blue felt, add smaller ovals of black felt and stick them above nose. Work other facial lines in thread as illustrated.

Dress: Cut a piece of fabric 40 by 60 cm (16 by 23½ in) then join short edges. Turn right side out and hem one remaining raw edge. Turn in and gather other raw edge round neck then sew to neck. Sew frill of trimming round neck. Run a gathering thread round dress 30 cm (12 in) from hem edge, pull up to body and fasten off. Now sew arms in place through dress at each side of body. For puffed sleeves cut two pieces of fabric 15 by 22 cm (6 by 8¾ in). Join short edges and turn right side out. Turn in one remaining raw edge and gather, then place round top of arm. Pull up gathers and sew to dress round arm. Turn in and gather remaining raw edge below elbow and sew to arm. Glue trimming round at this position.

Apron: Cut a piece of fabric 20 by 26 cm (8 by 10¼ in). Narrowly hem and sew trimming to all but one short edge. Gather this edge and sew to front waist. Cut a strip of fabric 6 by 50 cm (2⅜ by 19½ in) and fold in half along the length. Join long edges and across one short edge. Turn right side out and neaten short raw edge. Sew centre of strip to front waist of apron then tie ends at back.

Hat: Cut a piece of fabric 30 by 60 cm (12 by 23½ in). Join the short edges. Fold up one raw edge to meet the other, with right side of fabric outside. Gather raw edges tightly and

fasten off then turn hat right side out. Gather round hat 5 cm (2 in) from fold, pull up gathers to fit behind hair then fasten off. Stuff top of hat, sew to head through gathers then sew bow to front.

Abanazar

Make basic puppet as for Aladdin, using a piece of fabric 11 by 18 cm (4¼ by 7 in) for the head. Sew a triangle of contrast-coloured fabric to front of tunic as shown by dotted line on tunic pattern. Use a 3 cm (1¼ in) diameter circle of stockinette for nose, stuffing it into a sausage-shape. Use smaller ovals of black felt for eyes and short thin strips of black felt for eyebrows. Work other facial lines as illustrated. Cut two beard and two moustache pieces from felt. Oversew pieces together all round edges, pushing in a little stuffing before completing sewing. Sew to face as illustrated and catch moustache to beard where they touch.

Fez: Cut a 26 cm (10¼ in) diameter semi-circle of thin card. Form into a cone measuring 7 cm (2¾ in) across base. Cover as for Aladdin's hat then stick fez to back of head.

Turban: Use a piece of thin fabric about 25 by 80 cm (9¾ by 31½ in). Gather one end and sew to centre front at base of fez. Wind turban around head, catching in place with stitches and ending with a tail of fabric at one side. Sew on a feather and pin a brooch or sew a button to front of turban. Sew on curtain rings for earrings.

Scarf: Cut a piece of fabric 8 by 20 cm (3 by 8 in). Hem all edges and sew fringe to ends. Fold and drape round shoulders as illustrated and catch to puppet with a few stitches.

The genies

Use a different coloured thin fabric for each one. Use a coathanger, snipping off the top hooked portion only. Straighten out the bends, then bend round the ends of wire as for the wired hand on the other puppets and bind the handle with tape. Bend remainder of wire into an S-shape. Make head as for Aladdin, using a piece of stockinette 15 by 18 cm (6 by 7 in). Stuff head and insert padded end of wire as for bamboo rod. Cut strips of thin fabric and wind around wire to cover it, sewing it to head and handle at each end. For the 'curl of smoke' effect on the wire, cut 20 cm (8 in) wide pieces of fabric to make a 2 m (2¼ yd) length. Join long edges of strip, tapering seam towards one end. Trim seam and turn right side out. Slip this fabric tube over wire and sew wide end to head. Twist and pucker the fabric to fit over the wire as illustrated, then sew narrow end to handle.

Make nose as for Abanazar, using the thin fabric. Cut largest eye shapes from coloured felt, smaller shapes from black felt. Stick a sequin to centre of each then glue eyes in place. Stick row of sequins above eyes. Make beard and moustache from felt as for Abanazar, but using genie patterns. Before sewing these in place glue a small piece of black felt below nose.

Make turban as for Abanazar but using a little more fabric if necessary and starting by taking fabric from front to back of head to cover the top.

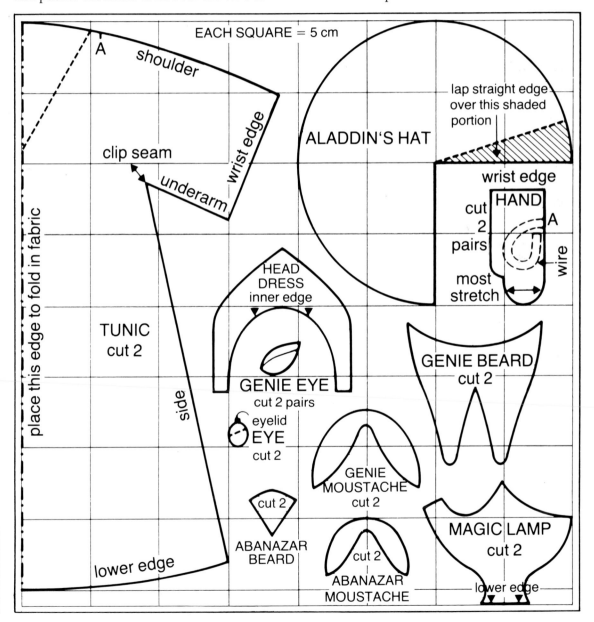

Funny Bunny

This cuddly bunny doubles as a teaching toy. He is dressed in clothes that have buttons and braces, buckle and laces, poppers and a zip fastner. He is 63 cm (25 in) high and his T-shirt is decorated with a clockface with movable hands – a fun way for any child to learn to tell the time

The rabbit

You will need: 50 cm (about $\frac{1}{2}$ yd) of Acrilan or Courtelle fleece fabric, 122 cm (48 in) wide; 500 g (1 lb) stuffing; scraps of stiff fabric such as Vilene interlining, to interline ears; scraps of red, black and pink felt, and black yarn for facial features; small pieces of fabric, felt, stiff card and a thick boot lace 91 cm (36 in) long for shoes; adhesive; metric graph paper.

Notes: 5 mm ($\frac{1}{4}$ in) seams are allowed on all pieces unless otherwise stated. Join pieces with right sides of fabric facing unless otherwise stated.

When binding raw edges with bias binding, turn bias completely to inside so that it cannot be seen on the right side of the garment.

On to metric graph paper copy the patterns square by square (each square on diagram equals 2 cm).

To make: From the patterns cut out body and ear pieces as directed, in fleece. For arms cut four fleece pieces 23·5 cm (9$\frac{1}{4}$ in) long by 7·5 cm (3 in) wide. Round off corners at one short end of each piece for hand.

Join body pieces round edges, stitching along line indicated between legs, leaving a gap in seam at one side, and leaving lower leg edges open as shown on pattern. Clip fabric between legs and clip seam at neck. Turn right side out. Stuff body and head firmly, then ladder-stitch opening in seam.

Cut shoe pieces in fabric. Join them in pairs at front and back seams; leaving upper and lower edges open. Trim seams and turn right side out. Cut two soles from card and place one inside each shoe at lower edge, matching points A and B. Glue lower edges of shoes 5 mm ($\frac{1}{4}$ in) on to card soles. Glue a felt sole to

each shoe to cover raw edges of fabric. Stuff shoes firmly.

Turn in upper edges of each shoe 5 mm ($\frac{1}{4}$ in), place these edges slightly overlapping lower edges of legs, with shoes turned outwards slightly, so that the rabbit will stand with toes apart, heels together. Slip stitch shoes to legs, adding more stuffing as you go to make legs and shoes quite firm.

Cut bootlace in half to make two equal lengths. Neaten cut ends by rolling strips of sticky tape tightly round. Sew centre of each shoe lace to each shoe in a triangular shape (as shown in illustration), so that ends are free to be knotted and tied.

Tie strong thread as tightly as possible round rabbit's neck to shape it, then sew thread ends into body.

Using black yarn, mark mouth in long straight stitches: begin about 9 cm (3$\frac{1}{2}$ in) up from neck and work a fairly long stitch downwards, then make shorter stitches for lower part of mouth as shown in the illustrations.

For a nose cut a 3 cm (1$\frac{1}{4}$ in) long oval of red felt and sew this in place covering top of first mouth stitch. For eyes cut two 2·5 cm (1 in) diameter circles of black felt; pin them in place each side of nose, about 4·5 cm (1$\frac{3}{4}$ in) apart, then work black eyelashes before sewing the eyes in place. Cut two pink felt circles 5 cm (2 in) diameter, and sew them in place to make cheeks.

Join ear pieces in threes, placing one interlining piece against each pair of fleece pieces (right sides facing) and leaving lower edges open. Trim seams and turn right side out. Turn in lower edges and slip stitch, pulling thread tight to gather slightly. Ladder stitch ears firmly in places shown on pattern.

Join arm pieces in pairs, leaving short straight edges open. Turn right side out and stuff to within 5 cm (2 in) of top. Tie strong thread round wrists 6·5 cm (2½ in) up from hands as for neck. Turn in upper edges of arms, bringing seams together, and slip stitch pulling thread to gather slightly. Sew arms to body at each side, 4 cm (1½ in) below neck.

The rabbit's clothes

T-shirt

You will need: 30 cm (about ⅜ yd) of fabric 91 cm (36 in) wide; bias binding for neatening raw edges; a strip of Velcro touch and close fastener, 18 cm (7 in) long; scraps of white Vilene interlining, felt and a button for clock motif; adhesive.

To make: Cut two T-shirt pieces from fabric as shown on pattern, then cut one open on fold line for back opening of shirt.

For the clock face cut a circle of Vilene 7 cm (2¾ in) diameter; mark numerals round it with a ball-point pen. Stick, then sew clock face to a 7·5 cm (3 in) diameter circle of felt, then stick and sew a 5 cm (2 in) diameter circle of felt to centre of clock. For clock hands stick a small piece of felt on to Vilene, then cut out two 5 mm (¼ in) wide strips, one 3 cm (1¼ in) long and the other 2·5 cm (1 in) long. Cut ends of hands to a point, and make a small hole at opposite end of each hand, with scissor points. Sew hands to clock face, taking thread through these holes, through the button and back again through the holes. The hands can now be moved to any position. Stitch clock to centre front of T-shirt 4 cm (1½ in) down from neck edge.

Join T-shirt front to backs at shoulder seams, then sew one edge of bias to sleeve edges. Join underarm and side seams, stitching twice to reinforce, then clip seams as shown on pattern. Finish off binding sleeve edges then bind lower and neck edges. Turn in back edges 5 mm (¼ in), and sew on Velcro strips to fasten.

Pants

You will need: 20 cm (about ¼ yd) of fabric 91 cm (36 in) wide; scraps of leathercloth or felt for braces; two large buttons.

To make: Cut two pairs of pants pieces from fabric. Join them in pairs at centre seams, clipping curves in seams. Join these pairs to each other at side seams, then inside leg seams. Turn in waist and lower edges 5 mm (¼ in) twice, and hem.

For braces cut two strips 41 cm (16 in) long by 4 cm (1½ in) wide. (If felt is used stitch together two layers for strength.) Round off one end of each strip and cut a large oval slit in these ends, starting 2·5 cm (1 in) in from the ends, to fit buttons easily.

Sew buttons to pants at front, where shown on pattern. Put pants on rabbit and loop buttonhole ends of braces on to buttons. Take braces back over each shoulder, cross them over at centre back and tuck ends inside back waist edge of pants, pinning and adjusting length to fit neatly. Take off pants and sew back edges of braces in place, trimming off any excess length.

The jacket

You will need: 70 cm (about ¾ yd) of fabric 91 cm (36 in) wide; an open-ended zip fastener long enough to be cut to fit jacket; bias binding for neatening raw edges; a buckle; metal eyelets (optional).

To make: Cut two jacket pieces from fabric as directed on pattern, then cut one piece in half along fold line for centre front opening. Cut two pockets from fabric. Turn in upper edges of pockets 1·5 cm (½ in) and stitch. Turn in remaining raw edges 5 mm (¼ in) and tack. Sew pockets to front of jacket as shown on pattern.

Open the zip fastener. Turn in centre front edges of jacket fronts 5 mm (¼ in) and tack them each side of zip fastener, with lower edges of zip 1·5 cm (½ in) above lower raw edges of jacket fronts. Cut top ends of zip level with neck edges. After this *do not* close the zip right up until the collar is sewn on or the slide fastener will come off.

With the zip fastener undone, machine one half of it to each front edge of the jacket, then remove the tacking stitches.

Join jacket fronts to back at shoulder seams. Sew one edge of bias to lower sleeve edges. Join side and underarm seams, sewing twice to reinforce, then clip seams at underarms.

Finish off binding on lower sleeve edges then bind lower edge of jacket.

Cut two collar pieces and join them leaving neck edges open. Trim seam, turn right side out and press. Tack raw edges of collar to neck edge of jacket, lining up the ends of the collar with the centre front edges of the jacket. Stitch bias binding over the join on inside of jacket, taking care to stitch between zip teeth.

Note: To avoid striking zip teeth with machine needle, one or two teeth can be pulled right off the fastener.

For the belt cut a strip of fabric 69 cm (27 in) long, and twice as wide as centre bar of buckle, plus 1·5 cm ($\frac{1}{2}$ in). Join long edges of strip and sew across one end, making a V point. Turn right side out and press. Attach buckle to other end of belt, making a small hole for prong. Pin belt to jacket 5·5 cm ($2\frac{1}{4}$ in) above lower edge, with buckle at centre front. Sew belt to jacket to within 2·5 cm (1 in) of centre front edges. Put eyelets in end of belt, or cut small holes and buttonhole stitch to neaten.

Carrots

You will need some scraps of orange and green fabric and stuffing; a large snap fastener.

As a pattern use one quarter of a circle 20 cm (8 in) in diameter. Cut two carrots in orange fabric. Join straight edges of each piece, turn right side out and stuff. For each carrot top, fray out one long edge of a small strip of green fabric. Roll up the strips and put one inside each carrot top, unfrayed edges downwards. Run a gathering thread round each carrot top, pull up tightly turning in raw edges, and fasten off thread securely. Put one carrot in jacket pocket. Sew half a snap fastener to remaining carrot and other half to rabbit's hand.

Scarf

Use a strip of fabric 15 cm (6 in) by 91 cm (36 in). Fray out the short edges then join long edges of strip. Turn right side out. Press, then stitch across short ends above fringes.

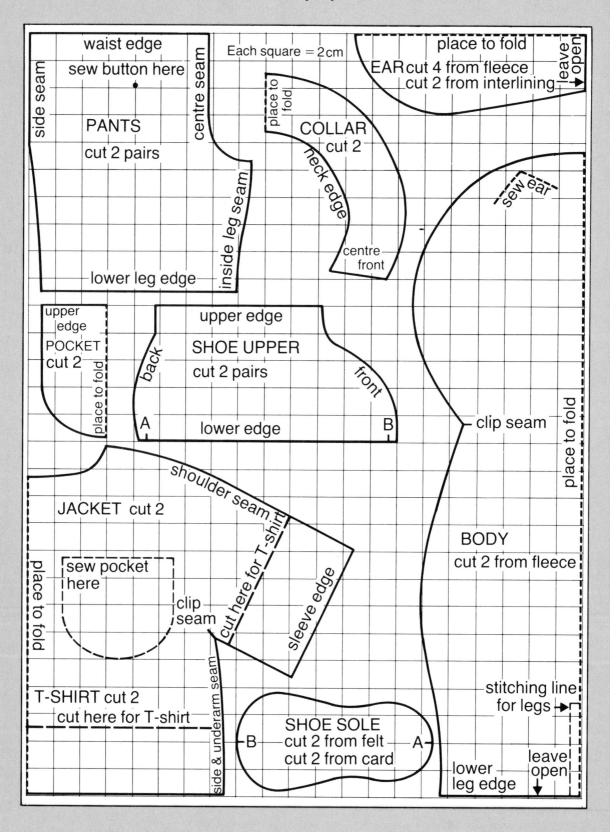

waist edge

sew button here

side seam

centre seam

Each square = 2cm

place to fold

EAR cut 4 from fleece
cut 2 from interlining

leave open

PANTS
cut 2 pairs

place to fold

COLLAR
cut 2

neck edge

inside leg seam

sew ear

lower leg edge

centre front

clip seam

place to fold

upper edge

POCKET
cut 2

place to fold

upper edge

SHOE UPPER
cut 2 pairs

back

front

A

lower edge

B

BODY
cut 2 from fleece

shoulder seam

JACKET cut 2

cut here for T-shirt

clip seam

sleeve edge

place to fold

sew pocket here

T-SHIRT cut 2
cut here for T-shirt

side & underarm seam

B

SHOE SOLE
cut 2 from felt
cut 2 from card

A

stitching line for legs

lower leg edge

leave open

Dancing Clown

This floppy clown, about 97 cm (38 in) tall, is the perfect dancing partner for a small girl when the elastic loops on his feet are slipped over his partner's shoes. He also makes an ideal mascot doll for older children and adults

Clown

You will need: 1·10 m (1⅛ yd) of cotton stockinette – tubular knit 57 cm (22½ in) wide, opening out to 114 cm (45 in) width, (see List of Suppliers on page 254). Alternatively you can use cuttings off discarded plain-knit vests and T-shirts as explained in the notes below. 500 g (1 lb) stuffing; 2 m (2 yd) of 1·5 cm (½ in) wide tape (to tie round neck and wrists and to anchor hair); a 5 by 50 cm (2 by 20 in) strip of cotton fabric (to reinforce body where arms are sewn on); 50 g ball of chunky knitting yarn for hair; two 1·5 cm (⅝ in) diameter black trouser buttons for eyes; scraps of pink felt for nose; black, blue and red thread for facial features; red pencil.

Notes: If you are making the doll from discarded vests or T-shirts, the garments available may not be large enough to cut out the pieces given in the instructions. However the pieces can be joined as necessary to make up the sizes required. For example a 38 by 56 cm (15 by 22 in) piece is needed for the body and head; this could be made up by cutting two 38 by 28·5 cm (15 by 11¼ in) pieces then joining them along one 38 cm (15 in) edge taking a 5 mm (¼ in) seam. Do take care to cut out the pieces so that the most stretch in the fabric lies in the direction stated in the instructions.

For safety, when making the doll for a very young child, use felt circles instead of buttons for the eyes and pompons in place of bells. Take 5 mm (¼ in) seams on all the doll pieces.

Body and head: Cut a 38 by 56 cm (15 by 22 in) piece of stockinette with most stretch in the fabric going across the 38 cm (15 in) width. With pencil, mark a line for neck 20 cm (8 in) down from and parallel to one 38 cm (15 in) edge, on right side of fabric – this edge will be the top of the head. Join long edges and turn right side out. Gather the top 38 cm (15 in) edge tightly and fasten off thread.

Stuff head very firmly down to neck line, then stuff remainder of body slightly more loosely, making a sausage shape 46 cm (18 in) in circumference. Turn in remaining raw edge 5 mm (¼ in), bring edges together and oversew for lower end of body. Note that the 56 cm (22 in) seam should be positioned to come at centre back of doll. Tie a length of tape as tightly as possible round marked neck line – the head should flop slightly above neck.

Face: Mark on centre position of each eye 9·5 cm (3¾ in) up from neck and set 5 cm (2 in) apart. Work a blue cross stitch, 2·5 cm (1 in) square for each eye with the mark at the centre of the cross. Work two black eyelashes in one quarter of each cross as shown in illustration.

Using a darning needle and very strong thread sew on buttons for eyes, taking thread through head from back close to one side, then through each button (with right side of button against face), then back through head; knot securely, pulling thread tight to depress buttons slightly into face.

From pink felt cut a 5 mm by 1·5 cm (¼ by ½ in) oval for nose and sew in place. With red thread work a U-shaped mouth in back stitch, 5 cm (2 in) up from neck, then oversew, working back through each stitch. Colour cheeks with pencil.

Hair: For fringe cut a 13 cm (5 in) length of tape. Wind yarn four times round two fingers of one hand, slip loops off fingers then machine stitch one end of loops to the tape. Repeat this, machining loops to tape as they are made until tape is covered. Sew tape to forehead with loops ending about 1·5 cm (½ in) above eyes.

For remainder of hair cut a 33 cm (13 in)

length of tape; make as for fringe, winding yarn round four fingers instead of two to make longer loops. Sew tape round head at back to meet fringe at front of head. Note that remainder of head will be hidden by hat later on.

Legs: For each leg cut a 20 by 46 cm (8 by 18 in) strip of stockinette with most stretch in the fabric going across the 20 cm (8 in) width. Join the long edges of each strip then turn right side out. Gather each leg tightly at one end for ankle then fasten off thread.

Stuff legs lightly so that they are flexible. Turn in top edges 5 mm ($\frac{1}{4}$ in), bring them together and oversew, then sew tops of legs securely to lower edge of body.

Arms: For each arm cut an 18 by 41 cm (7 by 16 in) strip of stockinette, with most stretch in fabric going across the 18 cm (7 in) width. Join long edges of each strip then continue stitching round one short end rounding off corners to make hand. Trim fabric at corners then turn arms right side out.

Stuff arms and finish off remaining raw edges as for legs. To make wrists, tie lengths of tape tightly round arms 10 cm (4 in) from ends of hand. Make thumbs by taking a stitch round through each hand.

To reinforce body before sewing on arms, sew the strip of cotton fabric round body about 2·5 cm (1 in) down from neck. Now sew tops of arms to each side of body 4 cm ($1\frac{1}{2}$ in) down from neck.

The clothes

You will need: 1·90 m (2 yd) of 91 cm (36 in) wide striped fabric (it doesn't matter whether stripes run across width or down length of fabric – see diagrams 1 and 2); 1·40 m ($1\frac{1}{2}$ yd) of 91 cm (36 in) wide contrast fabric for frills and rosette trimmings; 23 cm ($\frac{1}{4}$ yd) of 91 cm (36 in) wide fabric for shoes, hat band and rosette trimmings; small pieces of card and felt for shoe soles; stuffing for shoes; 1·40 m ($1\frac{1}{2}$ yd) of ric-rac braid; 30 cm (12 in) of 1·5 cm ($\frac{5}{8}$ in) wide elastic; 5 bells; adhesive; metric graph paper.

Notes: The shoe patterns are printed full size and can be traced directly off the page. To make the full size tunic pattern, copy the pattern shown in the diagram, onto graph paper noting that one square on the diagram equals 5 cm on the graph paper.

Take 1·5 cm ($\frac{5}{8}$ in) seams on the tunic pieces; other seams as stated in the instructions. Join all pieces with right side of fabric facing unless otherwise stated.

Shoes: Cut two pairs of shoe uppers. Join them in pairs taking 5 mm ($\frac{1}{4}$ in) seams at back and front. Clip seams at curves then turn shoes right side out. Cut two soles from card and two from felt. Place a card sole inside each shoe matching points A and B. Glue lower edges of shoes 5 mm ($\frac{1}{4}$ in) onto the card soles.

Stuff shoes firmly and glue the felt soles to the card soles to cover raw edges of shoe fabric. Turn in upper edges of shoes 1·5 cm ($\frac{1}{2}$ in) and place each shoe at ankle edge of each leg. Tuck gathered leg ends inside upper edge of each shoe and oversew top edges of shoes to legs.

Cut two 15 cm (6 in) lengths of elastic; sew ends of each elastic to sides of shoes (as shown on shoe upper pattern) to make loops. Now glue ric-rac braid round shoes to cover ends of elastic.

Tunic: Cut out two pairs of tunic pieces using the pattern (placing pattern on fabric as shown in diagram 1 or 2 according to direction of stripes). Join each pair of tunic pieces at centre front or back seams, then join the pairs to each other at overarm, underarm and sides. Finally bring centre seams together and join inside leg seams. Turn tunic right side out.

Wrist frills: Cut two 13 by 40 cm (5 by 16 in) strips of contrast fabric. Join short ends of each strip, then fold strips in half with right sides outside bringing long raw edges together. Sew a frill strip to each wrist edge of tunic with right sides facing, raw edges level, and taking a 5 mm ($\frac{1}{4}$ in) seam. Press seam towards tunic.

Ankle frills: Cut two 13 by 50 cm (5 by 20 in) strips of contrast fabric. Make and sew to ankle edges of tunic as instructed for wrist frills.

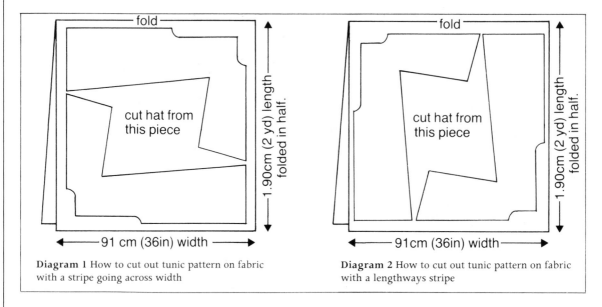

Diagram 1 How to cut out tunic pattern on fabric with a stripe going across width

Diagram 2 How to cut out tunic pattern on fabric with a lengthways stripe

To assemble doll and tunic: Place tunic on doll, turn in neck edge 1·5 cm ($\frac{5}{8}$ in) and, using strong thread, gather round close to folded edge. Pull up gathers tightly to fit neck then fasten off. Gather wrist and ankle edges in same way, running the gathering threads round through frill fabric close to seams. Catch frills through gathers to wrists and ankles all round.

Neck frills: For widest neck frill use a 23 by 136 cm (9 by 54 in) strip of fabric, joining pieces as necessary to make required length. Join all short edges then fold strip as for other frills. Turn in remaining raw edges 5 mm ($\frac{1}{4}$ in) and run a strong gathering thread round close to this edge through all thicknesses. Put frill on doll then pull up gathers to fit neck and fasten off.

For next neck frill use an 18 by 91 cm (7 by 36 in) strip, and for smallest frill use a 13 by 91 cm (5 by 36 in) strip. Make frills and sew to doll as before.

Hat: Cut two 23 by 28 cm (9 by 11 in) pieces of striped fabric and two 5 by 28 cm (2 by 11 in) strips of fabric to match shoes. Sew the narrow strips to hat pieces along the 28 cm (11 in) edges taking 5 mm ($\frac{1}{4}$ in) seam (to form band at lower edge of hat). Sew ric-rac to centre of each narrow strip of fabric. Now join side edges of hat pieces, then tightly gather up top edge and fasten off thread. Turn hat right side out.

Put hat on doll's head to cover upper looped ends of hair, turning in lower edge of hat 5 mm ($\frac{1}{4}$ in). Slip stitch lower edge of hat to head all round. Let the hat flop to one side then sew in position with a few stitches to hold in place.

Rosettes: Cut a 15 cm (6 in) diameter circle of contrast fabric for a rosette. Turn in raw edge 5 mm ($\frac{1}{4}$ in) and gather all round, pull up gathers tightly and fasten off. Sew this to gathered top of hat with a bell.

Make four more rosettes in same way – two from 18 cm (7 in) diameter circles of contrast fabric and two 10 cm (4 in) diameter circles of fabric to match shoes. Sew these in pairs to front of tunic, then sew a bell over each rosette.

For shoes, make two rosettes as for hat rosettes. Sew one to point of each shoe with a bell.

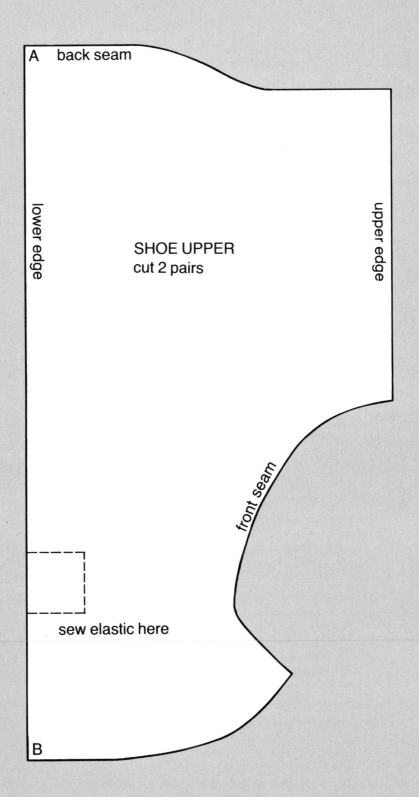

A back seam

lower edge

SHOE UPPER
cut 2 pairs

upper edge

front seam

sew elastic here

B

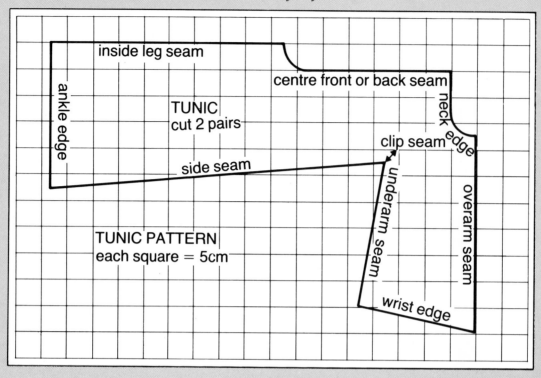

inside leg seam

centre front or back seam

ankle edge

TUNIC
cut 2 pairs

neck edge

clip seam

side seam

underarm seam

overarm seam

TUNIC PATTERN
each square = 5cm

wrist edge

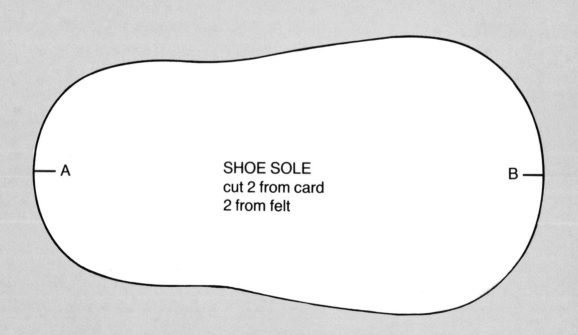

A

SHOE SOLE
cut 2 from card
2 from felt

B

Teaching Teddy

This 35·5 cm (14 in) tall teddy stands securely on a stiffened circular base and she wears clothes that a toddler can learn to take off and put back on. There's how to tie a bow (the bonnet ribbons), fasten a snap fastener (on the knitted shawl), handle hooks and eyes (on the apron), cope with a button and zip fastener (on the skirt), and make that lovely tearing noise with Velcro hook and loop fastener on the underskirt.

You will need: For body and sleeves, 40 cm ($\frac{1}{2}$ yd) of 91 cm (36 in) wide fabric (this amount will make the apron too); 1·2 m ($1\frac{3}{8}$ yd) of 3 cm ($1\frac{1}{4}$ in) wide lace edging; for head and arms, 30 cm ($\frac{3}{8}$ yd) of 138 cm (54 in) wide fur fabric (enough to make two toys); 375 g ($\frac{3}{4}$ lb) of stuffing; strong card for the base (glue several layers of thin card together if necessary); strong thread for gathering; scraps of blue and black felt for facial features; metric graph paper; adhesive.

Notes: Copy patterns off the diagram on page 239 on to graph paper, square by square; each square on diagram = 2 cm. Mark on all details.

Cut out fur fabric pieces with the smooth stroke of fur pile in the direction shown on each pattern piece. 5 mm ($\frac{1}{4}$ in) seams are allowed on fur fabric pieces, and 1 cm ($\frac{3}{8}$ in) seams on all other pieces unless otherwise stated. Join pieces with right sides facing.

The teddy

Body: Cut a 28 by 45 cm (11 by $17\frac{3}{4}$ in) strip of body fabric. Join short edges. For the base cut a 13 cm ($5\frac{1}{8}$ in) diameter circle of card and a 15 cm (6 in) diameter circle of body fabric. Gather round raw edge of fabric circle, place the card circle at centre, pull up gathers tightly and fasten off thread.

Turn in and press one remaining long raw edge of body, then oversew this edge to the fabric round edge of base. Turn body right side out. Stuff body, run a gathering thread round the remaining raw edge, then pull up gathers tightly and fasten off.

Head: Cut a pair of head pieces from fur fabric. Cut the head gusset across the width of fabric, testing the pile of fur fabric for the smoothest stroke before cutting.

Mark mouth lines on wrong side of the head pieces, and also mark centre point of eye on each piece with coloured thread on right side of fabric. Machine stitch along each marked mouth line six times, using black thread, to make a thick line.

Join head pieces at centre front, then insert head gusset between top of head pieces, matching points A. Turn head right side out and stuff firmly, especially at snout. Gather the neck edge of head in same way as for body. Clip the fur pile short above and below the mouth line and around the snout.

Place head on top of body, matching gathers, and hold it in place with darning needles pushed through the head and body fabric. Ladderstitch the head to the body where they touch, working round two or three times to make them secure.

Ears: Cut four ear pieces from fur fabric and oversew them together in pairs, leaving lower edges open. Turn right side out. Oversew lower edges of each ear together, pulling stitches tightly to gather slightly. Sew the ears to sides of head, with inner edges touching gusset seams.

Face: Cut two nose pieces from black felt and glue them together. Sew nose in place at end of snout.

Cut two pupils from black felt and work a highlight on each one in white thread, as shown on pattern. Cut two eyes from blue felt, then stick pupils to eyes. Trim fur pile short around the marked centre points for eyes, then stick eyes securely in place.

Arms and sleeves: Cut two pairs of arm pieces from fur fabric. Join them in pairs, leaving upper edges open between dots, as shown on pattern. Turn arms right side out and stuff lower portions, then fill each upper part very lightly. Oversew upper raw edges of each arm together.

For each sleeve, cut a 9 by 20 cm ($3\frac{1}{2}$ by 8 in) strip of the same fabric as used for the body. Cut two 30 cm ($11\frac{3}{4}$ in) lengths of lace edging. Turn in one long edge of each sleeve and gather lace edging pieces to fit, then sew in place. Turn in remaining raw edges of sleeves and press.

Slip a sleeve over each arm so that top edge of arm is 5 mm ($\frac{1}{4}$ in) below the top edge of sleeve (see diagram). Now catch the sleeve to arm at the position shown in the diagram, with strong oversewing stitches.

Bring top edges of sleeves together and run a gathering thread along through all sleeve thicknesses. Pull up gathers to measure 3 cm ($1\frac{1}{4}$ in) and fasten off. Gather round lower edges of sleeves at tops of lace edging, pull up to fit arms and fasten off. Sew gathers to arms. Sew the gathered top edges of sleeves securely to each side of the body, 2 cm ($\frac{3}{4}$ in) down from neck.

For neck frill, cut a 60 cm ($23\frac{1}{2}$ in) length of lace edging. Join the ends then slip it over Teddy's head. Gather lace up round neck, then pull up gathers tightly and fasten off.

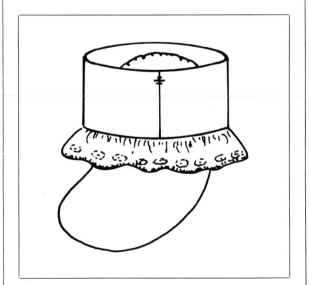

Catch each sleeve to an arm at top of seam, at position of the three small stitches

The clothes

Bonnet

You will need: 30 cm ($\frac{3}{8}$ yd) of 91 cm (36 in) wide fabric; a small piece of firm Vilene iron-on interfacing; 70 cm ($\frac{3}{4}$ yd) of 2·5 cm (1 in) wide ribbon.

To make: Cut two bonnet brim pieces from fabric and two from interfacing, placing the edge indicated on pattern to a fold each time. Iron interfacing pieces on to fabric pieces. Join brim pieces, taking a 5 mm ($\frac{1}{4}$ in) seam and leaving inner edges open. Trim seam, turn right side out and press. Tack raw edges together. Stitch round, 1 cm ($\frac{3}{8}$ in) away from outer edge of brim.

For bonnet side piece, cut a 9 by 70 cm ($3\frac{1}{2}$ by $27\frac{1}{2}$ in) strip of fabric. Narrowly hem short edges. Gather one long edge to fit inner edge of brim and stitch it in place, taking a 5 mm ($\frac{1}{4}$ in) seam. Trim seam, then bind it with a 2 cm ($\frac{3}{4}$ in) wide bias strip of fabric.

Cut bonnet back piece, placing edge of pattern indicated to fold in fabric. Narrowly hem lower edge. Gather the remaining raw edge of bonnet side piece to fit curved edge of bonnet back piece, and stitch in place. Trim and neaten this seam.

Cut ribbon in two pieces and sew one to each side of bonnet on outside, just behind the brim, forming the end of ribbon into a small loop.

Petticoat

You will need: 30 cm ($\frac{3}{8}$ yd) of 91 cm (36 in) wide fabric; 1 m (1 yd) of lace edging; a small piece of Velcro hook and loop fastener.

To make: For the skirt, cut a 20 by 91 cm (8 by 36 in) strip of fabric. Fold over one long edge 5 cm (2 in) and press. Stitch along, 5 mm ($\frac{1}{4}$ in) away from fold to make the first tuck. Make another tuck in the same way, 2 cm ($\frac{3}{4}$ in) above first. Narrowly hem long edge nearest to tucks and sew on lace edging. Join short edges of skirt strip from hem edge, leaving 7 cm ($2\frac{3}{4}$ in) open at top of seam. Press seam open and neaten raw edges of opening. Gather waist edge of petticoat to fit around Teddy.

For waistband, cut a 5 by 48 cm (2 by 19 in) strip of fabric. Bind the gathered edge of skirt with waistband strip, taking 5 mm ($\frac{1}{4}$ in) seams and letting the excess length of waistband extend at one end of skirt opening, for overlapped fastening. Sew Velcro to this overlap.

Skirt

You will need: 30 cm ($\frac{3}{8}$ yd) of 91 cm (36 in) wide fabric; 1 m (1 yd) of ric-rac braid; a 2 cm ($\frac{3}{4}$ in) diameter button; a 10 cm (4 in) zip fastener.

To make: For the skirt, cut a strip of fabric 18 by 91 cm (7 by 36 in). Cut waistband as for petticoat. Stitch ric-rac along skirt strip,

2 cm ($\frac{3}{4}$ in) away from one long edge, which will be the hem edge of skirt. Join short edges of skirt from hem, leaving 10·5 cm ($4\frac{1}{4}$ in) open at top of seam for zip fastener. Insert zip into open edges.

Narrowly hem lower edge, then gather waist edge and attach waistband as for petticoat. Make a buttonhole in the extended end of waistband and sew button to other end, to correspond.

Apron

You will need: Fabric left over from making body; 1 m (1 yd) of narrow braid; two large hooks and eyes.

To make: For apron, cut a piece of fabric 12 by 18 cm ($4\frac{3}{4}$ by 7 in). Round off corners at one long edge. Narrowly hem edges, except

for long straight edge. Sew braid round the hemmed edges. Gather raw edge to measure 10 cm (4 in).

For waistband, cut a strip of fabric 6 by 48 cm (2½ by 19 in). Turn in all raw edges 5 mm (¼ in) and press. Fold the waistband in half down length and stitch edges together, inserting gathered edge of apron at centre of waistband. Sew hooks and eyes to ends.

Shawl

You will need: A small ball of 4-ply yarn; a pair of 5½ mm [No 5, USA 8] knitting needles; one large snap fastener.

To make: Cast on 90 stitches. Work in garter stitch (every row knit), decreasing 1 stitch at each end of every row until 2 stitches remain. Knit these 2 together then fasten off. Sew snap fastener halves to points.

Shopping bag

You will need: Scraps of fabric, iron-on interfacing and trimming.
To make: Cut two 10 cm (4 in) squares of fabric and two of interfacing. Iron interfacing pieces on to fabric pieces. Join the squares, taking a 5 mm (¼ in) seam and leaving one edge open.

Keeping the wrong side out, open up and flatten seams, then at each lower corner, bring side and lower seams together and stitch across at right angles to seams, 1·5 cm (⅝ in) away from corners. Trim off corners. Turn in remaining raw edge 1 cm (⅜ in) twice, and stitch in place. Turn the bag right side out and sew on trimming as shown.

For the handle, cut a strip of fabric 4 by 18 cm (1½ by 7 in). Turn in all raw edges 1 cm (⅜ in) and press. Bring long edges together, then stitch all round strip. Sew the ends of the handle to the top of the bag at sides, inside the top edge.

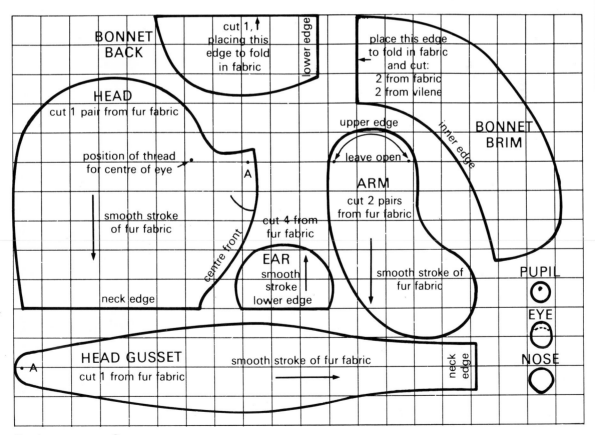

Each square = 2 cm

Easter Bunny Puppet

This soft toy bunny, just 28 cm (11 in) high, also doubles as a hand puppet. The body is lightly stuffed, with an opening at the back allowing a hand to be put inside, so that the fingers and thumb can work the bunny's hands. There are also plenty of clothes for dressing up the toy.

You will need: Oddments of the following – fur fabric; thin cotton fabric for lining body and dress; printed fabrics; ribbon and trimmings for dress, bonnet, nightdress and pop-over pinafore; stuffing; brown and black felt and black embroidery thread for facial features; white fur fabric for tail; four small buttons and short lengths of elastic.

Notes: 5 mm ($\frac{1}{4}$ in) seams are allowed on all pieces unless otherwise stated.

The patterns are printed full-size on pages 244–6 for tracing directly off the page, but note that body front, base and dress front should be traced on to folded paper, placing fold to dot-and-dash line on pattern. After tracing, cut out and open up the folded pieces to give full-size patterns.

Cut out fur fabric pieces with smooth stroke of fur pile in the directions shown by arrows on the patterns. When cutting a *pair* of pieces, be sure to reverse the pattern when cutting the second piece.

The bunny

To make the body: Cut one body front from fur fabric and one from lining fabric. Mark arm darts on wrong side of fur fabric piece only, then stitch and trim darts. Tack lining and fur fabric pieces together round edges, wrong sides facing, except for lower edges.

Cut a pair of body back pieces from fur fabric and a pair from lining fabric. At centre back edge of one fur fabric piece, sew a loop of elastic to right side of fabric as shown on pattern (check that the loop will slip over your size of button). Now join centre back edges of each lining to centre back edge of

each fur fabric piece, with *right* sides of fabric together. Turn linings over to wrong sides of fur fabric pieces and tack raw edges together except for lower edges. Join centre back edges of body back pieces by oversewing them together on lining side, from A to neck edge, and from B to lower edge.

Now join body back to front at sides, round arms to neck edges, with fur fabrics together. Clip seams at corners. Lay body aside.

To make the head: From fur fabric cut a pair of head pieces and one head gusset. Join head pieces from point C through point E to neck edge. Now insert gusset round top and back of head, matching points C on gusset and head. Turn head right side out.

To assemble body and head: Slip neck edge of head right through neck edge of body (*see diagram 1, opposite*), with head inside body and matching points D and E. Backstitch head to body at neck seamlines. Turn right side out.

Stuff head firmly through the neck opening. Gather round raw neck edge of head (you can do this through centre back edges of body), then pull up gathers tightly and fasten off, to hold head stuffing in place.

Stuff all body pieces very lightly and evenly, inserting stuffing through lower edges between fur fabric pieces and linings. Tack linings to fur fabric at lower raw edges.

To insert the base: Cut one base piece from fur fabric and one from lining fabric. Tack them, wrong sides facing, around raw edges, pushing a little stuffing inside before completing tacking. Turn body wrong side out through back opening. Pin, then backstitch base to lower edge of body, fur fabric sides together and matching points F, G and H. Turn body right side out and sew button to back edge to correspond with elastic loop.

To make the tail: Cut, gather and stuff a 6 cm (2½ in) diameter circle of white fur fabric. Sew it to centre back of body, between points B and H.

To make the feet: Cut four foot pieces from fur fabric and join them in pairs round outer edges. Turn and stuff firmly, then oversew inner edges together. Sew inner edges to edge of base and body at front, spacing feet about 2 cm (¾ in) apart.

To make the ears: Cut four fur fabric ear pieces and join them in pairs, leaving lower edges open; turn right side out and fold ears in half at lower edges, then oversew raw edges together as folded. Sew lower edges of ears to sides of head, about 2 cm (¾ in) below head gusset, then sew again at gusset seamline.

To make the facial features: First trim fur pile slightly shorter all over face area. Cut nose from brown felt and pin it in place at the end of head gusset. Using double embroidery thread, work a stitch for mouth,

2 cm (¾ in) below nose, starting and fastening off thread underneath nose. Sew nose in place. Cut two eyes from black felt and work a highlight on each one in white thread. Sew eyes in place 3 cm (1¼ in) apart, each side of nose.

The clothes

To make the dress: Cut dress front and one pair of backs from dress fabric. Sew elastic loop to right side of one dress back, where shown on pattern. Join front to backs at side edges, then sew on trimming above seam allowance at lower edge. Turn in seam allowance at all shoulder edges and press.

Cut and make dress lining in the same way, omitting elastic loop and trimming. Join lining to dress at centre back, armhole and neck. Clip curves in seams. Turn right side out and press. Slipstitch front shoulder edges of dress and lining to back shoulder edges.

For hem frill, cut a strip of dress fabric 5 by 60 cm (2 by 24 in). Make narrow hems on one long and both short edges. Gather the remaining long raw edge of frill to fit lower edge of dress and sew in place (leaving lining free), with right sides facing. Now turn in lower edge of lining and slipstitch it over seam. Sew button to back edge, opposite loop.

To make the nightdress: Add 4 cm (1½ in) to lower edge of dress front and back patterns, then make exactly as for dress. Sew trimming across yoke of nightdress and over armhole edges, then sew ribbon bow to front.

To make the pinafore: Use dress patterns but add 5 mm (¼ in) to side edges, trim 5 mm (¼ in) off lower edges of patterns and cut front neckline along dotted line shown on pattern. Make as for dress, but instead of frill at lower edge, sew on lace edging, easing it to fit round curve instead of gathering. Add ribbon bow.

To make the Easter bonnet: Draw and cut out paper patterns for bonnet and bonnet

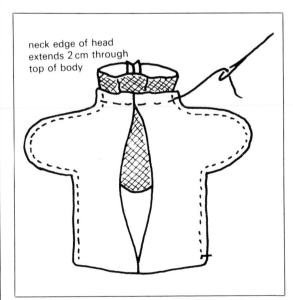

neck edge of head
extends 2 cm through
top of body

Diagram 1

back to sizes shown in diagram 2 (*right*). Cut earhole out of bonnet pattern as shown.

Now cut one bonnet piece from fabric, placing pattern to fold in fabric as indicated. Cut out earholes and bind them with narrow bias strips of fabric. Cut bonnet back from fabric. Join back edge of bonnet to sides and curved top edge of bonnet back, clipping straight edge of bonnet to fit round curves in bonnet back. Neaten seam to prevent fraying. Make a narrow hem on lower edge of bonnet to form casing for elastic. Thread elastic through to gather lower edge slightly, then sew the elastic to each end of casing.

For bonnet frill cut a strip of fabric 7 by 40 cm (2¾ by 16 in). Fold it in half down length, right side inside; join short ends rounding off corners at folded edge. Turn right side out, gather and sew raw edges to face edge of bonnet. Bind raw edges with a bias strip. Add ribbons to tie under chin.

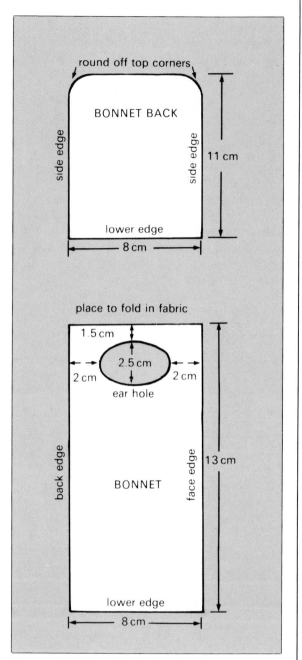

Diagram 2   Patterns for the bonnet

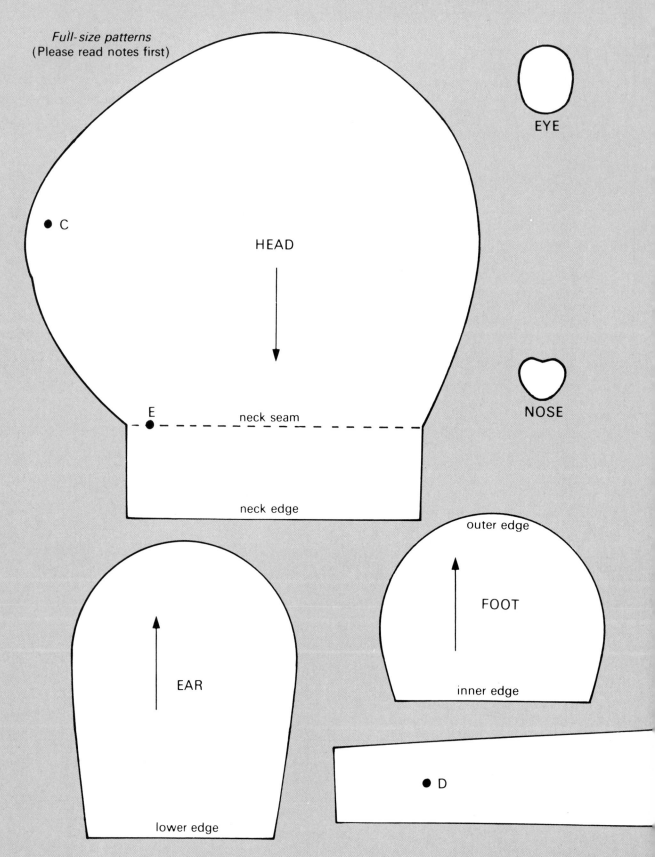

Full-size patterns
(Please read notes first)

EYE

● C

HEAD

NOSE

E

●

neck seam

neck edge

outer edge

FOOT

EAR

inner edge

● D

lower edge

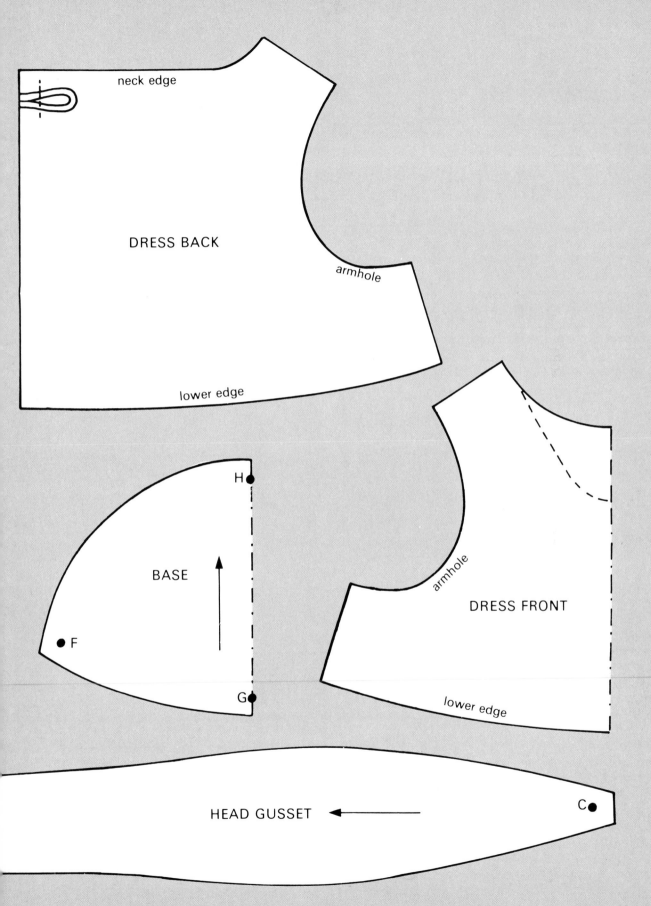

neck edge

DRESS BACK

armhole

lower edge

H

BASE

F

G

DRESS FRONT

armhole

lower edge

HEAD GUSSET

C

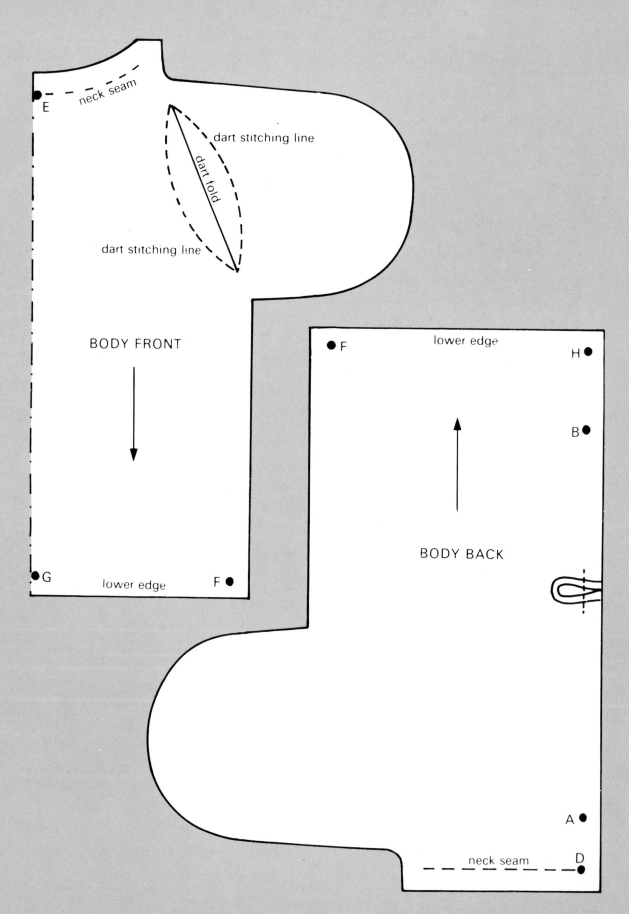

BODY FRONT

neck seam

dart stitching line

dart fold

dart stitching line

lower edge

BODY BACK

lower edge

neck seam

E

G

F

F

H

B

A

D

Bedtime Favourites

No more tears at bedtime! Granny the hot water bottle cover and Happy Clown the pyjama case will make bedtime funtime. Granny is about 46 cm (18 in) high and the clown is 53 cm (21 in) high; they are both easy to make from scraps of dress fabrics

Granny

You will need: 25 cm ($\frac{3}{8}$ yd) of 122 cm (48 in) wide white fleecy fabric; 35 cm ($\frac{1}{2}$ yd) of printed fabric and 1·40 m (1$\frac{1}{2}$ yd) of lace edging for the dress; small pieces of pink fabric for the face and hands; scraps of black and pink felt and plain fabric; red, black, white and brown thread for embroidery; a small piece of ribbon for the bow; 3 snap fasteners; metric graph paper.

Notes: Take 1 cm ($\frac{3}{8}$ in) seams and turnings except where stated otherwise. Join fabrics with right sides facing. Copy the pattern shapes separately on to metric graph paper. Each square on diagram equals 5 cm. Cut out the shapes and use as pattern pieces.

To make: Cut the face piece from pink fabric (following the broken lines on body pattern) and mark on all facial features as shown on the pattern. Clip the upper edge then turn it in and tack.

Embroider the facial features as follows: for cheeks, use red thread and small straight stitches worked in spirals radiating from the centres. Work spectacles in chain stitch using brown thread. Work the mouth in back stitch using red thread then work back, oversewing through each stitch. Cut eyes from black felt, sew in place then embroider a small white cross on each for the highlight as shown in illustration. Cut the nose from pink felt and sew it in place.

Cut two body pieces from fleecy fabric then sew the face piece to one of them with its top edge in the position shown on the body pattern and stitching round close to the edge. Now, using black thread, machine stitch lines on hair and bun as shown in illustration, on front and back body pieces. Hem lower edge of each body piece taking a 1 cm then a 2 cm ($\frac{3}{8}$ in then $\frac{3}{4}$ in) turning.

For the dress, cut two 26 by 34 cm (10$\frac{1}{4}$ by 13$\frac{1}{2}$ in) pieces of fabric. Turn in one long edge of each piece and gather until it measures 25 cm (9$\frac{3}{4}$ in). Hem the remaining long edges. Stitch the gathered edge of each dress piece to the body at position shown on body pattern. Tack side edges of dress to side edges of each body piece.

Cut four shoe pieces from plain fabric and cut two black felt pieces to shape (see dotted lines on shoe pattern). Sew these felt pieces to two of the shoe pieces. Join shoe pieces in pairs leaving upper edges open, trim seams, turn right side out then turn in upper edges and tack. Slip these upper edges 1 cm ($\frac{3}{8}$ in) under hem edge of dress at front, spacing them about 3 cm (1$\frac{1}{4}$ in) apart. Stitch upper edges of shoes in place. Sew lace trim to hem of each dress piece.

For each sleeve, cut a 12 by 20 cm (4$\frac{3}{4}$ by 8 in) strip of fabric. Join short edges of each piece and turn right side out. Cut two pairs of hand pieces from pink fabric. Join in pairs leaving upper edges open, trim seams and turn right side out. Turn in one raw edge of each sleeve and gather to fit 1 cm ($\frac{3}{8}$ in) over top of hand. Slip raw edges of hands in position inside sleeves and stitch through all

Each square = 5cm

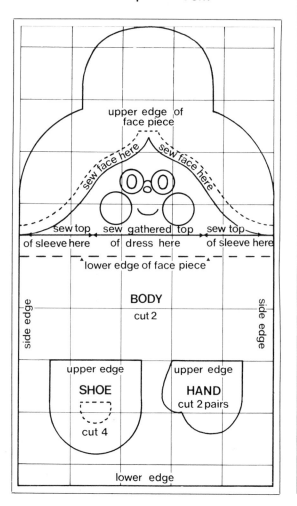

thicknesses at gathered edge. Sew lace trimming to gathers. Turn in remaining raw edges of sleeves and gather through all thicknesses to fit in positions shown on body pattern. Stitch top edges of sleeves in place then sew lace trim to neck edge of each dress piece.

Join body pieces all round, leaving lower edges open and catching side edges of dress in seams but taking care not to catch sleeves in seams. Sew snap fasteners to lower edges of body pieces and a small ribbon bow to front of bun.

The Clown

You will need: Small pieces of white stockinette for head and hands (cuttings from an old T-shirt can be used); 50 cm of 91 cm ($\frac{5}{8}$ yd of 36 in) wide fabric for body and sleeves; 40 cm of 91 cm ($\frac{1}{2}$ yd of 36 in) wide fabric for frills; small pieces of felt for hat and shoes; scraps of black, pink and red felt plus black, white and red thread for facial features; a bell or bobble for top of cap; three bobbles for front of body; 250 g ($\frac{1}{2}$ lb) of stuffing; 35 cm ($\frac{1}{2}$ yd) of trimming for hat; three large snap fasteners; chunky yarn for hair; adhesive; metric graph paper.

Notes: Make patterns as for Granny. Cut out head and hands with most stretch in stockinette in direction shown on patterns. Take 1 cm ($\frac{3}{8}$ in) seams and turnings throughout. Join fabrics with right sides facing.

To make the head: Cut two head pieces from stockinette. Join the side edges then run a gathering thread round 1 cm ($\frac{3}{8}$ in) from the top edge. Pull up gathers tightly and fasten off securely. Turn head right side out and stuff to measure about 36 cm (14 in) round. Bring neck edges together and run a gathering thread through both thicknesses along the dotted line shown on pattern. Pull up gathers until neck measures 5 cm (2 in) across then fasten off.

Cut nose from red felt, eyes from black felt and cheeks from pink felt. Work a highlight on each eye using white thread as shown in the illustration. Use dabs of adhesive to hold the features in position as follows: place nose 7 cm ($2\frac{3}{4}$ in) up from the neck edge; eyes at either side of the nose and 4 cm ($1\frac{1}{2}$ in) apart; cheeks below eyes as illustrated. Work a shallow W shape 2 cm ($\frac{3}{4}$ in) below nose using red thread. Sew all features in place then work four straight black stitches out from each eye to form a cross as illustrated.

For hair, wind yarn five times round three fingers then slip loops off fingers. Back stitch tops of loops to right side of head, covering the seam and level with top of eye. Continue making loops in this way round back of head to other side. Repeat this process making another row of loops 2 cm ($\frac{3}{4}$ in) above the first row. When you reach the other side of the head, continue making loops across the forehead, winding the yarn round two fingers instead of three for the fringe.

Cut four hat pieces from felt and join them in pairs at one side edge then join the pairs at the remaining side edges. Trim seams and turn right side out. Stuff top of hat and place on head lapping tops of yarn loops with lower edge of hat. Sew hat to head all round adding more stuffing to shape it if necessary. Sew bell to top of hat and trimming to lower edge.

The hands: Cut two pairs of hand pieces and join them leaving wrist edges open. Trim seams and turn right side out. Stuff hands then run gathering threads round wrist edges. Pull up gathers and fasten off.

The shoes: Make as for hands, gathering upper edges.

The body: Cut out body pieces and sleeves as stated on patterns. Join body back pieces from A to B and C to D. Press seam to one side then turn in and stitch back raw edges to neaten. Join sleeves in pairs at upper and underarm edges. Turn right side out and tack armhole edges of each sleeve together pulling stitches to gather to fit between points indicated on body pattern. Tack armhole edges of sleeves to side edges of front body piece having raw edges level. Now join body back to front at side edges catching armhole edges of sleeves in seams. Join front to back at inside leg edges then clip seam at point D. Turn body right side out and sew snap fasteners to back edges.

Turn in neck edge of body and gather. Pull up gathers to fit round gathered neck edge of head then fasten off. Sew gathered neck edge of body securely to neck all round. Turn in and gather wrist and ankle edges of body in the same way pulling up gathers to fit over hands and shoes lapping them about 2 cm ($\frac{3}{4}$ in). Push a little stuffing inside each sleeve then sew gathered edges of the clown's body to the hands and shoes all round.

Sew bobbles to front of body.

The frills: For neck frill cut a 16 by 91 cm ($6\frac{1}{4}$ by 36 in) strip of fabric. Join long edges of strip then turn right side out. Turn in short edges at ends of strip then slip stitch ends together. Run a gathering thread round the seamed edge of frill and place frill round neck. Pull up gathers to fit neck tightly then fasten off.

For each wrist frill cut an 8 by 35 cm (3 by $13\frac{3}{4}$ in) strip of fabric and for each ankle frill cut a 10 by 45 cm (4 by $17\frac{3}{4}$ in) strip of fabric. Make as for the neck frill and after placing in position sew gathered edges of these frills to the wrists and ankles of the doll.

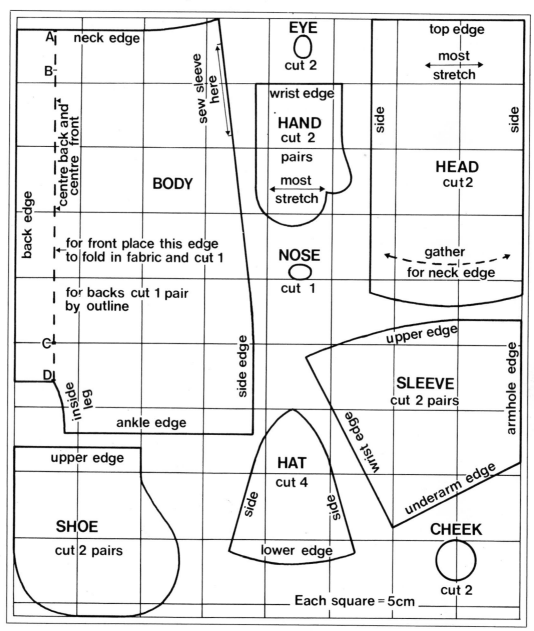

Christmas Tree Trims

These decorations for the Christmas season are fun, colourful and quick to knit. You can make them to hang on the Christmas tree or as amusing stocking fillers for the children. To give an indication of size, the lollypops measure 11 cm [4¼ in] in diameter and the garlands are 7 cm [2¾ in] in diameter.

You will need: Oddments of double knitting yarn in colours illustrated; a pair of 3¼ mm [No 10, USA 3] knitting needles; a little stuffing; large and small guipure flowers; flat wooden lolly sticks about 6 mm [¼ in] wide; adhesive.

Abbreviations: See page 17, as well as below – rev st-st, reverse st-st [P is right side of work]; m 1 – make one stitch by picking up horizontal strand of yarn lying between last knitted stitch and next stitch and knitting into back of it; sl 1, slip 1.

To make a twisted hanging cord
[optional] Cut a 120 cm [47 in] length of yarn and knot ends together. Secure knotted end to edge of a table with sticky tape. Insert index finger of right hand in folded end. Holding yarn taut, twist finger round and round in clockwise direction until yarn begins to curl tightly back on itself when relaxed. Bring ends of yarn together and knot, then smooth along length so that twists are even. Trim ends of yarn close to knot.

Christmas tree

Note that P side of work is right side of tree. Using green yarn begin at top and cast on 7 sts. St-st 2 rows.
Next row: Inc K wise into every st – 14 sts.
St-st 5 rows.
Next row: K 2, (m 1, K 2) to end – 20 sts.
St-st 5 rows.
Next row: K 2, (m 1, K 2) to end – 29 sts.
St-st 5 rows.
Next row: K 2, (m 1, K 2) to last st, K 1 – 42 sts *.
St-st 3 rows.
Next row: P.
Work dec for underneath tree:
** *1st row:* K 2, (K 2 tog, K 2) to end – 32 sts.
2nd and every following alternate row: P.
3rd row: K 1, (K 2 tog, K 1) to last st, K 1 – 22 sts.
5th row: (K 2 tog) to end – 11 sts. Break off yarn leaving a long end. Thread it loosely through remaining sts and leave.
For the tub, use red yarn and cast on 30 sts loosely. St-st 3 rows then cast off firmly K wise.

To make up
Gather up cast on sts of tree tightly and

fasten off. Join row ends as far as sts threaded onto yarn. Turn right side out, stuff, then pull up yarn length tightly and fasten off.
Roll up the tub strip tightly across width and sew row ends in place. Sew cast on edge of tub centrally underneath tree, then sew across rolled up cast off edges to hold in place. Sew two large guipure flowers glued together to top of tree then sew on a hanging loop. Glue on small guipure flowers to decorate tree.

Ice cream cone

Using fawn yarn work as for tree as far as *. G-st 4 rows. Break off fawn, join on white or pink yarn for ice cream and beginning with a K row, st-st 8 rows.
Shape top: Next row: (K 1, K 2 tog) to end – 28 sts.
Next row: P.
Next row: (K 2 tog) to end – 14 sts.
P 1 row then break off yarn leaving a long end. Thread it loosely through remaining sts and leave.
For the chocolate flake, use brown yarn and cast on 10 sts. G-st 22 rows then cast off.

To make up
Make up cone as for tree. Roll up flake strip tightly from cast off edge then oversew cast on edge to one of the g-st ridges. Sew across wound up ends of flake to hold in place. Sew one end of flake to ice cream as illustrated. Work a few chain stitches in white or pink yarn for dribbles of ice cream down the cone. Add a hanging loop.

Garland

Using green or red yarn on 10 sts and g-st 80 rows, slipping the first st on every row. Cast off loosely.

To make up
Oversew loops at row ends together, pulling up each st as you go, to curve the strip. Stuff

through ends. Join cast on and cast off edges by oversewing them together. Make a twisted cord and loop it round garland at join as illustrated.

Make a twisted yarn bow and sew to garland then add guipure flowers as illustrated.

Bell

Begin at top and using blue or yellow yarn cast on 7 sts.

1st row: Inc K wise into every st – 14 sts.
2nd row: P.
3rd row: As 1st – 28 sts. St-st 13 rows.
Next row: (K 1, inc in next st) to end – 42 sts.

St-st 2 rows. Break off blue or yellow and join on yellow or red yarn. Beginning with a K row, work 3 rows rev st-st. Break off yellow or red and join on black yarn. Beginning with a K row, st-st 2 rows.

Shape underside of bell: Work as given for tree from ** to end.

To make up

Make up as for tree, noting that K side is right side of work. Wind a tiny ball of yarn using red or green then thread end of yarn into a darning needle. Sew backwards and forwards through the ball to hold wound strands in place. Sew ball to centre of bell underneath, taking yarn up through centre of bell to top. Pull yarn to depress the ball slightly into base, then fasten off. Add a hanging loop and a twisted yarn bow as illustrated.

Candle

Using white or blue yarn cast on 14 sts and g-st 40 rows. Cast off.

For the flame, cast on 4 sts using red. Break off red and join on yellow yarn.

Next row: Inc K wise into every st – 8 sts.
Beginning with a P row, st-st 4 rows.
Next row: (P 2 tog) to end – 4 sts.

Next row: (K 2 tog) to end – 2 sts. Fasten off the 2 sts.

For candle holder use red or green yarn, cast on 36 sts and g-st 6 rows. Cast off.

To make up

Make up candle as for chocolate flake. Oversew row ends of flame together, right side outside. Stuff, then sew to top of candle. Wind the candle holder strip round base of candle and sew in place. Add a hanging loop to top of flame, or fix base of candle holder to branch of tree with a length of thread.

Lollypop

Using red or green yarn cast on 14 sts.

1st row: Sl 1, K to last st, turn,
2nd row: P to last st, turn,
3rd row: K to end.
4th row: Sl 1, P to end. These 4 rows form the stripe pattern. Join on white yarn and continue working the 4 row stripes using white and red or green alternately, until there are five red or green and four white stripes.

Last stripe [white]: Work rows 1 to 3 then cast off.

For the knitted strip which covers the stick, begin at top end and using fawn yarn cast on 6 sts. St-st 18 rows. Break off yarn leaving a long end. Thread it through sts, pull up tightly and fasten off.

To make up

Oversew cast on and cast off edges of lollypop together having wrong side outside. Gather up row ends at right hand side of work tightly and fasten off. Turn right side out and stuff.

Gather up remaining row ends tightly and fasten off, then take a stitch through centre of lollypop and back again, pulling tightly to make flattened shape. Fasten off.

Cut wooden lolly stick to 6 cm [2¼ in] in length. Having right side of knitted strip outside, oversew row ends together, enclosing the stick as you go. Sew cast on edge of stick to lollypop. Add a hanging loop.

STOCKISTS

The UK stockists listed will supply by mail order to the USA, Australia, etc. You can write for details, enclosing a stamped self-addressed envelope for a reply.

Beckfoot Mill,
Prince Street,
Dudley Hill,
Bradford BD4 6HQ
Tel. (0274) 651065
For fur fabrics, polyester toy filling, felt and many other toy making and craft materials.

Griffin Fabrics Ltd,
The Craft Centre,
97 Claremont Street,
Aberdeen AB1 6QR
Tel. (0224) 580798
For fur fabrics, polyester toy filling, felt and many other toy making and craft materials.

The Handicraft Shop,
Northgate,
Canterbury,
Kent CT1 1BE
Tel. (0227) 451188
For fur fabrics, polyester toy filling, felt and many other toy making and craft materials.

NOTES FOR THE USA

GLOSSARY

English	American
Cast off	Bind off
Fasten off	Secure end of thread
Fur fabric	Fake fur
Guipure flowers	Daisy lace, flower trim, flower decals
Iron-on interfacing or interlining	Non-woven fusible interfacing
Leather punch	Hole punch
Nylon tights	Nylon pantyhose
Plasticine	Reusable modelling clay
Polyester stuffing	Polyester fibrefill
Polyester wadding	Polyester quilt batting
Ric-rac	Rickrack
Snap fasteners	Snaps
Sticky tape	Transparent adhesive tape for sticking on paper
Stockinette	Cotton knit fabric
Stocking stitch	Stockinette stitch
Strong thread	Buttonhole twist
Tack	Baste
Tension	Gauge
UHU glue	Tacky glue or Slomons
Zip fastener	Zipper

USA knitting needles

Metric size	'Old' UK size	USA size
$2\frac{3}{4}$ mm	12	1
3 mm	11	2
$3\frac{1}{4}$ mm	10	3
$3\frac{3}{4}$ mm	9	4
4 mm	8	5
5 mm	6	7
$5\frac{1}{2}$ mm	5	8

Yarns

Knitters in the USA should substitute knitting worsted weight for double knitting and sport weight for 4 ply.

Yarn weight

See p. 17 for imperial and metric yarn weights.

Copying the patterns

See Metric – Imperial Conversion Chart, p. 7.

INDEX

Page numbers in italics refer to colour illustrations